A Thicket of Business

A Thicket of Business

A History of the Bowring Family and The Bowring Group of Companies

by

Peter Bowring

The Memoir Club

First published in 2007 by
The Memoir Club
Stanhope Old Hall
Stanhope
Weardale
County Durham

British Library Cataloguing in
Publication Data.
A catalogue record for this book
is available from the
British Library

ISBN: 978-1-84104-168-1

Typeset by TW Typesetting, Plymouth, Devon
Printed by CPI Bath

To all businessmen who have entered the tunnel
of commerce reluctantly and in darkness
and have emerged into the sunshine of retirement
fulfilled and unscathed.

Contents

List of Illustrations

Bowring vessels in St John's Harbour in the early 1900s

Edward Bowring's grave at the Unitarian Chapel in Moretonhampstead, where other members of the family and relations are also buried

Sir William Benjamin Bowring Bt, JP, 1837–1916, Chairman 1899–1916

The Bowring Library in Moretonhampstead, Devon, presented to the town by Sir Thomas Bowring

Sir Thomas Benjamin Bowring, 1847–1918

Sir William Bowring's Golden Wedding Anniversary, 13 June, 1911

Bowring Brothers' ship SS *Florizel,* built in Glasgow in 1909, seen here in occasional use as a sealer

An Anglo-Mexican horse-drawn tanker delivering Bowring's petroleum products in the early 1920s

An early petroleum rail tanker of the Bowring Petroleum Company

Between pages 178 and 179

Clink Wharf

Sir Frederick Charles Bowring, DL, JP, 1857–1936, Chairman 1916–36

Sir Matthew Drysdale

Sir Edgar Rennie Bowring, KCMG, 1858–1943

Eric Aubrey Bowring, CBE, 1884–1959

Sir Edgar Bowring with the Duke of Connaught at the opening of Bowring Park, St John's, Newfoundland in 1914

5 May 1969. Centenary of appointment of Bowring Brothers Ltd as Lloyd's Agent in St John's, Newfoundland

Frederick Clive Bowring, 1897–1965, Chairman of C. T. Bowring & Co. Ltd from 1957 until his death in 1965

Edgar Bowring and Fred Bowring

Harvey Bowring, Edward Stevinson and W.G. Pedley

Mrs Milling, Geoffrey Milling, Chairman of The Bowring Steamship Company, and Fred Bowring, at the launching of MS *Orlando,* August 1960

Fred Bowring presenting the Master and Officers of MS *Regent Springbok* to Her Royal Highness The Princess Royal, when she travelled on this Bowring ship to Trinidad in January 1953

Introduction

Although two excellent histories of The Bowring Group of Companies have already been written, I felt there was a need to bring the story up-to-date, especially because in 1980, after almost one hundred and seventy years of development in trading, shipping and insurance, the Group was merged with Marsh & McLennan Companies, Inc. of New York, and soon thereafter lost its identity. I have relied to a very considerable extent on the research carried out by the two previous authors, Arthur Wardle for his book, *Benjamin Bowring and his Descendants*, which was published in 1940, and David Keir for his later work, *The Bowring Story*, published in 1962. For the painstaking work carried out by these two well-informed writers I am extremely grateful. There is inevitably much repetition of some of their writing, but I have endeavoured to dig a little deeper and to provide some more detail about members of the Bowring family, especially their contributions, helpful and otherwise, during the last twenty years of the Group's existence.

My thanks are also due in large measure to the help I have received in St John's, Newfoundland. The Hon. Edward Roberts, Lieutenant Governor and Dr Axel Meissen, President and Vice Chancellor of Memorial University of Newfoundland both arranged contacts which have been invaluable. The help given to me by Greg Walsh of the Provincial Archives Division, and Bert Riggs and Heather Warsham, archivists at Memorial University, has been most useful and is greatly appreciated.

The information provided by John Cook on ships owned and managed by Bowring's since 1818 has been of outstanding help and for this, as for Mike Tarver's information on *Terra Nova*, I am most grateful.

Finally, I owe a considerable debt of gratitude to my wife Carole for her careful checking of the manuscript and to my son Antony in his unofficial but efficient capacity as family archivist.

Bermondsey, London, 2007

Chapter 1

As air canada flight 861 touched down at St John's airport on Monday, 27 October 2003, exactly on time after a smooth and comfortable five hours over the Atlantic, I remembered reading that, when my great-great-grandfather, Benjamin Bowring, arrived in Newfoundland from Exeter 187 years earlier with his wife and children, it was after a journey lasting several weeks in a small sailing vessel, battling against gales and tempestuous seas. At that time to arrive safely after such a journey might well have been seen as a triumph of hope over experience.

It is perhaps a little difficult to understand why Benjamin, a modestly successful watch and clockmaker, jeweller and silversmith, should decide in 1816, at the age of thirty-eight, to leave his native Exeter with his wife, Charlotte and their children, and emigrate to Newfoundland. After all Exeter seemed a prosperous enough city and, as far as one knows, there were no obvious reasons for him to want to make a quick getaway. One wonders, too, why Britain's oldest colony, with its uncertain economic future and doubtful climate, would have appealed as a haven of hope for a self-employed tradesman, with a young family, whose future in his native Devon cannot have seemed so unpromising as to persuade him to make such a brave, some might say foolhardy, decision. At this time, when commercial shipping was increasing, many merchant ships that undertook the frequently stormy crossing of the Atlantic were lost, as our intrepid emigrant would learn to his sorrow some years after his arrival at St John's.

There had certainly been Bowrings (Bouryngs, Bowringes or Bower-ings as it was and still is spelt) in the West Country of England since the beginning of the 14th century and one Stephen Bouryng held the manor of Bouryngslegh (today, Bowringsleigh) in 1303. The estate, near Kingsbridge in Devon, passed into the hands of the Ilbert family during the reign of Henry VIII and they occupied it for many generations. In his book, *Benjamin Bowring and his Descendants* (Hodder and Stoughton, 1938) Arthur Wardle asserts that the name Bowring is derived from an Anglo-Saxon word *buring*, said to mean *son of the farmer*. However, a

1

much more recent attempt to discover its origins by Desmond Holden, the results of whose researches were published in *The Peak Advertiser* on 8 March 1999, indicates that, among other possibilities, the name might have been interpreted as meaning 'one who lived in a group of hovels'!

There is, however, nothing to suggest that Benjamin's home and upbringing were other than reasonably comfortable. His father, Nathaniel, a serge maker in Exeter, was married to Susannah White of Moreton-hampstead, whose family were in the wool trade. Little more is known of him and he died in 1781 when Benjamin was but three years old.

Little is known, either, of Benjamin's early years. Born in Exeter in 1778, he was brought up and went to school in his mother's hometown. His early education, based on sound Unitarian principles, was at the school attached to the chapel in Moretonhampstead, which his cousin, Sir John Bowring (whose life and achievements will be referred to in due course), attended some ten years later. It is probable that Benjamin's brother, William, who became a prominent solicitor in Exeter and married Jenny Fouracre, went to the same school. He also had a sister who married William Tricks, whose unusual surname we shall come across again. At the beginning of the 19th century Moretonhampstead was quite isolated. There were no roads passable by wheeled carriages and everything – goods and passengers – was transported to and from Exeter on 'crooks' – bent tree branches, to which pack saddles were attached – drawn, presumably by horses. (Wardle; *Benjamin Bowring and his Descendants*)

After a simple, straightforward Unitarian education, imparted in the complete absence of urban distraction, Benjamin chose to enter the watch and clockmaking trade and was apprenticed to the elder John Tucker of Tiverton. (*Devon Clocks & Clockmakers*, by Clive N. Ponsford) His apprenticeship was successful and he opened a shop at 225, High Street, Exeter at the beginning of October 1803. On 6 October the following advertisement appeared in the *Exeter Flying Post*.

EXETER

B. BOWRING, Watchmaker, Silversmith, Jeweller and Engraver, begs Leave most respectfully to inform his Friends and the Public that he has opened a SHOP nearly opposite to St Martin's Lane, in the High Street, where he intends to carry on the above BUSINESSES in all their Branches; and he hopes by Assiduity and reasonable Charges, he shall merit and obtain their Patronage and continued Support.

It would not be unreasonable to accept this announcement as evidence of the beginning of the Bowring business, but throughout the life of the Trading, Shipping and Insurance enterprise that would eventually become known as The Bowring Group, the year of its founding has been considered to be the year in which Benjamin started trading in St John's, Newfoundland, and that has always been assumed to be 1811. That is the year during which he made his first visit to the colony, having been persuaded that there were opportunities for business in general and, possibly, for a clockmaker, there being no one established in that trade in St John's at the time. There can be little doubt that he made up his mind during this visit that he would, in due time, start a business there.

Bursting with pride and confidence, just six days after the *Exeter Flying Post* announcement, Benjamin married Charlotte Price, whose family came from Wiveliscombe in Somerset and whose father was a clock-maker. The marriage took place on 9 October at Wellington, some seven miles from the bride's home. The fact that they were not married in Wiveliscombe, at a time when travelling was anything but comfortable on rutted dirt roads, is explained by David Keir in his book *The Bowring Story* (The Bodley Head Ltd 1962). He writes that, in Wellington 'they were *allowed* (my italics) to marry under licence as Nonconformists'.

It is likely that Benjamin's new business at Exeter prospered during the next few years, though to what extent we have no knowledge beyond the fact that it was taken over by a Mr Henry Ellis in 1816 as a going concern when Benjamin finally emigrated to Newfoundland. That he made or, more likely, assembled a number of long-case clocks is certain and there are at least four still known to exist in the possession either of members of the Bowring family or of their business successors. But he is unlikely to go down in history as a great master of his trade, although he does merit a brief entry in *Watchmakers and Clockmakers of the World*. The other aspects of his business, as Silversmith, Jeweller and Engraver, are more likely to have provided him and his growing family with a reasonable livelihood.

The first of his five sons, William, was born at Exeter in 1804 and the second, Charles Tricks, in 1808. They were to be followed by Henry Price in 1815, Edward in 1819 and John in 1824. All would, in due course, make significant contributions to what was to become the international trading and insurance enterprise their father founded and built up in the ultimately successful but often frustrating and disappointing years ahead.

In 1811 England was suffering from widespread unemployment and strikes; the Luddites were destroying the new machinery, which was threatening their jobs. Benjamin detested the Tory government of the day, particularly because of their draconian methods in putting down dissent and rioting, and he might well, in such circumstances, have been looking westward where, judging from the increase in trade between Europe and British North America, he could discern the possibility of a brighter future for himself and his young family.

It appears, furthermore, that in 1810 a certain Mr Pitts, who had emigrated to Newfoundland, but who had previously lived in Exeter, came back to consummate a codfish deal and during his visit purchased three long-case clocks and other goods from Benjamin. There seems little doubt that a conversation with Mr Pitts persuaded Benjamin that, while Newfoundland was conducting a lively trade in fish and sealskins with Europe, the island had no established watch and clock business. Such an enterprise might well succeed at a time when the increasing number of St John's merchants was beginning to prosper. Whilst there may have been other considerations to influence Benjamin's decision to emigrate the factor, however, most likely to have dominated his thoughts was England's political and economic condition at the time. In addition, he held strong anti-slavery views, not shared by many of his fellow citizens in Exeter.

Benjamin's first visit to St John's in 1811 was followed by two or three more and in 1815 he spent several months there, no doubt putting the finishing touches to the establishment of his new enterprise. In 1814, in anticipation of his setting up in business permanently, he had arranged for an advertisement to appear in the St John's *Royal Gazette*.

It was in the spring of 1816 that Benjamin and his young family finally sailed into St John's, between the towering cliffs of the famous Narrows, after a cold and stormy passage lasting several weeks. I have often wondered, as no doubt have others, what thoughts would have passed through the minds of Charlotte and her children as the untidy and crowded harbour, which must have compared unfavourably with the ancient dignity of Exeter, came into view. And they may well have had their first view of an iceberg.

In spite of the enthusiasm and excitement that Benjamin surely felt now that he had his family with him and, henceforth, would be able to concentrate on building up his business, this was not to be for some time to come. Indeed, there would be moments when he must have wondered whether he should ever have left his native Devon. New-

> **BENJAMIN BOWRING,**
> *Working Watch-maker, Silversmith, and Jeweller—From EXETER,*
>
> MOST respectfully begs leave to inform the inhabitants of St. John's and its vicinity, that he has commenced Business in the above branches; and having been regularly educated for them, and had great experience in them, he presumes to hope, that by assiduity and moderate charges, he shall merit and obtain their patronage and continued support.
>
> He has taken a House in *Duckworth* Street, belonging to Mr. W. B. THOMAS, into which he expects soon to enter ; and in the mean time, he has lodgings at Mr. ANDREWS's, over Mr. STENTEFORD's shop, near the Lower Street, where he has for Sale an excellent assortment of Silver, and *some* Gold WATCHES, together with a few handsome Eight day CLOCKS, in mahogany and other cases, and where their commands will be thankfully received.
>
> Should he experience that support which he has been taught to hope for, it is his intention in the ensuing Spring, to enlarge his stock very generally ; and he pledges himself that the Articles he may have to dispose of, shall be selected from the best markets, and be of the first quality.—CYPHERS, &c. engraved.
> St. John's, 14th Sept. 1815.

An early press announcement by Benjamin Bowring following his having settled in St John's, Newfoundland

foundland was temporarily in the throes of economic depression following the end of the American war and many St John's merchants were facing ruin. The arrival of large numbers of immigrants from Ireland can only have added to the city's problems

Frustration and disappointment were all too often to be repeated in the years that lay ahead. Shortly after his arrival, the city was swept by a devastating fire, which destroyed the premises he had prepared for his business. Fortunately his stocks of merchandise, collected together during his last visit, were stored at his lodgings and escaped destruction. But he and his family must have wondered whether they had been wise to leave the comparative comfort and security of their home and a successful business in Exeter. One cannot but marvel at the courage demanded of them in the face of such depressing circumstances. The city was to suffer further such conflagrations and it is a testimony to Benjamin's indomitable spirit, and the fortitude of his young family, that he continued doggedly to build up the business he had created.

Such was the damage caused by this first fire, that it wasn't until September 1816 that he was able to announce that among the goods he had for sale, as described by David Keir in *The Bowring Story*, were: 'gold and silver watches, silver plate, fashionable jewellery, gilt and fancy ornaments, beads etc., cutlery, writing paper, prime English dip candles, soap, split peas, ladies' and gentlemen's fashionable wearing apparel'. The split peas seem a little incongruous but perhaps they were a harbinger of the varied nature of the trading in which the enterprise he had created would, in due time, become involved. A second disastrous fire broke out just over a year later in November 1817 during a particularly cold winter. Although St John's was in the grip of a deep economic depression, Benjamin, with characteristic confidence and courage, was sure that his business would survive and eventually prosper. There is no record of the extent to which his interests must have suffered as a result of this second fire; it is unlikely that he would have escaped substantial losses since no less than three hundred houses were destroyed and some two thousand inhabitants rendered homeless.

Notwithstanding these disasters and cruelly cold winters Benjamin's business grew, as did his influence on St John's life. In D. W. Prowse's *A History of Newfoundland*, Benjamin is described as being 'very active and intelligent' and he played a significant part in local politics. His wife, Charlotte, made a highly constructive contribution to the success of the business by recognizing some of the more pressing needs of the St John's housewives; she also added to the future management potential by presenting him with their fourth son, Edward, in 1819.

Whilst the watch and clockmaking, silversmith, and jewellery business continued to operate, the small but successful general store run by the enterprising Charlotte, and Benjamin's wider trading interests, soon overtook it.

In 1818 he felt sufficiently confident to fulfil a growing ambition. He became a shipowner, a natural consequence of his having purchased his own wharf. The first vessel in his fleet was *Charlotte*, 44 tons. Later he acquired *Eagle* and *Dove*. Both were 91-ton schooners and were built on Prince Edward Island, where, as a further indication of his confidence, business acumen and growing commercial success, he had purchased 3,000 acres of land, an impressively large slice of real estate to have acquired after only seven years in business in Newfoundland.

The little *Eagle* made several crossings of the Atlantic carrying general cargoes and, on one occasion at least, was laden with rum and molasses from Demerara to Liverpool, no mean passage for such a small vessel. Benjamin, from the beginning of his trading overseas, was able to make his purchases from England most advantageously through his numerous family connections in business there. At Exeter his uncles and a cousin were serge and woollen manufacturers; Bowring, Trist and Company, who flourished in London early in the century as wholesale haberdashers, were followed by John James Bowring, hatter, of Change Alley, while another cousin, Edward Bowring, carried on the business of silk, velvet and hat-shag manufacturer in Laurence Pountney Lane. Benjamin made numerous visits to England in order to purchase goods for sale in Newfoundland for which payment was usually made from the proceeds of sales of the island's produce, mainly salt-cod and sealskins, or by bills of exchange. However, owing to the prevailing currency problems, his purchases were sometimes paid for by the sale of coins. For one of his visits he had no fewer than thirteen parcels shipped to Liverpool containing Mexican dollars, Portuguese Crusada Novas, French coins and Irish silver bank tokens.

By 1824 the time had arrived for his eldest son, William, who had reached the age of twenty-one, to join the business, and Benjamin decided to name his company Benjamin Bowring & Son. This, surely, must have been a proud moment for the family. In spite of the many adversities already mentioned, the business was beginning to develop well. A fifth son, John, my great grandfather, had arrived and Benjamin must have held high hopes for the future, feeling perhaps that, with five sons to call on, succession was assured. Had he known, however, of some of the testing times that lay ahead, such confidence in the future of Benjamin Bowring & Son might have taken a serious battering.

Notwithstanding several years' absence, ties with their agents, friends and relations in Devon remained as strong as ever. In 1828 William sailed for England with the intention of marrying Miss Harriet Harvey of Moretonhampstead. This voyage of hope and expectancy aboard the brig *Matilda* turned out to be a major tragedy for the family, the business and, by no means least, the benighted Harriet herself. The vessel foundered before reaching England, never to be heard of again.

Although the loss of his eldest son at sea must have been a devastating blow to Benjamin's confidence in the future of his company and a sombre reminder of the uncertainty of Atlantic crossings, he nevertheless decided in 1830 to make the journey to Liverpool, presumably leaving Charles Tricks, now aged twenty-two, to run the business. He arrived there early in June accompanied, no doubt, by the customary baggage of diverse currencies in notes and coins. On this visit he took with him his two sons, Henry aged sixteen and Edward just eleven, with a view to placing them in a boarding school at Exeter where they would be assured of an education soundly based, no doubt, on strict Unitarian principles.

But there were other reasons for this visit to England. Having left his sons at a school kept by a Mr John Hookins, Benjamin returned to Liverpool where he became a member of the Liverpool Newsroom. Thereafter he travelled widely throughout the country in search of goods suitable for sale in Newfoundland. For several months following his peregrinations he concentrated on Liverpool as the most suitable commercial port in England through which to conduct the affairs of what he foresaw as an increasingly international enterprise. During the next year he appointed one John Cropper as his agent there to handle the exports to St John's and dispose of the inward shipments of Newfoundland's produce, consisting almost entirely of cod, cod oil, sealskins and seal oil.

For nearly five hundred years the catching and processing of cod, known locally simply as 'fish', was the staple industry of the people of Newfoundland. The established and well-tried method of salting and drying the fish, which for centuries had been available in seemingly unlimited quantities from the rich fishing banks off the island's coast, made it suitable for export to the warmer climates of Europe, the major customers being France, Portugal, England and the Basque country. The complex process of gutting, cleaning, washing, salting and drying, was known quite simply as 'making fish'.

I am indebted to Shannon Ryan who gives a clear description of 'making fish' in his book, *Fish Out of Water* (Breakwater, 1986): 'To process the cod into saltfish, it was split along the underside, and the head, offal, and part of the backbone were removed so that the fish lay flat, somewhat like a kippered herring (except that the latter is split along the back). It was then washed, salted in piles (saltbulk), and, later, spread on wooden platforms (flakes) or rocky surfaces to dry. When well dried, it could be stored almost indefinitely. Its keeping qualities and the comparative ease with which it could be transported . . . combined to make saltfish a useful and popular source of protein'.

The other important contributor to Newfoundland's economy in which Benjamin Bowring & Son would become involved was the Seal Fishery. During the 18th century the seals, which appear in great numbers each spring off the northeast coast of the island, were captured in nets laid close inshore. It wasn't until the very end of the century that the industry underwent a significant change inasmuch as schooners were used to visit the ice flows on which the seals congregated to have their pups.

The Aboriginal people of Newfoundland and Labrador had hunted seals for hundreds of years mainly in order to sustain their existence in harsh living conditions, the animals providing them with food, pelts for protective clothing and oil for cooking and lighting. When Europeans arrived, however, and settled in Newfoundland they saw the seal as an object of commerce, not survival. From the outset of their trading activities they recognized the value of the seal as an article of potential profit and it was not long before the pelts were being manufactured into various small items of clothing such as boots and caps, and the more progressive merchants showed considerable interest in acquiring sealskins for curing and exporting to leather manufacturers. Sealskin coats soon became a desirable, if not entirely fashionable protection against the rigours of Newfoundland winters. There was never much interest shown by settlers in seals as a source of food though the flippers were considered by some to be a delicacy. Others, however, will aver that the consumption of seal flipper pie throws an entirely new light on the meaning of dyspepsia. (A more comprehensive description of the Seal Fishery follows later.)

It was not, however, the pelts so much as the oil which was the product of the seal fishery providing the largest volume of trade in the middle of the 19th century. While the skins were salted down and sent off to tanners to be converted into leather the fat was rendered down into oil. To some considerable extent this was achieved by letting the fat rot naturally, a process which, in the warmer months, gave rise to an appalling stench, which did little to commend St John's as a desirable summer resort.

Benjamin, having strengthened his commercial ties with England, returned to Newfoundland in July 1831. The following year, though in many ways a momentous one in the family's history, started badly. In *The Bowring Story*, David Keir writes:

> Winter ice lasted long on the coast to the detriment of Benjamin's own little ships, any he may have chartered and those, in the course of his normal commerce, that usually brought goods from England and took

back cod oil and sealskin. His own immediate plans remained unchanged. If he was to alter the fabric of his business, which he was bound to do if it was to be enlarged on the scale of his ambition, then first things had to come first; and of these the most important was to get his son and heir, Charles, married and leave him firmly and happily established at St John's before he himself, as now seemed certain, left the colony.

At his father's suggestion, in the summer of 1832, Charles Tricks sailed for England on a twofold mission. Not only was he expected to perform the normal task of purchasing the now well-established range of merchandise, it was also anticipated that he would return with a wife. He was away for a year during which time he visited Moretonhampstead for long enough successfully to woo Miss Harriet Harvey in pursuit of whose hand, it will be recalled, his older brother, William, was intent when, in 1828, he was lost at sea. Their engagement no doubt delighted Benjamin. 'I think', he wrote to Harriet's father, 'that as far as Charles' character, disposition and prospects go you need not be under any anxiety respecting your daughter's happiness. He has become a partner in a concern which in confidence I may tell you has been a very profitable one and I believe with good management and industry is likely to be an increasing and permanent one. The concern is in debt, I believe I can safely say, to no one but myself, and although our stock is large and involves property to a large amount there is every prospect, if no accident happens, that he will in a very little while be free of me also'. Charles and Harriet were married at Moretonhampstead on 13 April 1833, possibly at the Unitarian Chapel in Cross Street, and they returned to St John's towards the end of May after a stormy passage, which lasted no less than five weeks.

Whilst Benjamin had not stood for legislative office in St John's, he was, nevertheless, much concerned with and played an active part in local politics. His particular bone of contention, understandably, was the lack of adequate legislation to combat the persistent and frequently severely destructive fires that so often came near to ruining his and others' businesses. Though not a candidate for election to the proposed new House of Assembly, he served on an election committee where he spared no effort in fighting his corner. His general interest in the political development of Newfoundland can be judged from the following tongue-in-cheek excerpt from a letter dated 5 January 1833 to John Cropper at Liverpool: 'I have by this opportunity sent on a St John's Newspaper giving an a/c of our Infant Legislature . . . We are all so much enraptured with the meeting of our fifteen honourable members that nothing else but politics are talked of. I am not quite sure but the results may surprise the world. It is not yet settled but the prophecy of one of the seers that the Vine and the Fig Tree shall grow and flourish in our hitherto bleak and snow clad hills may be realized and that our valleys may wave with golden corn. I wish the House of Assembly would begin by ordering off the Ice which has at this early season of the year already settled down on our harbour, for it is very annoying that our Vessels should be prevented from sailing as they now are.'

Early in 1833 there had been another dreadful fire at Harbour Grace, in Conception Bay, where some 600 people were left homeless. This tragic event had stimulated Benjamin's firmly held view that local legislature on the spot was necessary to enforce such measures as would at least reduce if not eliminate such disasters. One of the fairly obvious measures that would ultimately be enforced would be the requirement to use stone in the construction of buildings instead of the more readily available and probably more economical use of wood.

Unhappily for Benjamin Bowring & Son the proposed new precautions arrived too late. Although the new House of Assembly had been sitting since New Year's Day 1833, the necessary legislation had not yet been enacted. On 7 July 1833 another devastating fire swept through St John's, totally destroying the firm's premises. This must have been an overwhelming blow to Benjamin's hopes for the future of his business. But his powers of recovery and his determination to build upon what was left are apparent from the letter he wrote to his agent following the fire.

I am sure you will condole with me when I tell you that I have again been subjected to the destructive Element which has so often devastated this unfortunate town. We were alarmed on Sunday morning about 2 o'clock by the cry of Fire, which we found proceeded from the house of Mr J. B. Thomson, only three doors a way from us. We immediately endeavoured to save what we could and we were actively and nobly assisted by our Friends who came to our assistance, but as we had only about half an hour between the first alarm and the premises occupied by me being in full blaze we could of course do nothing. Our premises on the South Side of the Harbour were of great service as we moved whatever we could to save them, and a great part of our family are also there. I fear that the insurance I have made will by no means cover my loss within 12 or 14 Hundred Pounds, but in the confusion of the present moment this only amounts to conjecture. I and Mrs B. and my son and his wife are at private lodgings on the North side and my children are billeted upon our friends.

My plans as to futurity are hardly as yet arranged but I suppose I shall get into business here, as the concern of Benj. Bowring & Son is still solvent and our name and fame worth something. I think I can assure you that any balance we may owe you and a very few others is perfectly safe. No less than 56 dwellings were destroyed in less than 2 hours and a half. The worst part of the business, however, is that Mr Thomson (in whose house the fire broke out) and his daughter were both consumed in the flames.

This daunting situation must, yet again, have tested Benjamin's fortitude to its limits. There was, too, an element of weariness as can be detected from a letter he wrote to a business friend in Liverpool: 'I can assure you,' he wrote, ' that if it were not for my Son, I would not incur the hazard and trouble of beginning the world afresh, but he has lately married and brought out his wife under an expectancy of sharing in a business which has been far from unprofitable, and I am loth to leave him without that protection which I think my name and capital, small as it may be, will afford him.'

He had earlier given serious thought to returning to England in order to supervise the growing volume of business now emanating from Liverpool, which he had initiated on his previous visit and which Charles had fostered during the year recently spent there. A lesser man might well have hastened his leaving in such depressing circumstances. But he immediately postponed his departure for England for at least a year. He was now fifty-five, an age at which he might well have given serious consideration to taking life more easily and to distancing himself from any further possible devastating hazards of the kind that had done so much to test his resolve in the past. But Benjamin wasn't a quitter, and he was a man of firm decision when the need arose. He wrote to his insurers without a single day's delay, found, and immediately rented, temporary premises and, at the same time drew up plans for a new stone building. In less than a month he and Charles had put up for auction what remained of their salvaged stock and were offering for sale such a varied and eclectic range of goods as 'imported cognac in hogsheads, cast iron ware, window glass, black pepper in bags and mustard in kegs and a large assortment of Manchester goods received since the last fire'.

Further evidence of their energy and determination was manifest in their decision, in April 1834, to outfit 125 ships and 3,000 men for the annual seal hunt. Charles had shown himself to be sufficiently competent and confident during and following the recent crisis that his father felt he could now proceed with his plans to return to England, believing that he could safely leave the business in St John's in Charles' capable hands, with the assistance by now of his younger brother Henry Price. Work on the new stone building was going ahead, trade had picked up and they had taken the decision to buy, as soon as possible, the new ship that they were looking for to facilitate their growing transatlantic trading. On 20 June 1834, Benjamin Bowring, in the presence of his clerk, John Harris, signed a power of attorney in favour of Charles Tricks giving him freedom to run the St John's business, with the help of Henry, by now emerging from his teens. In addition Benjamin wrote a letter of instruction of which the following is part '. . . As far as regards the New Buildings I believe I need say no more than you and I have before said. You will of course adhere as nearly as possible to the plans I have left with you, making the heighth (*sic*) from the top of the Shop Floor to the top of the Dining Room Floor not more than eleven feet, the distance from the Dining Room floor to the Bed Rooms above eight feet six inches, and from that floor to the top of the Wall four feet six inches. . . Do not fail to write me by every Vessel for England so that very soon after I land I may hear how you get on. Direct for me to the care of Mr Cropper until you receive further instructions from me. . . . As soon as you hear from me of my arrival you will please send on by the first opportunity the Sealed Letter left to be opened only in the event of my death to such address as I shall then point out. I shall if I arrive safely look about to purchase a Vessel such as I think may suit our purpose and to avoid buying on both sides of the Water I wish you not to make any purchase of one here unless indeed you can buy the *Sophia* with all her materials as she came from sea cheap, say about £650 currency, that is if upon examination you find her *a faithful built vessel and well found* . . . I do not think I have anything more to remark on than generally request you will exert yourself to the utmost to conduct the Business now left to your charge actively, honourably and profitably, and to offer my ardent prayers to the Common Father of all for the health, welfare and happiness of you and every part of the Family. I am, my dear Charles, with sincere affection, Your friend and father, Benj. Bowring.' This letter bears the same date as the power of attorney and includes the slightly confusing postscript 'I do not think the *Sophia* will do!'

Towards the end of the month, with his wife, his youngest son, John and his daughter, also named Charlotte, Benjamin set sail for the last time from Newfoundland for the Clyde aboard the brig *Balclutha*, 182 tons, arriving on 15 July 1834 after a very stormy passage, encountering gales of such ferocity that Benjamin was moved to describe them as 'sufficient to split sheet iron'.

Chapter 2

BENJAMIN'S LIFE WAS ABOUT to undergo a profound change. He had left England some eighteen years earlier, a modest watchmaker and jeweller, but was now a merchant and shipowner, highly respected in Newfoundland, of some means and, though he could not possibly know it, the founder of what was to become a globally recognized, international, commercial group with wide-ranging trading, insurance and financial interests.

One can only imagine what their feelings may have been as he and his family party set out from the Clyde for Liverpool aboard the steam vessel *Vulcan* on a passage which took no less than ten days because the ship's boiler burst shortly after leaving Greenock. And this was not to be the last of their frustrating travel experiences. After Liverpool, the family went by stagecoach to London, Exeter and Moretonhampstead. Presumably access to the latter had improved since his childhood days when there were no roads. Having left Charlotte and the children there our dauntless traveller went back to London and thence set out on a buying expedition by boat for Hull, intending to go on from there to Leeds, Dewsbury and Manchester by coach. On 25 August 1834 he wrote to Charles from Dewsbury:

> The next morning (Tuesday, the 19th) I set off in the Steam Boat 'Yorkshireman' for Kingston-upon-Hull (in common parlance 'Hull') on my way to Leeds, being promised to arrive at 3 o'clock in the afternoon of the 20th. Our first misfortune was getting aground off Woolwich, which detained us about half an hour. We then got on very slowly but I had hoped surely until we got within about 30 miles of the entrance to the Humber, when the pipes of the Steam Boiler gave way, put our fires out and left us a mere log upon the water. The Engineers on board attempted to repair the damage and we were promised that we should soon have our paddles at work again. In the meantime, the Captain said he would attempt to beat her in with the use of sails, but 24 hours elapsed and it was clearly seen that the Boilers were irreparable, and that sails on such a leewardly beast were totally useless. The Captain would not hoist a signal of distress because he knew that if he did anyone coming to his assistance would claim salvage, and thus 120 Persons, men women and

children, were fixed with the Lincolnshire Shoals on one side and the German Ocean upon the other, with not more than one day's Provisions on board. Had the wind come on any way hard either from the Eastward or the Westward, what would have become of us is not easy to contemplate and we persuaded the Captain to take advantage of the tide and bring the Vessel as close as possible with the Lincolnshire shore, when I and three others volunteered to row to the land (distant fully 12 miles) and send off an express to Hull. We set off on this expedition but very fortunately the Captain of a Revenue Cutter, seeing the Steam Boat without his steam and without a signal of distress, and seeing us also leave her in a rowing boat, fancied that we were upon a smuggling expedition and determined to cut us off, which he did. When he was informed of the circumstances he promptly offered to go to the assistance of the Boat, and we went on board the Cutter which took the steamer in tow and absolutely dragged her up to Hull (a very stiff breeze having sprung up) so that we arrived, contrary to the expectations of every one, late on the Thursday night, having been towed fully 50 miles . . .

In much of his letter writing Benjamin shows signs of deep concern about the conduct of the business in Newfoundland and, although he clearly had complete confidence in Charles when he left for England he is, however, still deeply worried about the possibility of further fires in St John's. The new stone building was completed in August 1834 and he demonstrates his solicitude for the safety of the premises in a letter to Charles written on 27 October from Liverpool, where he was now lodging in a house in Mount Pleasant:

I wish (he writes) that your Shop Shutters were cased with thin Sheet Iron, and that Iron Shutters were made for the Front Windows . . . I think we shall be tolerably secure even if a Fire should happen on the other side of the street or above us or below us. I should not, if I were you, speculate in Board Lumber to fill up the yard. Balk, Scantling, Spars, I do not think there can be much danger with, but the Boards in event of Fire I am of opinion there would be a great deal, and that they would very likely conceal the source of a Fire . . . Fire is with me, under present circumstances, of the very first importance. Do not fail to impress upon the minds of everyone in your own house the necessity of carefulness, and do not go to Bed yourselves any night without seeing every Fire and Candle safe . . .

The new building in St John's, which cost Benjamin £3,000 of his personal funds (a considerable sum in those days) and for which

Benjamin Bowring & Son paid him rent, was to house not only the store but members of the family and, indeed, of the staff. So his continuing preoccupation with the possibility of further outbreaks of fire was perfectly understandable. As well as Charles Tricks, his wife Harriet and daughter, Charlotte Susan, also living in the building were John Harris their clerk, three apprentices (Charles Ayre, who would in due course start his own business in St John's, Philip Hutchings and Tom Snelgrove), Charles's two younger brothers, Henry and Edward, and a maidservant, who was likely to have been kept pretty busy. And Benjamin would certainly have been ever mindful of the fact that his fine new building stood on the ground where previously Mr Thomson and his daughter perished in the fire of 1833. But Benjamin's anxieties were not, however, confined to the safety from fire of his family and the burgeoning business. He became deeply concerned about the political future of Newfoundland and, in contrast to his earlier guarded enthusiasm for the establishment of representative government, he had developed a marked lack of faith in the island's legislation which can be measured in a letter written to Charles in October, 1834.

> I perceive (he wrote) that your House of Assembly, after having reduced themselves to the lowest pitch of Contempt by their absurd squabbles and pitiable proofs of a want of ability to legislate, are determined to do something to change the sneer into a curse. They appear to me to have adopted the language of Pindar as a motto: 'We'll triumph in death as we Catalines fall and go to the Devil together.' And so they are really determined to issue Exchequer Bills! To saddle the Island with the expense of an Interest upon debt which if *ever* paid must be paid now as at a future time. But who will take these Exchequer Bills forsooth? As one of the few concerned, I hereby enter my protest against having anything to do with them, no matter what Aegis or Discount.' To amplify further his deep mistrust of the legislature he adds, 'I would close the concern (Benj. Bowring and Son) altogether as far as my own interest goes rather than sell goods to be paid in such trash. I wish you to decline at whatever cost any Paper which is not regularly drawn on Great Britain and acceptable upon immediate presentation.

Having taken up residence in Liverpool after eighteen years in Newfoundland, Benjamin must have found the contrasting conditions depressing. The city, as a potential beneficiary of the Industrial Revolution, was attracting thousands of work-hungry men and women who mistakenly saw a better life than on the land in other parts of the

British Isles, notably Ireland. There were so many of them that their hopes of jobs in the expanding industries of the city could not possibly be fulfilled. As a result of the massive unemployment thus created, extreme poverty, hunger and crime belied the prosperous future that lay ahead for the city.

Notwithstanding these dreadful conditions, which were in stark contrast to the comparative tranquillity of the rocky fishermen's island he had just left, Benjamin's hopes for the business were buoyant. Although the city endured appalling slums, high mortality and disease, fearsome lawlessness and sectarian feuds, indeed some of the worst conditions in England, there were nevertheless hopeful signs of progress. In recent years new docks had been opened and Liverpool's shipping was increasing rapidly. There were grounds for optimism, a state of mind not altogether alien to our indomitable Benjamin although, as we shall soon see, his outlook was not always entirely positive.

Late in 1834 he bought the small brig, *Velocity*. It was with his personal funds that he paid for this vessel though he expected to be reimbursed by Benjamin Bowring & Son in due course. Built on Prince Edward Island, she was offered for sale by the Liverpool firm of Job, Bulley & Company (who also had significant interests in St John's) for £700. She was considered to be one of the finest vessels constructed on the island but required much expenditure to bring her up to the required A1 class at Lloyd's. Benjamin was fully occupied during the next few months supervising the fitting-out of his new acquisition and purchasing goods for Benjamin Bowring & Son in St John's.

It was at about this time that Charles announced that he sought to enter the seal oil business, a venture that did not appeal at all to Benjamin. He was without doubt wearied by the unexpected cost and amount of work that needed to be done on *Velocity*. In a letter to Charles he describes his proposal as one which 'with painful acuteness agitates and depresses my mind and spirits', but adds with a typical gesture of affection 'I do not wish you to alarm yourself too much about this'. Any thoughts that his sons, or indeed Benjamin himself, might have had that his departure from Newfoundland was an indication of his having considered even part retirement were emphatically dispelled. He was working and worrying as hard as ever.

A steady flow of letters during the early months of 1835 are full of warnings and advice and in some instances sheer frustration and gloom as is clear from one written during the fitting out of *Velocity*:

If you should ever have one tithe part the trouble with the *Velocity* which I have had in fitting her out, I think you will most deeply regret, as I do, the ever again having to do with Vessels; the expence(*sic*), enormous though it is, is but the least part of the annoyances. The having to battle day after day with the rapacity and roguery of the Liverpool Tradesmen, to endeavour to penetrate the mystery of iniquity existing under the name of discount, to set my back against further expence without success, and the noise and blackguardism of seamen, is more than I have been able to bear and the consequence is that it has produced an illness which I fear it will be some time before I get over.

It is probable that Benjamin had not foreseen the difficulties he would face with *Velocity* when, simultaneously with her purchase, he decided to open an office on 1 January 1835 at 32, King Street, Liverpool. A month later the following notice appeared in the *Liverpool Advertiser*:

BRITISH NORTH AMERICA
To sail from 1st to 8th of March
For ST. JOHN'S, Newfoundland.
The fine, new fast sailing A1 Brig,
VELOCITY

Thomas Blackstone, Master; 145 tons register; has room for a few tons freight, and good accommodation for passengers. For freight or passengers, apply to the Master, on board, Queen's Dock, or to

BENJ. BOWRING,
32 King-street

We have no knowledge of how many staff, if any, Benjamin employed at 32, King Street, but it is clear from the above advertisement that he was still, though now in his late fifties, likely to have been very much a 'hands on' businessman. It would have been with him personally that passages or cargoes were discussed; there is no mention at this time of any clerical assistance. But staffing, as the business grew on both sides of the Atlantic, was becoming a matter of some concern. In St John's, Tom Snelgrove, who had joined the firm as an apprentice in the early 1830s, proved to be unsatisfactory. He was found to be 'sulky and unsuitable'. There was some difficulty in finding a replacement and on 28 February 1835, Benjamin wrote to George Harvey, Charles Trick's father-in-law, in Moretonhampstead :

I should not trouble you at this moment but I have been in expectation of being able to obtain a Boy from the Blue School here, to send as an apprentice and which I had hoped to do by the *Velocity* to sail from this next week or the beginning of the week after. I am now, however, told that there is not a boy which can be recommended to me who has any wish to go abroad. As Philip Hutchings is coming home the now coming summer, I am sure it will be a great inconvenience to them if some assistant of this kind is not procured. I shall be much obliged if you or Mr Tricks [Benjamin's brother-in-law] would apply to the Master of the School of which C. R. Ayre was obtained to know if he can recommend us another such boy. We wish him to be bound as an apprentice for seven years for all purposes we may want him for, but he would have many advantages as he would be fitted for a Shopman or an Assistant in a mercantile office. We were very well pleased with the last boy and would prefer one from a School where the Scholars reside in the house and are not suffered out of the School to beat the streets.

Is this, perhaps, another manifestation, of Benjamin's firm adherence to strict Unitarian principles? He was always benevolently disposed towards his apprentices and in some of his letters to his sons in St John's refers to them almost paternally by their first names and he was known to send them gifts from time to time such as watches. It was his intention always, if at all possible, to choose them from 'respectable Unitarian families.

Velocity eventually sailed from Liverpool on 24 March 1835 with over 200 tons of general cargo and reached St John's some three weeks later. David Keir in *The Bowring Story* relates that 'by 13 August she was back at Liverpool, where Benjamin watched the dockers unload her cargo of cod and seal oil, sealskins, hides, blubber, hardware, bars of sheathing and 19 packages curiously labelled "Old Junk" '. So Charles had his way after all; he had made his first delivery of seal oil. With all the frustrations and worries that Benjamin experienced in getting *Velocity* ready for sea, he must have had mixed feelings about putting her up for sale some two years later, the more so because, under new ownership, she was wrecked off the Brazilian coast in August 1837.

In spite of the many and varied difficulties with which he was faced as the business took shape on both sides of the Atlantic, it seems that he managed to enjoy home and social life. In 1836 he and Charlotte had moved from their second house in Liverpool at Grove Street to larger premises on the Wirral across the River Mersey at Woodside, Birkenhead. Before leaving Grove Street he is reported to have attended a Grand Fancy Dress Ball in Liverpool attired in 'ancient Spanish dress' accompanied by Mrs Bowring who, unsurprisingly, appeared 'as a Spanish lady'.

During the mid 1830s expansion was fairly steady on both sides of the Atlantic and shipments from St John's to Liverpool continued to build up. They consisted mainly of seal and cod oils and were carried on Benjamin Bowring & Son's own two schooners *Dove* and *Eagle*. These vessels, considering the appalling weather and sea conditions they frequently had to face, and with a registered tonnage of but 91 tons, seemed, as mentioned earlier, frighteningly small.

Thanks to the expanding trade between the business in St John's and Benjamin's office in Liverpool, the firm had become one of the leading and more securely established mercantile houses in Newfoundland. Announcements were appearing regularly in the local press advertising the arrival of such varied imports, including manufactured goods from England, as tea, flour, butter in bulk, pearl barley and Westphalia hams. Growing quantities of Newfoundland produce were, at the same time, being exported on Bowring's own vessels as well as those of other shippers.

Although now permanently resident in England, Benjamin was still thought of in St John's, not without some justification, as a Newfoundland man. In 1839, after some five years absence, he had signed a petition to Parliament strongly advocating the removal of religious influences from local politics in the colony. This brought forth a lampooning reference by the editor of the *Newfoundland Patriot* who wrote:

B. BOWRING. Some fifteen years (*sic*) have elapsed since he first set foot on these shores – a decent, we believe, but a poor watchmaker; but if Benjamin was a poor man he was a knowing one, and we shall say that he proved himself a clever man, too; for from the selling of TRINKETS and PELTRIES and cleaning of old watches, he so managed to clean (honestly we mean) the pockets of his customers that he ultimately rose to the highest class of importing dried goods merchant and returned to Liverpool, leaving his shop to his sons – who will no doubt trace their father's footsteps to a hair, for at present they drive a lucrative trade and the whole 'tribe of Benjamin' are amply supported by it.

Edward, by now eighteen years of age, had been in England with his father for some eighteen months learning about the Liverpool end of the business, so the sons referred to in the satirical article that appeared in the *Patriot* were Charles Tricks, the eldest, and Henry. The youngest son,

John, was also in England attending school. The 'tribe' had been further increased two years previously by the birth of a son, William Benjamin, to Charles and Harriet.

There were two significant events in 1839, a change in the firm's designation and the purchase of a new ship. It was decided that the style of the firm in St John's should henceforth be Bowring Brothers, the name under which it operated for the next 140 years; and it was as Bowring Brothers that the order was placed for the building of the new fast-sailing brig *Margaret Jane*.

This little ship, of 103 tons, whose details have never been recorded in any shipping register, was to make many Atlantic crossings. She regularly bore cargoes of the marine products of Newfoundland to Liverpool, returning with salt for the fish-curers, chests of tea, barrels of sugar, spices, dried fruits and an assortment of ironmongery. She is reported to have carried, in 1840, four thousand Welsh slates, probably for the roof of the new Cathedral in St John's and, by a later passage some marble in unspecified form for the Bishop. The extent of the business being done by the year 1840 was such that, as well as using their own new vessel to the full, Bowring Brothers were shipping their merchandise across the Atlantic in five schooners belonging to other owners. It was in this year that *Margaret Jane* carried the firm's first major shipment to Liverpool of 2,136 sealskins, 110 casks of seal oil, which was sold for £30 per tun, and 44 cwts. of old junk. On a later voyage that year she carried 22 tons of dried codfish, this also being the first time that the firm had shipped such a cargo to Liverpool. And it was *Margaret Jane*, in the spring of 1840, that was the first of their vessels to be sent to the highly speculative seal fishery.

The extraordinary variety of cargoes carried by *Margaret Jane* and, no doubt, other vessels plying between Liverpool and St John's, can be gathered from the records regularly appearing in the Newfoundland newspapers. One such announcement lists these items available from Bowring Brothers:

> 50 half chests Souchong Tea
> Loaf Sugar in hogsheads and barrels
> 20 crates well assorted earthenware
> 250 bags Nails, Bar and Bolt Iron of Assorted sizes
> 4. M. Welch Slates
> Sheet Lead and Lead Shot
> Currents, Starch, Pepper

Together with

> A large and varied Assortment of
> MANUFACTURED GOODS

This announcement ends with the offer,

> for Freight or Charter,
> The Fast-Sailing Brig
> MARGARET JANE
> Will carry about 2,500 qtls. Fish in Bulk

Now over sixty years of age, Benjamin, through his correspondence with his sons in Newfoundland, is beginning to show occasional signs of weariness and uncharacteristic impatience. It becomes clear that he has little or no help in his Liverpool office and some small irregularity in a bill of lading causes a rather vexatious letter to Charles Tricks, dated 30 July 1840:

> I cannot tell you how much trouble even this simple incident occasioned me. I am sure it caused me to walk more than six miles yesterday in the only hot day we have had for summer, and even now I have fears whether I may not be disappointed. I must tell you I have not physical strength enough to get through all the laborious work which you throw upon me, and that without even a boy to assist me, having to attend the many difficulties of shipping goods, invoicing, writing letters, keeping the whole of your accounts here, together with many other calls upon me in every way. I am almost worn off my legs.

In the same letter he gives some idea of the minutiae of his involvement. It seems that a Mr Miflen had made a request for gingerbread, which he says he will attend to as soon as he has peeped through 'a thicket of business which lies before me'.

Another cause of irritation was a difference in interpretation of the accounts. In September 1840 Benjamin was at odds with Charles over entries in the books and wrote:

> You very coolly tell me that you hope I shall be able to agree with Henry about the false balance he has charged me with. Now it strikes me that it would have been just as well if you had looked into the account yourself . . . I strongly suspect some principle of error to a very dangerous extent has been at work in your method of book-keeping, and that you will ultimately find that your imaginary profits for the past year, although highly satisfactory, are illusory in a great degree.

He added later in the letter, pulling no punches, that the firm . . . 'cannot do without a book-keeper, and I shall be glad to hear that you have one who really knows something of the true principles of double-entry.'

While Benjamin was frequently quite demonstrative in his display of his deep affection for his sons, it is clear that, in his determination to ensure that they should not allow the heritage that he had created for them to weaken or fail, he could be stingingly direct in the delivery of his advice and instructions. The captain of any ship departing from Liverpool for St John's during the early 1840s would almost certainly be handed a letter for Charles Tricks, not only reaffirming previously issued instructions and containing fresh items of advice but also giving a lively report on the health and activities of the family in Liverpool where Edward with his father was learning about the business, prior to joining his older brothers in Newfoundland as a full partner of the firm.

It was on this subject that Benjamin wrote to Charles early in October:

> Edward has, as you will have known long before this, determined on not coming out this Fall, as he declares that he relies with confidence on your taking the stock in trade on 19 March next in every respect fairly; and as he has been of considerable service and indeed could not leave before the *Margaret Jane* went, I think he was perfectly right. I have been looking over the documents sent home by you relative to the alteration of the Firm and I find that the bond securing the third of the business to him from 19 March next, or indeed at any time, depends upon the contingency of his writing under his hand demanding and requiring to be admitted as such a partner.

Benjamin proposed that Edward should, indeed, adopt this means of securing his partnership and he further suggested, being as prudent as ever, that a duplicate of the formal application should be sent on a separate ship. He ended this rather typical no-nonsense letter on the somewhat lighter note that the two pairs of trousers that Charles had ordered were on their way!

Again, in mellower mood, Benjamin wrote in November to Henry, now twenty-six and beginning to make quite a name for himself in St John's business circles, on a topic of no commercial significance whatever:

> I cannot think what entered your head about Edward's being about to bring out a wife with him, for although I daresay if examined you would

find a score of indentations about the heart, yet I do not think any one of the them is of any depth. I do not know whether you have yet committed any overt act which will prevent *you* from entering the Society of Old Bachelors, but if you have do let me know; for although not a member myself, yet I shall take the right of proposing you if you do not make haste.

It seems that Benjamin was a little concerned that Henry had not yet found himself a wife, and would probably have been more so had he known that it would be another twenty-five years before he would get married, long after his worried father's demise.

The year 1840 had probably been the busiest and most successful in the company's history since Benjamin took up permanent residence and started the business in St John's in earnest some twenty-four years earlier. But since September the battle of the accounts had rumbled on and in his next letter on the subject Benjamin writes: 'I shall begin to think that some cloud of stupidity has fallen over you both if you do not explain yourselves'. And so the altercation went on into 1841, although he had indicated that he was partially satisfied with Henry's reasoning to the effect that the muddle was not after all disastrous. However, Charles and Henry still had some way to go if they were to calm the old man down completely. In *The Bowring Story*, David Keir writes:

> He again charged them with keeping unsatisfactory accounts protesting that he could make neither head nor tail of their explanations of the financial transfer from the original Bowring company to that of Bowring Brothers'. In a letter to Charles, Benjamin wrote, 'I find that the complicated interest calculations which the mixing up of my property with yours has caused, the anxiety about sales and shipping and receiving goods, and more especially the difficulty I have in making you understand my accounts when rendered, give more vexation than at my time of life I am disposed to, or am indeed able, to undertake. I shall therefore call upon you on 30 June next to close your accounts with me. I do not mean that after that I shall withhold my assistance either in money or advice which you may want or is in my power to give, but only that a balance shall be finally struck and your security given for such sums as may be retained by you at interest . . . You do not say how Henry's toothache is'.

From this latest letter it appears that Benjamin, now sixty-three, had his sights set on retirement and that he had, clearly in his mind, a date for handing over the business to his sons. On 4 February 1841 he wrote to Charles; 'As you are now about to start afresh, [presumably referring to his proposed retirement], if you were to adopt a different firm here than you have in Newfoundland it would make a distinction . . . Perhaps C. T. Bowring and Co. might be as well as any other.'

Meanwhile he had rendered his accounts to St John's for 1840 and had received a reply from his sons to which he replied on 18 February:

> Did you ever see an old man like myself hunting for his spectacles until he was vexed and tired, then finding them on his nose? I am not quite in such a case, but I confess I have for a long time half wished for a much better pair than I ever had to find out the riddle of the mistake which you say I had made in my account.

Charles, once again it appears, had some grievance over the appearance of certain of his father's figures on 'the wrong side of the ledger'. Benjamin's reaction was to repeat succinctly his earlier and frequently proffered advice that Bowring Brothers would do well to engage the services of an experienced book-keeper, an exhortation of which his sons were probably by now somewhat weary.

On 19 March 1841, however, there occurred an event that was likely, at least temporarily, to assuage such irritations as had arisen during the past few months. This was the day on which Edward, now twenty-one years of age, joined his two elder brothers as a partner in Bowring Brothers, notwithstanding the fact that he still resided in Liverpool. This milestone, which was the natural consequence of the change of the name of the firm to Bowring Brothers in 1839, was the manifestation of a true partnership and it encouraged Benjamin to write to his sons in words which would continue to be a source of inspiration to members of the family of succeeding generations as they became engaged in the business.

> I congratulate you all three on the new formation of the Firm of Bowring Brothers which takes place to-day, and which I most ardently hope will have every success which can be expected to result from combined industry, careful speculation and unanimous determination to forget the interest of the individual in the better interest of the whole.

Never able to exclude entirely from his mind the subject of accounts, he ends his letter: 'As I have before told you, I expect you to open books here (Liverpool) as Bowring Brothers after the 30th June next . . . Edward intends coming out on the first good vessel'.

It is becoming clear that the generation gap, which has been evident for a few years, is widening. It isn't difficult to glean from the correspondence between the sons and their father that there is, from time to time, only slightly veiled annoyance on both sides. I imagine sometimes the boys' reaction in St John's to the more critical of Benjamin's letters as ' what *is* the old man fussing about?' and on his part 'what *are* they up to; what *do* they think they are doing?'

In a letter to Henry in March, Benjamin repeated his earlier warnings about their deals in seal oil in which he felt they were trading too heavily. In a fluctuating market he was not only having difficulty in finding customers, but some of those he was able to secure defaulted on payment. 'I really do not know,' he wrote, 'where to look for safe customers here in the oil way . . . I cannot tell you how miserable these risks make me, and I can see scarcely a probability of selling for cash without ruinous sacrifices . . . The loss now sustained by you is so great that at least it ought to teach you that oil is no realization until actually in cash.'

In April, anticipating the changes that were due to take place on 30 June, he wrote to Charles Tricks in terms of undisguised acrimony 'when I shall require you to open accounts for yourselves . . . for I cannot consent any longer to manage so complicated a business as yours is now become with the certainty before me of having my accounts contested and explanations bandied about across the Atlantic from one to another at my time of life.' This letter contains yet further evidence of a rift between father and sons. Charles had apparently asked Benjamin to find out for him how he should go about installing gas lighting in Bowring Brothers' building. Benjamin, having stated that he hadn't been able to find out much about it, implied that this new-fangled invention would not only be expensive but, if installed by inexperienced colonials might prove troublesome. 'Upon the whole,' he wrote, 'I cannot but think that the scheme would never answer your purpose or come within any reasonable limits of expense, nor would the advantages be commensurate. There are, however, some newly invented lamps to burn common oil which I heard there is little or no trouble with, and which give a most brilliant light, at least equal to Gas, and even here cost about one halfpenny per hour in consumption.' Looking ahead, however, the brothers, with the same kind of initiative that distinguished their father from other settlers in the colony in earlier years, found their own way to overcome the difficulty. In 1844 Henry was one of a group of enterprising businessmen who launched the St John's Gas Light Company of which he was elected Treasurer. Such was the energy with which he played his part in bringing the new plant into operation and in making the Bowring store ready for this 'new-fangled' system of lighting, that within a year it became the first gas-lit store in St John's. Such was the general interest created that large crowds gathered in Water Street on the evening that the lamps lit for the first time.

In the meantime, however, having endured persistent troubles over the handling of seal oil and having made it clear that he did not wish to receive any further shipments, consignments continued to arrive. In a letter dated 12 April he issued a warning to Charles: 'If it should happen that I should receive any more on your account and I cannot sell for cash, I shall put it in store, insure it against fire and let it bye until I can do that, for I will not again trust them on bills.' With some regret he added, 'Perhaps you will think this is shutting the stable door after the horse has been stolen . . .' Well, maybe; but there is really no reason why Benjamin should reproach himself. The 'thicket of business' he described earlier was as impenetrable as ever and the weight of responsibility he bore might well have discouraged a younger man. Edward was on his way to join Charles and Henry in St John's and in Liverpool he had only his youngest son, John, now seventeen and probably not very experienced, to help him. The fact that he had not heard of Edward's arrival caused him anxiety and some irritation. On 3 May he wrote to Charles asking him to tell his young brother that 'unless the neglect is differently explained I think little dependence can in future be placed upon him'. However, it transpired that a letter written by Edward from St John's announcing his safe arrival was over a month late in reaching Liverpool. Meanwhile, on 20 June 1841 Charles left St John's for Liverpool in the hope of arriving in time to coincide with his father's withdrawal from active participation in the business.

Whilst Benjamin was never deeply involved in politics, National and Local Government affairs were frequently on his mind. This is apparent from a letter he wrote to Henry while he was awaiting Charles' arrival: 'We have been busy all this week', he wrote, 'in a bustle with the Borough of Liverpool, in which we poor Whigs have been most deplorably beaten, and we shall next week and the week after be as busy in the County. As soon after Charles' arrival as possible I am about to accompany Miss Charlotte (his daughter) on a tour of France, so that you may expect an account of her travels in two volumes quarto, to which on her behalf I beg leave to solicit your subscriptions.' Inevitably, as in so many of his letters, levity is tempered with sound parental advice:

I hope you and Edward will go on industriously, cautiously and steadily in the absence of your brother, and that you will be as successful as you can wish yourselves. You must recollect that your responsibilities are great, and that if anything goes wrong in consequence of your neglect, inattention or want of judgement you will have to reflect bitterly upon yourselves. Do not trust any more than you can help, and send home whatever you can realize. Above all, by some means or other let your books be kept correctly and every entry made directly and not left to memory.

It comes as no surprise that Benjamin should end this letter with a blend of his natural good humour and his affection for his sons: 'I should like to see how you two old boys get on without children about you.' (This alludes to the fact that, as Charles would now be devoting most of his time to the Liverpool end of the business, he and Harriet were taking their family with them.) 'Do make haste,' he continues, metaphorically wagging an admonishing finger at the two bachelors, 'and seek out helpmeets that your family might be better managed; but whilst one eye is searching let the other be examining, comparing and judging, so that your choices may be good ones.'

After the arrival of Charles and his family in Liverpool, the style of the business there was changed from Bowring Brothers to Charles T. Bowring and Company. It might well have been thought that, now, Benjamin could be released from the worries and the responsibility of being involved in helping to run a now rapidly expanding enterprise, the influence and reputation of which were being recognized in many parts of the world. That his sons should be showing the same enthusiasm and commercial acumen, as had encouraged him to found the business originally, must have been a source of pride and satisfaction to him.

In a letter from Woodside in September to his brother-in-law, William Tricks, Benjamin wrote:

I believe you know that Charles and his family returned here with the intention of settling in Liverpool or Woodside in order to manage the affairs of Bowring Brothers on this side of the water; and as the eruption of such a host of vandals (consisting of a man, his wife, five children and a servant) is quite enough to account for a poor fellow in such a small house as mine, being bamboozled and put out of his way, you will readily conceive that for the time they were here and before they could fit themselves into a house of their own, we were not much inclined to letter writing. So as our absence made a little more room my daughter and I set upon our travels and went by way of Southampton to Havre de Grace, upon the Seine to Paris (where we remained 13 days) and then went on to Brussels, Antwerp and home by way of Ghent, Bruges and Ostend to London ... Charles has now taken a house in Woodside not many minutes walk from our own, so that we frequently see one another. He is of course not yet thoroughly settled in, and is yet in a bustle buying furniture etc.

Notwithstanding his supposed retirement, Benjamin still kept a close watch on the fortunes of his sons in Newfoundland and his habit of writing to them regularly was unabated. In his letters to Henry, who was now in charge of the St John's business, he couldn't resist frequent repetitions of his advice on the advantages of cash sales over business done on credit. Edward was to receive similar counselling and in one of his letters he declared with feeling; 'I most sincerely wish the Bank had never been established.' But there was good news, which went some way, no doubt, to raising his spirits. The prices of cod oil and pale seal oil had improved and he wrote to Henry with this cheerful news in the hope that his letter would arrive before Christmas. In the same letter he promised to drink the health of his absent sons and said that he and his family would be thinking of Henry and Edward in their 'two old bachelorships, the one President and the other Vice, at your dining table that day. Do not forget us in your revels.'

The year 1842 started well. The good ship *Margaret Jane* carried a sizeable cargo of 2,500 quintals of cod to the Mediterranean and on her return was sent to the seal fishery in March with 34 men under the command of Captain Roche. This successful expedition resulted in a shipment to Liverpool of 3,560 packages of sealskins. This was also the first time that Bowring Brothers had shipped Newfoundland salmon – 191 tierces – to the Mersey. The volume of general trade was increasing at such a pace that the firm could not provide sufficient cargo space on its own vessels and it became necessary to charter ships from other owners for the St John's-Liverpool run. Two of these were the clipper schooners *Mantura* and *Joseph*, one of which returned to St John's with 500 hogsheads of Cheshire salt for the Newfoundland codfish industry.

Later in 1842 Benjamin felt that it would be a good idea if Charles were to make a return visit to St John's so that Henry might spend some time in Liverpool, acquainting himself with that end of the business and purchasing goods for sale in Newfoundland. He wrote to Henry in the meantime, on 4 April, a letter which goes a long way to defining his political views:

> Mr R. Peel is again about to impose upon Trade that iniquitous and inquisitorial Tax on Income which was so universally rejected by the whole Nation even under the old Tory system, whilst a tax on property, which certainly ought upon emergencies to be the first resorted to, is in a great measure rejected by our governing clique of landowners . . . I hope there is still spirit enough to convince this man of money that he cannot thus befoul the nest in which his fortune was hatched with impunity.

This succinct and gritty expression of his firmly held political stance was, no doubt, that of many contemporary merchants and shipowners trading overseas and most of them would certainly have shared his spirited advocacy of Free Trade. In this he was a staunch supporter of his famous cousin Sir John Bowring, also a passionate champion of Free Trade and closely associated with the Anti-Corn Law League. Though both born in Exeter, it is unlikely that the cousins would have met until after Benjamin's return from Newfoundland and, indeed, there was quite a difference in their ages Benjamin being the older by some fourteen years. However, Sir John was a frequent visitor to Lancashire, particularly to Liverpool, Manchester and Bolton, for which he was elected Member of Parliament in 1841, a seat which he held until 1849.

In *The Bowring Story*, David Keir writes of him,

> In the long history of the family there can hardly have been a more remarkable figure than Sir John Bowring. To look again at his family ancestry, he was the great-great-great grandson of the 17th century Sir John whose patent of nobility was allegedly eaten by hungry mice behind a wainscot. His grandfather, also called John, went into the wool trade, and at one time professed such strong sympathies for the American colonists and their cause that an Exeter mob burned his effigy in the cathedral yard. Sir John Bowring's father, Charles, was an exporter of coarse woollens to Spain and China, and it was he who purchased the Larkbeare property at Exeter from the Baring family, and erected the buildings afterwards used as the judges' lodgings there.
>
> The future Sir John, born at Exeter in 1792, showed in early life that he was a man of remarkable talents. Within four years of leaving school he mastered French, Italian, Spanish, Portuguese, German, Dutch and later added sufficient Swedish, Danish, Russian, Serbian, Polish and Bohemian to let him translate works in those languages with facility. Later still he added Magyar, Arabic and Chinese. When he became editor of the

Westminster Review he wrote not only political articles on Free Trade and kindred subjects, which Benjamin naturally applauded, but articles on the culture of Finland, the language of the Netherlands and the poetry of Hungary. He was invited by various governments to advise on their finances. In 1835 he was returned to Parliament for the Clyde Burghs, lost his seat two years later and then travelled in Egypt, Syria and Turkey on commercial visits. Having spent some time in Nubia, Aleppo, Acre and Constantinople he came back to Manchester, where he helped Cobden to form the famous Anti-Corn Law League, another of Benjamin's enthusiasms. With Benjamin's approval again, he crossed to Prussia in the hope that his free trade arguments would persuade the Prussian authorities to reduce their tariffs on English goods. On this occasion his efforts proved abortive since the Prussians not unnaturally took the view that it was fruitless to expect them to reduce their tariffs on British manufactures so long as Britain's Corn Law imposed prohibitive import duties on foreign grain. As member for Bolton, however, he continued his campaign at home, and eventually had the satisfaction of seeing the Corn Law repealed in 1846. Unfortunately his parliamentary career came to an end when the grave depression of 1847 so reduced his financial resources that he had to resign his seat and take up an appointment as British Consul at Canton. Later he was appointed plenipotentiary to China, and made Governor, Commander-in Chief, and Vice Admiral of Hong Kong and its dependences: he was also accredited to the courts of Japan, Siam, Cochin-China and Korea. It is hardly surprising that such manifold services should have been recognized by a knighthood.

On his way home from China on retirement Sir John Bowring survived shipwreck in the Red Sea and three days' exposure, on a coral reef, all without lasting effects on his remarkable vitality. Back in England he continued to pursue his enthusiasms through such organizations as the British Association and the Social Science Association. He delivered lectures, contributed to many reviews, wrote poems and hymns, and translated poetry from a variety of languages. Even shortly before his death in 1872, when he was nearly eighty, he was still in full cry addressing an audience of some 3,000 people at Plymouth.

Much more could be told about Sir John, by no means least concerning his radical views, such as were held by so many of his contemporaries, especially those involved in commerce and shipping who were striving to expand their businesses throughout the world by their vociferous and energetic support for the principles of Free Trade.

Chapter 3

IT BECAME QUITE CLEAR in the early 1840s that Benjamin's 'retirement' had become somewhat mythical. In spite of the fact that Charles Tricks was functional head of the business, his father obviously found it difficult to loosen his grip on the reins. Whilst naturally showing signs of physical fatigue on occasions, his mental energy seemed unabated and his sons could expect to be surprised from time to time by his up-to-the-minute knowledge of the firm's day-to-day activities. However, in April 1842, he probably astonished them all by announcing a new career for himself in a letter written to Henry (still at St John's) congratulating him on his birthday:

> Having performed this important duty', [the birthday message] I shall proceed to inform you of what I daresay you will be surprised to hear, that I am about to leave Woodside and turn farmer. Yea, verily my dear Henry, when you visit us in June next it is probable that you may find me in the bushes coolly calculating whether I have enough peas for my dinner, how my grass gets on and what quantity and kind of vegetables I am likely to get out of the earth. Were I romantically inclined here is a good opportunity to descant in glowing and Arcadian tones upon the beauties of a country life, especially to an old man and his wife whose years are nearly approaching the common term of humanity.

He continued in light-hearted vein, hoping that when Henry arrived in England, he would be able to give him a 'draft of buttermilk' and ended with his usual warm parting: 'Give all our best love to Edward and tell him that your Mother and Charlotte are very busy getting their milk pails and their pig buckets ready.'

However, these thoughts of a rustic, perhaps to Benjamin and Charlotte even an Elysian way of spending the later years of their lives were to come to nought. It was only a couple of months before he decided to let the property at Little Sutton, about half-way between Birkenhead and Chester, 'even at a sacrifice', having decided that what he described as his 'rural settlement' was not in fact what he wanted. In a letter to Edward, unusually replying to one from him (Edward was a notoriously bad letter-writer), Benjamin, who seldom showed signs of indecision, remarked: 'We are now very likely to rust the short remainder of our lives at Woodside.'

On Charles Tricks' arrival at St John's, where he temporarily took charge of the Bowring Brothers' store and the small but growing fleet of trading vessels, Henry set sail for Liverpool in order to become more acquainted with the firm's expanding activities there and to seek out a broader and more varied selection of goods to be sold in Newfoundland. Although he was unwell shortly after his arrival he soon recovered sufficiently to be able to visit London and several European cities. These journeys seem to have been quite successful and it was not long before newspapers in St John's were advertising a larger and more varied assortment of articles for sale by Bowring Brothers than ever before. In fact, in September 1842 no fewer than four vessels arrived with goods for the company, and for some of their associates in such out-ports as Harbour Grace. The cargoes included iron, tinplate, nails, soap, hogsheads of red wine from Sicily, Geneva from Holland and Souchong tea.

Whilst serenity and success seemed to characterize the progress of the business during the latter months of 1842, a domestic situation arose which was to cause a mild disturbance in the family. Charles Tricks wrote to his wife Harriet, who had not accompanied him on his temporary visit to St John's, asking her to pass on, confidentially, to his mother the disquieting news that Edward was playing fast and loose with an 'unsuitable local girl'. Charlotte, quite naturally, passed this on to Benjamin, who immediately wrote to Charles, first excusing himself for doing so since the information was not addressed to him, and thereafter expressing deep fatherly concern.

'A false step taken by him in a matter of such importance,' wrote Benjamin, 'may drive him ultimately from the station which has been secured for him and lead to his ruin. What indeed could result from his alliance with an ignorant and uneducated girl, who has had set before her no example of feminine worth and respectability, and with no other recommendation than the fickle fancy for a face?' He foresaw the possibility of Edward's being 'saddled with an almost pauper family' if, as he put it, this misalliance were allowed to take place. But Benjamin showed that he was concerned also for the hapless girl. 'The mere attention paid to her,' he asserts, 'is an act of cruelty and injustice on his part.' But it appears that this was not the first time that Edward's amorous pursuits had caused cardiac flutters in the family. Apparently he had been 'flirting about' with another girl in Harbour Grace and could not, in the circumstances, expect much sympathy from his family. However, the fact that he was brought back to England six months after this correspondence is not thought to have been an expression of censure.

But Benjamin's concern about Edward's past waywardness lingered. He wrote to him in early May 1843 to tell him that Henry was on his way back to Newfoundland and he added: 'I know that you are very susceptible on the score of the ladies, so I shall inform you that Emma White is about to pay us a visit, Lucy Harvey is on a visit to Charles at this present moment, and Jane's marriage to Mr Charles Willmer came off on 22 April.' In *The Bowring Story* David Keir captures the mood of the moment,

> Perhaps Benjamin knew what he was about when he so playfully dropped in his letter the name of Emma White; for it was she whom Edward, within a year, was to meet again and with whom he fell deeply in love. Within three weeks of Edward's arrival in Liverpool towards the end of June 1843, Benjamin and Charles had invited Emma White to their house. Charles, also back from St John's, obligingly arranged at the same time for Lucy Harvey, his wife Harriet's young sister, to be brought forward as well for Edward's inspection.

In a letter to Henry from Woodside, Benjamin seemed a little uncertain as to whether or not these oblique manoeuvres would be fruitful. 'I cannot yet learn that if either of them (Lucy or Emma) has made an impression on Ned's heart, which it cannot be denied is a very volatile one.' Nevertheless, in August Edward went to Moretonhampstead with both of these young ladies and his sister Charlotte. In his letter to Henry, Benjamin suggests that he should have no difficulty in guessing the purpose of the visit and continues, 'I should not wonder if he were to bring out a companion.' And he seemed to have got it right. By November Benjamin was telling Henry that Edward seemed to be 'desperately deep in his attentions and,' he added, 'I hope in love.' Edward eventually abandoned his bachelorhood and married Emma White in 1844. After their marriage they departed for Newfoundland aboard the new Bowring schooner *Harriet*, arriving at St John's on 10 June. (*Harriet* was the first Bowring vessel to be constructed at a British yard and was reserved for transatlantic trading. She never went to the seal fishery; more will be heard of her.)

While affairs of the heart were occupying the minds of some members of the family some of the time, the business was far from being neglected and, indeed, considerable progress was being made in all aspects of trading. The brig *Margaret Jane* was still making rapid crossings between Liverpool and St John's as well as attending the seal fishery. But the increasing volume of trade still made it necessary to charter in additional tonnage from other owners.

Benjamin continued to withhold his support for entering the seal fishery as full participants, but Charles, Edward and Henry held the unanimous view that to become totally involved, notwithstanding the occasionally unpredictable nature of the business, would in general be to the firm's advantage. To do so, however, would require more ships; there had been no additions to the fleet since the *Margaret Jane* was acquired in 1839. The determination of the brothers to become engaged in a trade which, unlike today, had few opponents, drove them to ordering a new vessel, a 125-ton brig named *Symmetry*, which they had built for them on Prince Edward Island in 1842. Before being used in the seal hunt, this was the ship on which Charles returned to Liverpool in 1843 after spending a year in St John's. By the year 1845 the time had come for Benjamin's youngest son, John, now twenty-one, to follow in the footsteps of his brothers and leave for Newfoundland. He was by now well acquainted with the business carried on in the Liverpool Office, having received his training there at the hands of his father Benjamin and his brother Charles.

Benjamin's health was beginning to fail and his family were deeply concerned. The years 1845–6 were troublesome enough for Liverpool where housing and employment problems were aggravated by the arrival of Irish immigrants during and following the potato famine, and conditions became further unsettled as Anti-Corn Law agitation increased. On 1 March 1844 Benjamin, who had moved into a house in Clarence Terrace, Everton, wrote to Henry a letter which must have lowered the brothers' spirits. It had been quite clear to them for some time that his zest and vigour were in decline as the letter all too clearly shows:

> I told you in my last letter that I thought I had got rid of my doctor. I am sorry to say I was obliged to send for him again about ten days since, my speech being almost taken from me and my strength much impaired. I think all these attacks must end fatally, and although I pick up again a little occasionally and improve a little, yet I have no confidence in their continuance.

Although Benjamin lived for a further twenty-seven months, this was the last of his letters to survive. It seems as though he had probably suffered a stroke and he died on 1 June 1846. He was buried at the Protestant cemetery at Liverpool, known as the Necropolis, which has since vanished. However, before it was covered up to make way for housing, the tombstones were recorded and the legends preserved. His wife, Charlotte, survived him by nearly four and a half years and shared his grave over which the tombstone bore the simple legend:

IN MEMORY OF
BENJAMIN BOWRING of LIVERPOOL
Who died June 1st, 1846, aged 68 years,
Also CHARLOTTE BOWRING, relict of the above
Died October 30th, 1850, aged 69 years.

Benjamin died just eight days before one of the worst fires ever experienced in St John's. Thirteen years had elapsed since the previous very serious fire of 1833, in which Benjamin Bowring & Son lost practically everything when their premises were engulfed in the flames. At that time Benjamin was in two minds as to whether or not he would abandon the business, but his courage and determination prevailed and the recovery that followed ensured that he would continue to pursue his destiny. There had been two further fires in 1839 and 1840, neither of which was sufficiently widespread to endanger the business seriously.

It was on the morning of 9 June 1846 that this latest devastating and all engulfing blaze broke out. It was caused when a pot of glue boiled over in the workshop of Mr Hamlin, a cabinet maker, setting alight the upper storey of his premises on the west side of the town. The extent of the conflagration can be judged from extracts of a letter which arrived in Glasgow on 18 June, brought by the schooner *Gazelle*:

> . . . in a short time (the fire) spread in all directions with frightful rapidity. It soon embraced both sides of Queen Street and came raging towards Water Street in a fiery torrent. It now became apparent, from the increased force of the fire and wind, that nothing could save Water Street, the fire engines not having the least effect . . . The scenes as now witnessed from the water were awfully terrific – masses of fire ascending high in the air, then stretching forth and seizing everything within its reach, but still unshackled, rushing on with destructive energy.

There had been a very long period without rain and the wooden buildings, especially, were tinder dry. The flying sparks quickly touched them off. But buildings of stone were not to be spared either as the blaze increased and the flames drove fiercely on. Whilst there was some hope that a group of stone buildings in Water Street might have halted the fire's progress, burning debris reached large vats of seal oil, close to these buildings, which instantly burst into flames, further aggravating an already hopeless situation. The wind, which had blown steadily from the west, increased in strength as the day wore on until it reached almost gale force, and this brought to an end any hope of saving the rest of the city. In spite of the gallant efforts of artillerymen from the local garrison who attempted, by blowing up a building, to create a fire-break, the major part of St John's was destroyed from end to end. All that the now homeless inhabitants could do was to try and rescue some of their possessions with which they huddled, throughout the night, surrounded by wreckage and desolation.

Accurate assessments of the extent of the damage are hard to come by. One report estimated that between 1,500 and 2,000 houses were completely destroyed and that the number of the population rendered homeless was of the order of 7,000, mostly women and children since the majority of the males were absent at the fishing grounds. In spite of an immediate grant from the British Government and other relief funds raised through public subscription, hundreds of people were to remain homeless throughout the following winter. To make matters worse, a very severe storm of wind and rain hit St John's in September, reckoned by some to have been the worst the city had ever experienced. It wrecked much of the rebuilding work that followed the fire, washed away three bridges and blew down many of the new houses and temporary stores that had been completed.

While Benjamin's sons were counting their losses and endeavouring to assess the extent of the damage suffered by the business, news reached them of Benjamin's death, a devastating blow to their already shattered expectations. If there could have been any good to come of this accumulation of misery it would surely have been the fact that Benjamin, in his poor state of health, was spared the dreadful news that the business which he founded and which he struggled so hard to build up, might well have been ruined by that 'destructive Element' to which he so graphically referred in his letter to his agent in Liverpool after the 1833 fire, and with the potential dangers and prevention of which he was always so deeply concerned.

Notwithstanding the profound sense of loss felt by Benjamin's sons they, with their inherited resilience and determination, set about picking

up the pieces and getting themselves back into business with as little delay
as possible. By 30 June the following notice was appearing in the local
newspapers:

THE SUBSCRIBERS

HAVING now nearly completed their temporary premises (opposite those
of Mr Clift) beg to inform the public that they intend opening the above
on WEDNESDAY next, when they will be able to offer the Goods saved
from the late Fire at their usual low prices.

Also

Just arrived per mail from Liverpool a large and var Assortment of
MUSLIN, BALZARIN, RIBBONS, etc. for the present season.

BOWRING BROTHERS

It was, no doubt, that indomitable spirit which spurred Benjamin on
through so many disappointments and disasters to persevere with building
up his business, that also inspired his sons to soldier on with tenacity and
confidence. In *The Bowring Story*, David Keir honours Benjamin so
appropriately:

> So Benjamin's voice which, through his letters, can be heard so clearly . . .
> was stilled at last. He had identified himself with the firm to the last. For
> several years after effective control had passed to his sons he remained a
> positive influence over the management of its affairs. But this could hardly
> have been otherwise, for Benjamin was a man of rare spirit, a typical
> English merchant of his time: adventurous, thrifty, indomitable, and
> endowed with admirable judgement. He never accepted the establishment
> of his times, nor sought to become part of it. He voted Whig and
> worshipped Unitarian . . . Benjamin's true memorial is neither a covered-
> up churchyard nor a commemorative plaque. It lies, rather, in the whole
> fabric of integrity and sound business that grew from the foundations he
> laid, and the principles that he laid down in that memorable letter of 19
> March 1841 when he wished his sons '*every success that can be expected to
> result from combined industry, careful speculation and unanimous determination to
> forget the interest of the individual in the better interest of the whole*'.

Now that all four of Benjamin's sons were working together in the
business – Henry, Edward and John in St John's, and Charles Tricks in
Liverpool – it is perhaps appropriate to take a broader view of the
company's activities as they expanded after the recovery from the
dreadful havoc wrought by the fire of June 1846. Perhaps the most
significant development was the full-scale entry into the seal fishery,

about which some reference has been made earlier. Although Bowring Brothers were hitherto involved to the extent of organizing and equipping ships of other owners to participate in the annual seal hunt, and playing a considerable part in marketing the catch, they had not yet sent their own vessels and crews to the ice. As we know, Benjamin was always strongly opposed to full involvement, otherwise entry might have been earlier; but, the main reason for not yet having taken part was probably the company's lack of suitable ships. Had they been in a position to do so the firm would almost certainly have become fully involved earlier.

European settlers on the northeast coast of Newfoundland had become familiar with and interested in the North Atlantic Harp Seal in the early 18th century. Unlike the indigenous inhabitants, particularly the Beothuks (the island's then declining aboriginal Red Indian tribe) whose interest in seals was to provide them with food, clothing, housing, heating and light, the settlers saw the seal as an important object of trade.

Harp seals, so called because of the shape of the large black patch on the back of the adult males (sometimes described as being horse-shoe shaped), have always been the type of seal to attract commercial interest because they are gregarious and can be found in large communities, which makes them easier to catch than other species which tend to be more dispersed, generally travelling in small family groups. Settlers from England, when they started to winter on the northeast coast of the island, were quick to recognize the potential commercial value of the harps. Having spent the summer in the high Arctic, the seals migrate south in great herds to the coasts of Labrador and Newfoundland where they feed for several months. In February they climb onto the drifting ice where the females have their pups and where they remain nursing their young for a few weeks. It is usual for each female to have just one pup; twins are rare.

In the earliest days of commercial sealing the catch, mainly of adult seals, was caught from the shore. There were three ways in which this was carried out. The method most frequently adopted was to intercept the seals by the use of nets in narrow passages or off headlands, wherever they passed close by the shore. Secondly, if the wind blew the ice floes close inland, it was possible to walk out to the catch. The third method was to hunt the seals in small boats without venturing too far from the shore.

The first of the sailing vessels to enter the seal hunt set out from St John's in 1793 after which, at the beginning of the 19th century, large fleets of schooners, frequently over 100 of them carrying anything up to 4,000 men between them, would leave for the ice. These were small vessels of about 45 tons pioneering, with their intrepid crews, an industry which was to last nearly 200 years. Building these boats, as the seal fishery grew in importance, became a significant local industry and it wasn't until the middle of the century, when the size of the boats increased to around 100 tons, that the major participants in the hunt decided to have them built beyond the island's shores, in the Maritime provinces, probably because of the of the lower costs prevailing there.

Notwithstanding the increasing size of the schooners, the perils of the seal fishery could be overwhelming. During the period when the hunt was on, the treacherous weather and navigational hazards of the North Atlantic could be particularly severe. The combination of gales, snow and hail could reduce visibility to nil. Formations of splintered moving ice, fog and mist, which would freeze on the rigging and running gear, and the general instability of the weather all contributed to the awesome dangers encountered by the brave crews of these small vessels. Perhaps the greatest of the perils faced by them arose when they had to jump on to the ice, in freezing temperatures, sometimes in the face of gales or blizzards, and encumbered by gaffs, skinning knives and ropes, in order to pursue their quarry, which would be reached by leaping from one ice floe to another. Once they had killed a seal by a blow to the head with the spiked gaff, the skin and fat were removed from the carcase and dragged to the ship to be carefully stowed. The plump little whitecoats were the most sought after catch, because their oil was more highly valued and they were easier to kill. Adult seals were usually shot since it was difficult to get near enough to them to club them and, in any case their skulls were too hard to be crushed by a blow from a gaff.

A successful sealing season could bring handsome rewards to owners and crews and the latter could expect extra bonuses depending on the size of the catch. It should be mentioned, however, that there were also unsuccessful seasons when schooners returned with empty holds or sometimes failed to return at all and lives were lost. Nevertheless, between the 1820s and the 1840s the industry prospered. In 1820 the exports of sealskins amounted to 213,679, but by the late 1830s the numbers were nearer 400,000 and in 1840, a good year, which certainly played an important part in influencing Bowring Brothers to become fully involved, more than 600,000 sealskins were shipped abroad. The value of seal products exported during the early 1840s represented about a quarter of Newfoundland's total exports and in the 1850s the figure was nearer one third. Towards the end of the 1850s no less than 14,000 men aboard nearly 400 vessels were taking part in the seal fishery. This meant that 11 per cent of the male population of the colony was away from their homes between early March and the end of April experiencing extreme discomfort and considerable danger. Living conditions aboard some of the sealing vessels were atrocious. The schooners carried 40 to 50 men each, their quarters having been described as 'filthy, often saturated in oil, and crew and skipper live and lie together in a narrow dark cabin of the smallest possible dimensions, and the fewest possible conveniences'.

Problems arose in the industry during the first half of the 1850s. In the previous twenty years serious inroads had been made into the size of the harp seal herds and, as a result, the size of catches declined. In spite of the fact that prevailing values for seal products remained buoyant, financial returns diminished. In these circumstances Bowring Brothers, heeding the advice of the founder concerning the risks of the seal trade, decided in the late 1840s and early 1850s to reduce the number of ships sent to the ice and to concentrate more on building up a fleet of tramp vessels which in due course would be seen on many oceans trading under the Bowring red cross house flag. (In 1855 the International Flag Code came into general use having been introduced by the British Board of Trade. It seems that Bowring Brothers, when they decided on a red diagonal cross on a white background as their house flag, were unaware of its significance; it means 'I am in distress and in need of help'!) In 1855 there was a change of mind. In that year, although their determination to increase the size of their merchant fleet was in no way impaired, the firm sent six ships (presumably chartered) and 270 men to the seal fishery, no doubt encouraged by the fact that, the previous year, larger catches than anyone could remember were landed. Bowring Brothers' attendance at the annual seal fishery would continue for many years. But, in the second half of the nineteenth century, the firm was beginning to branch out in many directions and was developing varied trading activities in other parts of the world.

The staple contributor to the Newfoundland economy was, and had been since the colony was founded, the cod fishery. In the earlier years the main markets for cod and cod liver oil were Canada and the United States, but during the 19th century the demand spread to the Mediterranean, various South American countries, notably Brazil, and to the

British West Indies. It has been suggested that part of the reason for these areas becoming interested in importing salt cod was religious in origin; there was a need for ample supplies of fish at any time of year to meet the disciplines of fast days and the demand invariably increased before and during Lent. Whatever the reason, or indeed the season, the Newfoundland merchants found that they could rely on a steady demand. In return for their purchases of cod the customers would ship cargoes of their own countries' produce such as wine, coffee, fruit, and the salt required to cure and preserve the fish of which they would be taking further supplies in due course. In Portugal the popular dish called *baccalao* is made from salt cod. After deliveries from Newfoundland of the vital ingredient, the ships would often return with a cargo of casks of port, which acted as useful ballast for the return voyage. It seems that the time spent in a hold, in cask, at the bottom of the vessel during the crossing of the Atlantic had such a beneficial effect on the wine that, when it was allowed to mature in cellars in St John's, it did so to such good effect that it became well known to connoisseurs for its outstanding quality.

In his book, *Fish Out of Water*, Shannon Ryan, gives a helpful description of the manner in which dealings between the merchants and the fishermen were conducted at the time when Bowring Brothers were becoming more deeply involved in the trade. 'In purely organizational terms' he writes, 'the production of codfish for export was (also) relatively straightforward ... The merchants generally supplied the fishermen in advance for the summer fishery and received the fishermen's complete catch in the autumn. Ideally, the catch was sufficient to pay off the debt to the merchant and also pay for the fishermen's winter supplies.' That sounds straightforward enough, but later in his excellent treatise Shannon Ryan writes:

> The fishermen caught and cured their fish according to their own expertise and inclinations, and the finished product was a combination of qualities and sizes. In the autumn, the merchant fixed the price of the fishermen's catch, deducted the sum owed, and gave winter supplies for the balance. Often there was very little balance and sometimes merchants were forced to advance further credit – if only to prevent the fishermen from starving or emigrating.

In the worst cases, during times of depression, which bedevilled Newfoundland from time to time, fishermen did, indeed, emigrate and some merchants went bankrupt.

During these middle years of the 19th century, when Henry, Edward and John were struggling to make a success of the business, they, along with other merchants, had to face the fact that the colony had very little opportunity to diversify. In 1841, as Shannon Ryan quotes in *Fish Out of Water*, the St John's Chamber of Commerce wrote:

> The resources of Newfoundland are entirely external, and consist alone in her fisheries; she is dependent for almost everything upon foreign importation; nearly all her provisions, both salted and fresh are imported. The great exertions which of late years have been made to introduce agriculture have succeeded in extending it no farther than to the immediate neighbourhood of the fishing settlements, from whence offal fish can be carried for manure; the growth of grain, except oats in small quantities, which when grown are for the most part cut down for fodder, is almost unknown among us; and even of potatoes, the only article of human subsistence produced in any quantity, we are forced to depend for large supplies upon England, Ireland, Scotland and the neighbouring colonies . . .

It is against this rather unpromising background that Bowring Brothers sought to expand their business and to concentrate on increasing the size of their fleet of ships, and, whilst continuing to participate in the cod fishery, in their capacity as merchants in the manner described above, to broaden their general trading activities. During the ten years from 1850 to 1860 fifteen new ships, ranging in size between 124 and 544 tons, were added to the fleet, some of them, for the first time, being of iron construction. All of them were built in England, the work being shared between a number of different yards including Lumley Kennedy & Co. of Whitehaven, John Cox & Son and Elias Cox of Bridport, Stothart & Fripp of Bristol, Cato Miller & Co. of Liverpool and others.

Earlier sailing vessels, *Margaret Jane*, built in 1839 and *Symmetry*, 1842, were colonial built brigs of 103 and 125 tons respectively. They were followed by the first vessel to be built in England, the schooner *Harriet*, 124 tons, named after Charles Tricks' wife. She was launched at Shoreham in 1843 and cost £2,279. She served the company until 1860 when she was sold to Hodges & Co. of St Ives. As mentioned earlier, she remained with Bowring Brothers on the transatlantic run as a cargo and passenger vessel, recording some rapid passages. *Harriet* survived until 1879 when she was wrecked in September of that year at the River Volta. Also launched at Shoreham in 1849 was *Emma*, 207 tons, named after Edward's wife. To coincide with the imminent growth of their fleet, the company, having subscribed for the first time to Lloyd's Register listed, as their current fleet, the names of five vessels – *Titania, Emma, Kyanite* and *Symmetry*, all brigs, and the schooner *Harriet*. It will be recalled that Benjamin named his first little schooner, *Charlotte*, after his wife and subsequently, the names of Charles's and Edward's wives were used. But the number of Bowring wives was not increasing at the same rate as that of ships being launched. So a new nomenclature was sought. This resulted in a large majority of Shakespearian names being adopted and used for well over a century. The first was *Titania*, 221 tons, followed by *Oberon*, 279 tons, *Prospero*, 289 tons and *Miranda*, 314 tons, all barques; *Hermione*, 426 tons and *Imogene*, 387 tons, were the first of the firm's iron ships, the latter being sunk in a collision after only one year twenty miles off Holyhead while on passage to Pernambuco. These were followed by *Prospero* (II), 309 tons, *Imogene* (II), 312 tons, *Cymbeline*, 220 tons, *Trinculo*, 310 tons, *Romeo*, 403 tons and, to revive a family name, a second *Harriet*, 186 tons. There was also the somewhat incongruously named *Fanny Bloomer*, 142 tons, owned by Edward Bowring. One wonders whether there might perhaps have been some nostalgic connection with the 'unsuitable local girl', object of his youthful flirtations. No explanation for choosing the name *Symmetry* can be found, but the rather unattractively named *Kyanite* owes her identity, for obscure reasons, to a certain J. H. Kyan who, it appears, achieved distinction by inventing a product to preserve wood from dry rot. During the second half of the century cargoes for South America were usually carried in larger ships of around 1,000 tons, whereas trade with Europe called for the smaller vessels such as those currently being built for Bowring Brothers. For their shipments of fish to Brazil, however, they would charter the larger ships, as also would other St John's merchants such as Job Brothers, James Baird and Baine & Johnson. These early Bowring ships all carried apprentices, who remained with the company for five years and whose rates of pay ranged from 9 shillings per month for the first year to a princely 22 shillings and fourpence at the end of their apprenticeship.

In 1847 the Liverpool office was moved to No. 8 Chapel Walks and in the same year Charles Tricks moved from his Birkenhead home to Oakleigh, West Derby Road, at that time a residential suburb of Liverpool. In his book, *Benjamin Bowring and His Descendants*, Arthur Wardle notes that on 17 October 1849, the secretary of the Liverpool &

London & Globe Insurance Company reported to his directors that 'he had seen Mr Bowring, who was willing to undertake the Agency for his House in Newfoundland.' This date is significant; it is the first time that we have any knowledge of the company becoming involved in the Insurance business. One wonders whether Charles could have had even the slightest notion, much concerned as no doubt he was with the conduct of the growing enterprise on both sides of the Atlantic, that Insurance would eventually eclipse all the Company's other activities. It is apparent, however, that Insurance was an aspect of business in which he had become personally interested. He began marine underwriting on his own account in the 1850s.

Benjamin's widow, Charlotte, died on 30 October 1850 at her home in Richmond Terrace, Everton. She had been a most active and supportive wife, not only in playing a significant part in the development of the Company, but as a constant supporter of charities in Liverpool, Newfoundland and Exeter. There is no doubt that, in the early days in St John's, Charlotte, by recognizing the needs of Newfoundlanders, contributed to the growth of the business by helping Benjamin to broaden the scope of his trading beyond being a clockmaker and silversmith, of which little is heard after their first few years in the colony. Benjamin's own description of their marriage as a 'happy joint pilgrimage' seems to be a wholly sincere and appropriate sentiment.

The later 1850s and early 1860s turned out to be something of a mixture of good news and bad, of some successes and some failures. As well as being a decade in which the firm built more ships than in any similar period previously, incurring considerable capital expenditure, there were also the losses of *Prospero* in 1854 and *Imogene* and *Emma* in 1856. The loss of *Emma* was particularly inauspicious. She was thirty days out of Liverpool with a cargo of salt from the Cheshire salt mines destined for the Newfoundland cod fishery and was within ten miles of St John's when, in heavy seas, she became unmanageable and ran aground near Flat Rock. There she became a total wreck. In *The Bowring Story*, David Keir describes the dramatic circumstances of the crew's rescue:

> To try and save his fellows, a brave Italian cook, who had probably signed on at Leghorn or some Italian port of call, jumped overboard among the rocks and lost his life trying to get a line ashore. Captain White and his crew, however, got on to a ledge on a cliff face where in the darkness for

many hours they kept up a barrage of shouts for help. These providentially attracted a dog who heard the shouting on his prowls, and was intelligent enough to run from the cliff edge to his master's house some distance away. Having wakened his master, a fisherman, and his two sons, by barking loudly and scratching at the door, he led them to the top of the cliff where he had heard the voices. There they lowered a rope and the seamen were duly drawn up the cliff face to safety.

To give an example of the extent to which the business was now growing, it is recorded that in the year 1857 no fewer than 28 ships, 16 of them Bowring owned and others on charter to the firm, sailed out of Liverpool, destined ultimately for St John's, but in some cases, no doubt calling at other ports en route as the rapidly widening trading pattern would now demand. In the following year the new *Trinculo* (II) was completed for trading between Liverpool and Brazil and there was a marked increase in the amount of insurance business transacted as a result of the firm's representation in Newfoundland of the Liverpool & London & Globe Insurance Company which had been assumed some years earlier. Two new ships were added to the fleet, the wooden barque *Imogene* (II), built at Bridport and the iron brig, *Cymbeline*, built at Chester; and Bowring Brothers were appointed agents for the North Atlantic Steam Navigation Company whose two powerful iron screw steamers ran a regular service between Liverpool, St John's, Halifax and Portland. Finally, by way of assuring continuity, John Bowring's two eldest sons, Frederick Charles (later Sir Frederick) and Edgar Rennie (later Sir Edgar) were born in 1857 and 1858 respectively.

It was also in 1857 that Charles Tricks, who had not hitherto shown any particular interest in public affairs, decided to stand as the Liberal candidate to represent the St Peter's Ward on the Liverpool Town Council. He was, by now, well known in the city's commercial circles, but his political interests were not widely recognized. Nevertheless, although the ward was a Tory stronghold and the retiring councillor, Harmood Banner, a forceful and extremely popular representative of the Conservative Party, Charles Tricks fought his corner with such vigour and conviction, against extremely long odds and contrary expectations, that he secured the seat by a majority of twenty-one votes. Though not believed to have been a particularly fluent orator, his energy, foresight, financial wisdom and absolute integrity ensured that he would hold the seat until almost the end of his life.

In 1860 Charles Tricks established a line of vessels plying regularly between Liverpool and Rio de Janeiro and Bowring ships became quite celebrated for the speed with which they were able to complete this journey. The company's *Imogene* was known to have made the 4,000-mile voyage in thirty-three days. This for a sailing vessel of the time was considered to be good going. In this year Charles Tricks became a director of the Liverpool Chamber of Commerce. He also decided that his eldest son William, now in St John's, should go to New York in order to establish a United States branch of the company.

Now that a new generation is beginning to assume responsible positions in the company, it might be helpful to take a look at how the size of the family was increasing alongside the development of the business. Charles Tricks and Harriet had ten children, four boys and six girls. Of these, seven were to contribute to the business, either directly in the case of the boys, William Benjamin, Charles, Henry and George Edward, all of whom made significant contributions to the company's progress or, where the girls were concerned, Charlotte Susan, Harriet Jane and Edith by marrying husbands who either joined the company themselves or whose sons did in due course. Henry Price's son did not work for the company, but his grandson did; of Edward's family of four, one son and two daughters were involved either directly or indirectly, and John's family of eleven children (eight boys and three girls) provided three sons and one daughter, Charlotte Rennie, whose son and grandsons joined the business.

William Bowring arrived in New York towards the end of 1860, but his efforts to establish a branch of the parent company were frustrated by the outbreak of the American Civil War and it wasn't until 1862 that he was able to blazon the nameplate of Bowring and Archibald on the door at 29 Broadway. The name of the enterprise derives from the partnership he formed with Brenton Archibald, the son of Sir Edward Archibald, then Consul General in New York. Sir Edward and Benjamin had been close friends some thirty years earlier at the time when he was appointed the first Clerk of the Assembly in Newfoundland's Bow-wow Parliament. (This odd name for the island's first House of Assembly owes its origins to a drawing by John Doyle who depicted its members as a pack of unruly dogs.)

Once established, the New York branch soon began trading. Its main activity was to purchase various commodities for shipment to Liverpool and St John's. These included wheat, flour, beef, and pork and beans.

Soon the business was to expand in other directions. Bowring and Archibald were appointed Lloyd's Agents at New York; they became managers of a Bowring shipping service, recently started between New York, Halifax and Newfoundland, and they began shipping petroleum products, an activity which in due course would give rise to much wider involvement in this very young but rapidly growing trade.

William Benjamin, clearly of a resourceful nature, would not let the postponement of his plans to open his New York office interfere with other pressing thoughts he had in mind. He hastened to St John's in 1861 where he married Miss Isabel McLean Jarvis. In the following year Charlotte, eldest daughter of Charles Tricks, married Laurence Stoddart, who was one of the partners of the Liverpool firm of shipowners and brokers, Stoddart Brothers. A number of their family of later generations would, as we shall see, pursue distinguished careers with Bowring companies of the future.

But the year 1861 will be remembered also for less agreeable events. In Newfoundland there had been two years of poor results from the cod fishery, the island's main economic prop. This understandably led to uncertainties and dissension throughout the colony, especially since it followed a period of relative prosperity. In his book *The Bowring Story*, David Keir writes of this setback: 'There was conflict between Protestant and Catholic, merchant and fisherman, Governor and Government; the local newspapers, editorially, were at each others throats; and the political scene became so volatile that there were even serious disturbances between rival Catholic candidates during the election. And in many parts of the island there was looting and destruction of property.'

It was inevitable that sooner or later the bickering and lawlessness would lead to political troubles. In the early spring the Liberal Premier, John Kent, accused the Governor, Sir Archibald Bannerman, of plotting with the Opposition to throw out a Government Bill. The Premier refused to withdraw the charge, whereupon the Governor dismissed the Government, having dissolved the House of Assembly, and asked the Opposition to form a new executive.

During the general election that followed, a fierce row broke out as a result of two rival Catholic candidates at Harbour Main claiming the seat. When both factions accused their opponents of intimidating the returning officer, riots broke out during which one man was killed and several others were injured. Rioting continued up to, during and after the inauguration of the new House by the Governor, who was jeered by angry crowds. The Colonial Building, which housed the Assembly, was besieged by an unruly mob which tried to break in.

Although civil disorder on the scale of the inauguration-day riots was not repeated, conditions in St John's continued to be very unsettled and frayed tempers tended to be aggravated during an exceptionally hot July. Some thirty-four years later the Newfoundland historian D. W. Prowse observed:

> Out of evil sometimes comes good; the direct result of all this rioting and violence, all this storm of violent partisanship and sectarian strife, was to put an end for ever to religious ascendancy on both sides. After a short respite, it became the settled rule in the formation of our Government that all religious parties should be fairly represented in the arrangement of an administration and in the distribution of offices. As a direct result, sectarianism in politics, bigotry, and intolerance, have year by year diminished.

After the relative prosperity of the late 1850s, Bowring Brothers' fortunes were to suffer to some extent following the disturbances of the early 1860s. The island was more than ever dependent on the cod and seal fisheries, each as unpredictable as its weather. Whilst the business remained active, profitability was elusive, notwithstanding the energetic marketing of the imported needs of Newfoundlanders. It seems that, unless you were inured to a diet of salt-cod and seal flipper pie, practically everything needed to keep body and soul together had to be imported. Cargoes of beef, butter, tea, salt, sugar, even bread, to say nothing of rum and brandy, and quantities of cotton and other materials, leather (a little surprising, perhaps, since the seal and the caribou could presumably have provided this), and hardware, were arriving regularly after a transatlantic crossing that could take anything up to forty days or more. Losses at sea were frequent. Most of these cargoes were still carried in sailing vessels, the steamship still being a rarity. Navigation aids were primitive compared with those of today and negotiation of the Newfoundland coastline and the prevalence of pack-ice and icebergs rendered these voyages exceptionally hazardous. The plight of the Irish brigantine *Perseverance* and her crew as related by David Keir emphasizes these dangers:

> This little 195-ton ship – small by modern standards even for coastal shipping – sailed from Hamburg for St John's early in 1861 with a large consignment of ship's biscuits for Bowring Brothers. Thirty-five days and

about 3,000 miles out of Hamburg, with only another two days' sailing ahead (or so it seemed), *Perseverance* ran into heavy pack-ice, split in two within a few minutes and began to sink. The crew of ten managed to get clear in an open boat, but had no time to stock it adequately with food and fresh water. They had, however, thrown on board a few bags of ship's biscuits and some meat: enough, as they thought, to make short rations for ten days at most. Their drinking water came from the ice around them.

The ship had struck on Tuesday 9 April. On Friday the first man died. A week later three more of the crew succumbed to hunger and exposure, by which time the remaining men had barely the strength to throw the bodies of their dead shipmates overboard. Nor had they the strength to live. At the end of another week only *Perseverance's* master, Captain Wilson, was alive when a passing ship sighted the boat and came to the rescue.

By this time Wilson, who was to make a remarkable recovery ashore, had been afloat in near-arctic conditions for 18 days. Beside him lay two dead members of his crew. He had tasted not a single morsel of food for almost a week. How many times he must have recalled, with a feeling of gnawing frustration, the bags of ship's biscuits in his cargo intended for Bowring Brothers. But undoubtedly his worst moments were those when he had seen other ships pass by, always out of hailing distance and too far away to catch sight of his small boat in the ocean swell. He had also suffered not only the agony of watching his entire crew dying before his eyes but the horror of some of them being driven insane by pain and privation before they died.

There were many such wrecks off the Newfoundland coast in those days and in 1864 the British Government sought an official report concerning the losses incurred between 1861 and 1863. Deeply depressing though these losses at sea must surely have been it was the partial and sometimes total failure of the cod fishery and the uncertainties of the seal hunt which were to bring eight years of hardship and anguish to the island.

But it was not only Newfoundland that was suffering. At Liverpool and, indeed, in much of Lancashire, the outbreak of the American Civil War created widespread economic recession. The abrupt stop to the imports of cotton plunged the Lancashire mills into idleness and, as a result, thousands of workers found themselves unemployed. Charles Tricks Bowring was among the Liverpool City Fathers who organized a relief fund which raised almost £100,000 to help those who had lost their jobs and for whom there was little if any alternative employment. For C. T. Bowring and Co. the effect of these conditions was less

Exeter in the early 19th Century

*Mrs Benjamin Bowring (née Charlotte Price of Wiveliscombe, Somerset).
No picture of Benjamin has ever been traced*

*One of Benjamin Bowring's clocks from the days in the early 1800s before he emigrated
to Newfoundland, when he was a jeweller and clockmaker in Exeter*

St John's town and harbour, Newfoundland, July 1831

Water Street, St John's looking west, in 1837

A model of the schooner Charlotte, *Benjamin Bowring's first ship*

Charles Tricks Bowring

Desdemona – *iron ship, built at Liverpool in 1875*

Bowring Brothers' Waterside premises at St John's

Charles Tricks Bowring and his family, on the 50th anniversary of his marriage to Harriet Harvey of Moretonhampstead, Devon, 13 April 1883

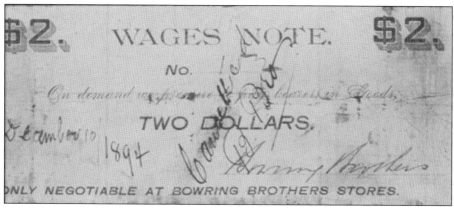

Monetary note issued by Bowring Brothers when the Newfoundland banks closed in 1894. It was acceptable throughout the country

St John's, Newfoundland. The wooden town was repeatedly destroyed by fire in the 19th Century. This picture shows the devastation in 1892

damaging than for those businesses directly affected by the lack of cotton imports; the cotton merchants and manufacturers were, of course, extremely badly affected. The fact that C. T. Bowring had in recent years concentrated on building up its shipping interests helped to broaden the scope of its trading worldwide and the construction of yet more new ships was planned. The privations caused by the war in America, though not entirely without their impact, did not by any means cause Bowring's growing enterprise seriously to falter. It might even be said that concentration on building up the shipping activities on both sides of the Atlantic was the start of what was to become a new expansive era in the fortunes of the company and a diminution in its dependence hitherto on the capricious nature of the cod fishery and the seal hunt.

Because of the partial failure of the cod fishery in 1860, an indifferent result in 1861 and what has been described as 'almost complete failure' in 1862, the people of Newfoundland were reduced to extreme poverty and these conditions were not to improve until the end of the decade. There was substantial emigration to Canada and the United States in the meantime. And the seal hunt fared no better.

In the spring of 1862, a persistent northeast wind drove huge floes of ice on to the coast of the island. The sealing vessels were unable to leave port and for the shipowners this spelt absolute disaster. To the inshore fishermen along the coast, however, this was a benign happening. At Green Bay, for instance, thousands of seals congregated on the massive rafts of ice where they were clubbed and skinned for days on end to the financial benefit of the inhabitants.

But, alas, this could only be seen as a local bonanza and was to the benefit of but a very small number of people. For the next two years misfortune continued to overshadow the seal fishery. R. B. McCrea in *Lost Amid the Fogs* (published in London, 1869) gives an account of the disaster suffered by the St John's sealing fleet in the spring of 1864:

> Four-five-six long weeks passed by, and not a vestige of news reached the trembling city from the north. It was sickening to behold the anxious, long-drawn faces at the doors watching the staff on the Signal Hill, from which, sad to relate, the pennants for the returning fleet were never to fly. But the ill-tidings came at last. The ships had never struck the seals at all; but, caught by easterly gales between the ice and a lee-shore, had been jammed until they had been crushed like walnuts in that iron grip. The men, poor wretches! had escaped on shore; and the news came that they were starving in the out-harbours to the northward, from which the

miserable, broken-looking wretches came down by driblets, and slunk away to their equally miserable lairs. Down tumbled insurance companies, never to raise their heads again; and old-established houses, of undoubted strength and reputation, shook and trembled under such terrific blows.

A somewhat inflated description, maybe, but there can be no doubt that the disaster could hardly be overstated. Twenty-six vessels were lost at the seal fishery that year; altogether 140 were jammed in the ice off Green Bay and no fewer than 1,400 shipwrecked sailors were brought ashore.

These disasters caused great distress in the boardrooms of the St John's commercial houses, Bowring Brothers by no means least among them. As they contemplated their losses they were possibly heartened by the knowledge that the days of sending vulnerable sailing ships to hunt the seal were nearly over; they would no doubt have been comforted by the fact that the introduction of steam propulsion was at hand.

Although Bowring's hopes and aspirations were increasingly towards a wider field of commercial pursuits, the hunt for seals remained predominant in the ever-broadening range of their activities, in spite of the inherent uncertainties and the possibility of serious financial losses in the bad years. In 1865 the firm purchased in Liverpool a 283-ton ex-naval gunboat, HMS *Plover*, which they renamed *Hawk*. She was the first of their steam driven ships. She sailed for Newfoundland a few days before Christmas and arrived in plenty of time to be sent to the ice in March. This first attempt with a steam vessel was a triumph; she returned to St John's with 10,700 seals, accompanied by the diminutive schooner *Sarah Ann*, also operating for Bowring Brothers, with 2,500. Many owners had experienced a disastrous season, over 40 ships being caught in the ice in Bonavista Bay, eventually to return empty. *Hawk* went sealing annually until 1876 when she was lost in the ice. She was commanded successively by two members of one of the most illustrious families known to Newfoundland sealing, the Jackmans. Notwithstanding the dangers and discomforts of joining the seal hunt, it was the ambition of practically all young Newfoundland men to join one of the vessels heading for the ice, especially if it was commanded by either William or Arthur Jackman, both of whom were well known for their skill at locating the seals and for their successes in returning to St John's with impressive catches. Incidentally, in 1867 William Jackman performed an act of outstanding bravery and endurance. The schooner *Sea Clipper* was wrecked off Spotted Islands in a blizzard and gale force winds. In spite of huge seas running inshore, William, who happened to be nearby, swam with a line around his waist some 200 yards from the rocky coast no less than twenty-seven times in order to save the lives of all the passengers and crew. For this amazingly courageous deed he was awarded the Royal Humane Society's medal and diploma.

The variations in wind and tide from one year to another had great influence on the position of the ice floes on which the seals might be found and from reliable records these floes, of anything between 60 and 80 square miles in extent, could be anywhere in an overall sea area of some 200,000 square miles. One of the Bowring skippers, Captain Abram Kean (pronounced Kane), as well as the Jackmans, was famous for his skill in locating the seals within ten days to three weeks of leaving port. It was not unknown for Captain Kean to trick less able skippers, who would follow him out of port, by leading them astray and changing his course during the night to where he believed, more often than not correctly, the seals would be found.

As the seal fishery played such an important part for so many years in the life of Bowring Brothers we shall be returning to it again, but in the meantime, it is worth recording the views, as described by David Keir, of a parson called Philip Tocque, who in 1846, when the firm was taking a more serious look at becoming fully involved in sealing, published a book in which he did his utmost to give the sealers a thoroughly bad character. 'The seal fishery', he said:

> . . . is not only a dangerous and hazardous enterprise; it not only causes the sighing of the widow and orphan, but it is moreover, in too many instances, a sink of iniquity, where every principle of morality is laid prostrate, and the heart shrivelled up to the narrow dimensions of gain . . . The sanctity of the Sabbath is disregarded with but few exceptions. How carefully are the vessels insured that are engaged in the seal fishery, which are only the inventions of mechanism, destined to float a short time on the ocean wave and then sink into annihilation. Not so the immoral spirits who are engaged in the voyage; they will live through the revolving periods of eternity. But alas! We fear few apply to the Insurance Office of Heaven before they proceed to the perilous and icy ocean.

In fact, observance of the Sabbath was not entirely ignored by the seal hunters, rough lot though they may have been, and indeed, Captain

Giles of Carbonear made it clear that members of his crew would not be required on a Sunday to perform any duties other than those necessary for the safety of his ship. Other masters followed suit and on Sundays divine service was held on their vessels more often than not. The reverend gentleman also had something to say about the serious drinking indulged in before the ships left for the ice: 'Look at the drunkard's swollen face, his burning eyes, ready to burst from their sockets, and his quivering frame ready to sink into the jaws of death; what a host of diseases wait upon him to hurry him to his long home!'

It had not been a rewarding decade, but in 1871 the new steam vessel *Eagle*, under command of the formidable Captain William Jackman, made three successful visits to the ice, returning with a total of 27,553 seals, an achievement which no doubt brought cheer to the Water Street office. Alternating success and failure continued to be the pattern of the firms sealing ventures. In 1873 *Eagle*, after three trips, landed nearly 40,000 seals valued at £23,420, whereas the following year, because measles swept through his crew, the admirable Captain Kean put in to Greenspond with a very disappointing 4,700.

Chapter 4

WHILE THE CAPRICIOUS FORTUNES of the cod and seal fisheries were occupying the time and thoughts of the Newfoundland based Bowrings, the minds of those in Liverpool during the 1860s were concentrated on building up the company's shipping interests. This was a period during which the name of the company would become known more for the worldwide progress of its growing merchant fleet than for any other aspect of the business. The diverse nature of the maritime activities now being engaged in can be judged from the wide variation in the types of the 19 vessels, for example, bought or built during the 1860s, which ranged between small schooners, of the sort which characterized the earlier ships owned by the company, to 1,200 ton iron clippers. The 1870s saw the inevitable move towards steam. During that decade a further 21 ships were added, of which five were steamships. As the move towards the use of steam hastened, so the proportion of sailing vessels being ordered by Charles Tricks and his fellow-directors was reduced. In the 1880s, 22 new ships were ordered of which no fewer than 14 were steam-powered. Over a period of thirty years some 62 new ships had joined the Bowring fleet, of which 19 were steamships However, the age of sail was by no means over – nor, one hopes, will it ever be – and for a number of years yet Bowring sailing vessels would be seen gracing the oceans of the world. It would be many years before steam took over the major trade routes from sail. Small steamships were not yet suitable for long passages in deep waters and the schooner would be plying the main trade routes for many a decade to come. And so they continued to do during the 1860s and 1870s, though how many were Bowring's own ships and how many were on charter the scarce records of the day do not state.

It was not unknown, however, for Bowring ships to be chartered on occasions by other operators. For instance, in 1868 the Bowring owned 1,243 ton iron clipper, *Juliet*, was launched from the Belfast yard of Harland and Wolff and immediately chartered to James Baines, Taylor & Company for service with their Black Ball Line between Liverpool and Australia. It was apparent from the announcement of her forthcoming departure that *Juliet* was 'one of the finest iron clippers afloat . . . her accommodation for all classes is of the most superior description, she affords an unusually favourable opportunity for passengers, and is a most eligible opportunity for shippers of fine goods.' She made this maiden voyage to Melbourne in eighty-two days, and on her return journey to Liverpool, brought 31,205 sacks of wheat from San Francisco. It is not unlikely, on those occasions when C. T. Bowring either chartered out one of their vessels to other shippers or chartered in ships of other owners to carry their merchandise when they hadn't available sufficient tonnage of their own, that they would have engaged the services of Charles Tricks' third son, Henry, who had set up on his own account in 1866 as a ship and insurance broker. He occupied an office in Rumford Street, Liverpool, where he also held an agency for the Liverpool & London & Globe Insurance Company. In the same year, William Benjamin returned from New York to help his father and uncle, Henry Price, in the Liverpool office and took up residence at 13, Devonshire Road, Prince's Park. In due course his duties at New York were to be taken over by his cousin Thomas Benjamin, the son of Edward Bowring.

In 1869 two iron barques, *Romeo*, 641 tons, and *Viola*, 590 tons, were launched for the company. Built by Thomas Royden & Sons of Liverpool, they were both also placed immediately on the Liverpool–Australia run. The two earlier built iron ships, *Oberon* and *Ophelia*, both built by John Reid & Co. of Port Glasgow, were making regular passages to India. In spite of the increasingly rapid introduction of steam, the company continued to add more sailing vessels. By 1870 Bowring's sailing fleet amounted to some 36 ships, in sizes appropriate for worldwide trading. But it is interesting to note that there are records, albeit somewhat lacking in detail, indicating that in St John's Bowring Brothers corporately and, in a number of cases, the partners individually owned over 30 much smaller vessels ranging in size between 25 and 165 tons, most of these probably being used in the seal fishery.

In the late 1860s and early 1870s Liverpool was enjoying a period of expansion and prosperity. In fact between 1837, when Queen Victoria came to the throne, and 1871, there was a dramatic increase in the shipping tonnage handled at the port from less than 2,000,000 to substantially over 6,000,000, and the harbour dues had increased by over 300 per cent. Liverpool was the port of registration for one seventh of all shipping throughout the world and by 1871 was handling a third of the exports and a quarter of the imports of the United Kingdom.

For much of the information concerning the affairs of the businesses on either side of the Atlantic during these years we are grateful for the fact that Charles Tricks kept a diary. Once again there is good news and bad, as will always be found in the chronicles of maritime concerns. During the early part of 1873, the diary tells us that *Imogene* is at Pernambuco (now Recife) and *Eagle* (II), an auxiliary wooden sealer built by Alexander Steven & Sons of Dundee in 1871, is at Halifax, Nova Scotia, about to join the seal hunt in the spring with *Hawk*. *Romeo*, the fast wool clipper on the Australia run, has just completed a voyage. *Harriet* (II) has arrived at St John's, *Bianca* is at Hamburg and *Oberon* is loading at Calcutta for New York. So much for some of the good tidings. It was probably on *Harriet*'s next voyage that news was received of her stranding on the Bar at Oporto. Although her crew and part of the cargo were rescued, *Harriet* was declared a total loss.

More disagreeable news was to follow. From the diary we learn that during the year one of the company's captains died of yellow fever at Pernambuco; the carpenter and one of the mates of another ship were reported dead and a third ship arrived at St John's with one of her crew in a straitjacket. In his diary Charles Tricks meticulously noted the movements and related incidents of all his ships whether their voyages took them to Melbourne or Cardiff, or to Hamburg or Valparaiso. At the end of the year the diary records the dismal news that *Oberon's* Captain has had his ticket suspended for six months following a collision between his ship and another vessel. Whereas blame for the accident did not rest with *Oberon*, it was the fact that her captain failed to make sufficient effort to rescue members of the other ship's crew that cost him the temporary loss of his ticket.

On 1 August 1878 one of the company's finest ships, *Juliet*, was wrecked on an island, in severe weather, while rounding Cape Horn on a passage from London to San Francisco. Heavy seas were breaking over the ship's sides and the crew had but one option to escape being washed overboard – to scramble up into the rigging. There they managed to cling on for no less than 14 hours, watching a German brig, the *Thetis*, which, though standing-by, could do nothing to help in such appalling conditions. Eventually, the weather moderated enough for an attempt to be made to lower a boat, but no sooner was this tried than a vast wave picked it up and smashed it against the ship's side. This happened three times, leaving only one last boat on which the lives of the crew now depended. However, good fortune prevailed and all the crew, except for one apprentice, who was washed overboard during the third attempt, managed to scramble aboard and heave themselves away to the German vessel which had been lying in safer waters until such time as she might have been able to send her own boats to the rescue.

A few months later the brigantine *Titania* (II) met her end on North Rock, Co. Down in a snowstorm and, following an official enquiry, her master's certificate was suspended for six months. These gloomy reports would undoubtedly have caused despondency in the Liverpool office, but there was good news from other vessels and the company's overall profitability was now improving, especially by the transportation and distribution of American and Russian oil products, their involvement in which will be referred to later.

In the mid 1870s St John's seems, from the accounts of visitors, to have presented a down-at-heel appearance, except for the major stores on Water Street, and Warrington's, an hotel, which, from those who stayed there, was said to have 'resembled the best type of English hostelry with its comfortable bedrooms, quiet dignity and good food.' For the rest of the town, however, there was little good to be said. As one contemporary visitor comments:

> Through the streets drive little fish carts drawn by diminutive, shaggy horses. Burly red-whiskered men in blue guernseys walk along trailing heavy cod in their hands. A knot of bulky, black dogs are snarling over some fish refuse. There are scores of dogs. You see them prowling about the streets, romping with the children or sunning themselves in the doorways. No matter where you go you are always knocking against some bass-voiced dog or other. Everybody owns one . . . You walk on rough cobble pavements, and climb steep, foul by-ways, with rocks cropping up in the middle of them. You see rickety houses, all out of straight, shored up with long poles . . . You come upon rows of squalid dwellings, the narrow doors cut in half with only the lower leaf shut.
>
> No matter how decayed or wretched the house, it possesses a little shop for the sale of confectionery and tape. Hens dance in and out behind the counter. Nets, sails, oil-tuns, and anchor chains lie on all hands. Long-legged pigs, goats and scraggy cows dispute supremacy with bare-legged, bareheaded children who play at 'ringba-jing' and other games in the middle of the street.

This was the St John's to which Edgar, second son of John Bowring, came in 1875, at the age of seventeen. Edgar, who later in life was to receive a knighthood and who became one of the most influential and generous citizens of St John's, arrived in the colony at a time when the gradual transition from sail to steam manifested itself in a development which had its origins back in the 1860s. It was in March 1860 that the House of Assembly voted a subsidy of £3,000 per year for a coastal steamship service north and south from St John's and a further £1,200 for a service to be based on Conception Bay. In the early days of this service Bowring Brothers participated in part of it with *Hawk*. However, in 1876 they were awarded the entire service, and two ships, *Curlew* and *Plover* were ordered by Charles Tricks and built at Liverpool. Launched in 1877 at Queen's Dock Slipway, they were identical 473-ton composite mail steamers and were brought into commission later that year. Capable of almost 11 knots, they could safely negotiate most of the creeks and could load and discharge their cargoes and passengers at the small piers and jetties by virtue of their comparatively shallow draft; and they were equipped with steam winches.

While both cabin and steerage passengers had free meals included in the fare, quenching their thirst seemed to offer rather limited options. In March 1877 Charles Tricks records in his diary:

> Gave instructions that the tickets printed for passengers by the s.s. *Curlew* and *Plover* should be printed with the condition, 'no wines, spirits or intoxicating liquors should be found by the ship, or would be sold on board.

I wonder whether Charles Tricks' orders were based on a personal leaning towards temperance or a precaution against possible unruly behaviour at sea. The generally accepted beliefs regarding inherited frailties lead me to the conclusion that he was more likely to have been concerned for the safety of his ships and their passengers.

Of the two ships, *Plover*'s career was not a happy one. She was involved in a collision on her arrival at St John's on 17 May and needed to have much of her keel replaced. As a result of the mishap several people were drowned. A few months later she went aground, though we are not told where. After some years she was wrecked again and finally, after her coastal service was over, she was lost at sea. Once again we are indebted to Charles Tricks' diary, which indicates that whilst in summer the operation seems to have been profitable, the lack of passenger traffic in winter and, on occasions severe ice conditions, would soon give rise to managerial headaches. The ships still had to be maintained notwith-standing the lack of profitable bookings.

On both sides of the Atlantic the early 1880s were years of disappointment and, in some cases, disaster. On 10 April 1880, *Falcon*, built in Germany in 1878 for an unknown owner and subsequently purchased by C. T. Bowring for Newfoundland operations, was damaged in the ice without having caught a single seal. She had to be towed back to port by a rival company's ship which was carrying some 6,000 skins. *Plover* was trapped in ice off Trepassey; the seal fishery was generally so bad that *Eagle* and *Kite* between them could only account for just over 2,000 seals; fishing for cod on the Grand Banks was very poor and, because *Falcon* was engaged in both fisheries, she could barely earn her keep. At the same time there was much criticism in the newspapers of the coastal service being run by Bowring Brothers and, to make matters worse, widespread unemployment was having a serious effect on sales at the store.

But there were some heartening developments in the offing. On 29 April 1881 the Newfoundland government, having sat from 11.00 a.m. until 3.00 a.m. the following morning, agreed a proposal by the Blackman Syndicate to construct a railway. Work started in August of that year. With the exception of a few foremen and supervisors, the work was carried out with local labour and, as the then Prime Minister, William V. Whiteway was able to point out, the enterprise gave a tremendous boost to the island's economy. There can be no doubt that Bowring Brothers' store and other activities would have benefited from this important development. In addition to the railway, work was begun on a new dry-dock, capable of accommodating the larger steamships that were now visiting St John's.

There were at Liverpool, too, ground-breaking advances. In a letter to his brother Henry, dated 21 April 1880, Charles Tricks wrote:

> The telephone has been going all day, first to one person and then to another. It is really a very useful instrument and saves much time and we can now work it very well.

Early in 1880, Charles Tricks placed an order with Raylton, Dixon & Company of Middlesbrough for a new iron steamer to be named *Titania*, the third vessel of this name to be owned by the company. Of 2,436 tons gross, she was to be placed on a regular service, under command of Captain Walter Williams, between Newcastle-on-Tyne and New York. She was to be followed in 1881 by a sister-ship, *Juliet*, built by the same company. The previous *Titania*, it will be recalled, was wrecked off the Irish coast in 1879. I have wondered whether Charles Tricks, when giving this new ship a name that was associated with misfortune, might have felt that he was tempting providence. But it is more likely that at the time of the naming ceremony, he would have been much more concerned about *Hamlet*, 130 days out of New York on a voyage to Ceylon. After 141 days, nothing having been heard of her, she was presumed lost. But there was good news from *Titania*; she had reached Newcastle on 22 June with a cargo of sheep and cattle, all in good order.

Arthur Wardle, in his book *Benjamin Bowring and His Descendants*, gives a helpful explanation of what was the accepted practice at the time when these ships were launched: ' As customary in those days,' he writes, ' each vessel was nominally owned by a single-ship limited liability company, and the following is a typical memorandum of registration:

JULIET STEAMSHIP COMPANY LIMITED

Registered 11th June, 1881, with a capital of £20,000 in £1shares, to acquire the steamship, *Juliet*. The subscribers, who take one share each, are C. T. Bowring, 25 Castle Street, merchant; W. B. Bowring, 25 Castle Street, merchant; E. Bowring, 25 Castle Street, clerk; J. Congdon, 5 Newstead Road, Liverpool, master mariner; J. S. Wellings, 25 Castle Street, clerk; Messrs. C. T. Bowring & Co. are appointed managers.

Charles Tricks was now well into his seventies and, not unlike his father, had reached a stage in life when unbusinesslike behaviour by any members of the company would invoke his thinly disguised displeasure. He still maintained a strong grip on all aspects of the business and misdemeanours seldom escaped his notice. It was sometime during 1880 that he became aware that all was not well between the American office and Lloyd's. David Keir in *The Bowring Story* takes up the saga:

A few months later he was admonishing Bowring and Archibald at New York. Apparently someone in the New York office – it is not clear who – had written ineptly to Lloyd's in London about insurance agency business, and in turn a resentful Lloyd's Committee had passed the letters on to Charles Tricks for his view. The New York office, we should recall, had long been Lloyd's agents and had achieved considerable prestige in consequence. Naturally therefore Charles Tricks tried to clear the matter up with his nephew Thomas Benjamin Bowring, who had joined the New York office in 1870 and was later to go to London.

Forthrightly Charles Tricks told his nephew that he thought the Committee of Lloyd's had reason to complain. He went on: 'To write grumbling letters to Lloyd's Committee and try to get them to interfere to throw commissions into Bowring and Archibald's is curiously absurd and unbusinesslike. Lloyd's Committee have no right or desire to force people to do their business through their agents alone. It is for these agents to do work committed to them so well as to make it patent to all that no other firm could do the work better. If the Agency is really no profit to you, I can conceive of no way you would get it taken away from you than such letters of Bowring and Archibald to the Secretary of Lloyd's.

'The letters complained of are, in my opinion, unless there are some facts existing that have not come to my knowledge, most offensive and unbusinesslike. Do let me know who wrote them, and immediately write to Lloyd's trying to do away with the injurious impression they were calculated to make and have made on Lloyd's Committee . . . The writer of these letters evidently thinks that Lloyd's Register of Shipping and Lloyd's Committee are the same people and the ungentlemanly way in which many remarks are made is calculated to give great offence . . . To try to get Lloyd's Committee to force the shipowners, owners of cargo and underwriters to place their interests in Bowring and Archibald's hands, is an absurdity that I should have credited the youngest clerk in your office to be guilty of.'

Charles Tricks was at this time beginning to suffer severely from gout and his wife, Harriet, had become so ill as to require constant nursing at home. He might be forgiven therefore if, under the strain of his domestic life at this time, he should occasionally find himself at odds with the younger generation across the Atlantic with whose managerial ability he was becoming less than satisfied. In the spring of 1881 he was convinced that they had lost their grip on the business, and it was apparent that Bowring Brothers were losing money. There were a number of reasons for this. In the first place both the seal and cod fisheries had, for the past few seasons, been unproductive; the firm had been giving too much credit and the bad debt situation had become serious.

Indeed, Charles Tricks was becoming disenchanted with the Newfoundland business as a whole. He had become preoccupied with recent diversification involving the growth in marine insurance commitments, developments in the firm's interest in the petroleum trade and increasing concentration on adding more steamships to the fleet. Furthermore he was exercising serious doubts about the island's politics, which as described by David Keir, 'had become so raucous'. In fact his son,

Charles, who had become a member of the Newfoundland House of Assembly and of the Legislative Council, was the subject of a strongly worded and abusive article in the press which expressed the view that surely men could differ without referring to each other as 'liars and thieves'.

As 1881 wore on Charles Tricks, ageing, plagued with gout and both he and Harriet far from well, wrote on 16 August to Charles probably the strongest manifestation of discontent and disappointment in his long and dedicated business career:

> My dear Charles, your uncle John is writing the business letter in the absence of William who is in Shropshire shooting – so I shall not say anything on business matters. Indeed I find that anything I have said lately has been paid little or no attention and therefore I shall very probably take very little trouble to write you much more.
>
> If I could only haul my capital out of the Newfoundland business I should be only too glad to do so and pay no more attention to it for I believe under present management it is a decaying business and not worth anything as a backing. This year with a good cod fishing and a fair seal fishing ought to turn out well if any year will, but I confess myself without hope of the future of the business and believe that nothing I can say will get you out of the vicious grooves you have got into.
>
> You tell me that your uncle John's being in Newfoundland has done no good and reduced none of your filthy debts. What then can be done? I see that any advice is like jigs whistled to mile-stones and of no use whatever and I shall cease to give it.

On the same day as this letter was written, Charles Tricks wrote another, this time to the New York office, once again venting his displeasure over a matter that, with some justification, had annoyed him. Normally he was a man of even temper and the spirit of these letters, being so out of character, can only be ascribed to a combination of his increasing frailty and what he saw as growing incompetence in the handling of the business.

During the summer of 1881 *Juliet*, on what must have been one of the earliest of her voyages, called at New York where Bowring and Archibald had arranged for her to take on board a large cargo of bacon and a consignment of molasses. It was unfortunate that the casks of molasses were stowed on top of the bacon; they leaked! It wasn't apparent at the time that this might have been the accidental birth of sweet cured bacon. The bacon backs were saturated and, on hearing of it, Charles Tricks was furious and wrote on hearing of the incident:

I never heard of a grosser case of mismanagement. The Captain was to blame for allowing it to be stowed in this manner, the stevedore and whoever is your vat-manager equally so. I do not suppose that this act of folly ever came to the knowledge of either of the principals of the concern, but whoever saw it and did not energetically protest against it participated in the fault. Do ascertain and let us know who the culprit is. I expect the claims will be large and swallow up nearly all the freight.

It was some weeks later that Charles Tricks wrote to his nephew, Thomas Benjamin, at the New York office. He was believed to have acquainted himself with the sequence of events leading up to the unintentional and unfortunate fusion of bacon and molasses.

'I have seen,' he wrote:

> ... a letter written by Fred (his nephew and the eldest son of John Bowring) attempting to exculpate the folly of stowing Molasses *over* Bacon in *Juliet* and *Titania*. He says in it, it is evident that Molasses or Treacle is most dangerous stuff to carry and that you must be careful of it for the future. Surely it did not take the experience of a man of twenty-four years of age to come to this conclusion. I should have thought any boy out of petticoats would have known this and avoided taking the wretched stuff. I blame the Captain very much indeed for ever signing Bills of Lading for it, no matter what pressure was brought to bear to make him sign ...
>
> The tale they tell, and Captain Williams believes the tale, is this – that with regard to *Juliet* the Molasses was brought alongside in such a state that the quay was covered with the leakage from the casks so badly that your people on shore were obliged to get a large quantity of sawdust to cover the leakage and it was by this means hidden. However the Captain says that he pointed out the state of the casks and refused to take them on board. He says that he was told by 'Mr Fred' that the Molasses was booked and must go and that he insisted on its being taken on top of the Bacon and taken it was, with an exercise of stupidity which to my mind is marvellous. The result is that we have to pay damages for the injury done to the bacon, which I understand will be very large and we also today received notice of action from the receiver of the Molasses for loss and injury to the casks causing leakage and loss. Where it will end no one can tell.
>
> Williams tells me that at the bottom of *Juliet*'s hold the Molasses was so thick as to be over his shoes and I see the complaint of the owners of the stuff is that the casks had broken chimes, some of the staves bulged in and there was every evidence of bad usage. They also say the Molasses being for Dundee was obliged to be removed at Newcastle to deliver goods for

that place and thus the casks were damaged . . . It is very disgusting to lose money by such folly.

However, the company met its obligations and Charles Tricks' final observation on the unfortunate incident was that 'one of the many people involved in the whole transaction turned out to be a scoundrel and a scamp'. There has been, over the generations, an uncomfortable feeling that his reference was to my great-uncle Fred, of whom there will be more to be said.

There followed a series of misfortunes affecting *Titania*. On 21 August news was received that, on a passage to Dundee, she had run down a small fishing boat, and that one of the fishermen was drowned. Two months later a cable from Halifax brought news that she had sprung a leak as a result of her spare screw breaking adrift, and this led to a salvage claim for £25,000 from the owners of the vessel that had taken her in tow. But the worst was to follow. The bad luck that had dogged the two earlier *Titanias* was to strike again. On 22 January 1882 she sailed from New York bound for Newcastle upon Tyne with a crew of 40 and a cargo of provisions. *Titania* was never heard of again.

It is understandable that such news should put Charles Tricks in a melancholy mood. In a letter dated 4 July 1882 to his son Charles in New York, he spells out his growing disenchantment with ship owning following this serious loss.

> The Board of Trade are holding an enquiry today in the cause of the loss of the s.s. *Titania* and have summoned William to give evidence in the case. I do not think they can find anything wrong in our management or equipment of the ship and I think they are quite right to hold an enquiry: indeed I think that a kind of coroner's inquest should be held on every lost ship. I do not think there is any inducement to replace *Titania*, for freights are now so low and the production of iron ships is now so great that I do not believe that either of the partners in the concern in England wish to extend their operations in steam.

The court of enquiry found no fault with the management of the vessel nor with her equipment and no one was found responsible for her loss.

The familiar pattern of gains and losses continued throughout the 1880s and 1890s and damage to ships or their loss by various causes continued. For instance, on 14 February 1882 the iron barque *Romeo* was lost between Cape Everard and Ram Head, off the coast of New South Wales on passage to Hamburg. Her master had his ticket suspended for six months for faulty navigation. (*Romeo* was, perhaps, an unfortunate name for a ship to be lost on St Valentine's Day). But, on a happier note, an extensive building programme of new ships was envisaged notwithstanding Charles Tricks' expressions of doubt expressed earlier. His uncertainty of outlook was probably as much a manifestation of the inexorable advance of old age as for any other reason. He was now approaching seventy-five, an age at which, after such an energetic and, at times, exhausting life, he might well have been enjoying a more relaxed *modus vivendi*, especially since his health had been in decline for some months. A letter written after he had received the depressing news of an indifferent 1882 seal fishery gives an indication, at least at that time, of the extent to which his spirits and, indeed, his state of health had deteriorated:

> I do not now take much on myself in the way of business, and therefore have not much knowledge of what is going on for my opinion to be of much use. A very little now tires me and I feel I am an old man. The remains or the results of the last attack of gout have made me very crippled in my feet and knees so much as to make it difficult for me to walk either much or fast or long. I can only creep about at a snail's pace and consequently ride almost everywhere.

A couple of weeks later, the agonies he was suffering struck even harder when he insisted on going to his office. He had experienced severe pain in his foot earlier in the day and, on arrival at his home later, it was so much worse that he had to be carried from his carriage on an invalid chair and, in his own words 'and in the night upstairs to bed by four women.' Fortunately, the attack did not last very long and he was away from the office, on this occasion, for only one day.

But, in addition to his physical suffering, Charles Tricks was faced in the early months of 1883 with the depressing news of a further loss at sea. In March, the iron barque, *Jessica*, one of the company's older vessels, built at Glasgow by J. Reid & Co. in 1863, had to be abandoned off Cape Horn during a storm when bound for England with a cargo of wheat. Her crew found refuge on the Falkland Islands where a court of enquiry exonerated the master, Captain Sergeant, from all blame. These cargoes of grain from the Pacific coast of America to the Thames and the Mersey had become a regular feature of Bowring's growing maritime involvement. In the autumn of that year the iron sailing ship, *Othello*, sailed from San Francisco for Liverpool with a wheat cargo of 48,851 centals (a unit of measurement for which I have been unable to find a present-day equivalent) valued at £83,046. She was followed by the barque, *Cordelia*, with 20,228 centals of wheat worth £32,264. It would be more than thirty years before the Panama Canal was completed and for these sailing ships negotiating Cape Horn was extremely hazardous.

By the spring of 1883, Charles Tricks seems to have been in better health. His seventy-fifth birthday was in March, and he and Harriet celebrated their golden wedding anniversary in April. This, in his own words, 'was an unclouded day for us and seeing so many of our children around us was a perfect pleasure.' It was, by all accounts, a memorable occasion with nine of his ten children present, the only absentee being Henry who was in New York. We do not know how many of his thirty-five grandchildren managed to be present; he considered their numbers to be 'alarming'. In addition to this memorable family occasion he records that he '. . . gave the clerks and captains a nice dinner at the Reform Club which the persons who were at it say was very enjoyable and cheerful without any excess.' Following the celebrations he wrote to Henry, no doubt expressing his disappointment that he couldn't be present, but also telling him about the flood of telegrams that had arrived: 'I did not know we had so many friends in the world . . . Love to each of your children and wishing that you may be able to spend your golden wedding day as happily as we did, I am my dear Henry, your affectionate father, C. T. Bowring.'

From letters such as this we can catch glimpses of the character of a man who was never shy about expressing his affection for his family. But we have seen the other side to his nature, too. In the conduct of the business, he would not tolerate any vestige of slackness on the part of the younger generation in matters of detail, in which he himself was seldom, if ever, to be found at fault. His innate sense of business discipline would occasionally cause him to react reproachfully if he observed any matters that, in his judgement, were being dealt with inefficiently. There were, at this time, clerical errors in the St John's office with regard to a certain cargo contract and a bank guarantee, concurrently with the arrival and departure of *Juliet*, whose movements were not reported to the Liverpool office; it was not known whether the ship had gone to Sydney or Halifax. Charles Tricks was provoked to write forthrightly: 'These irregularities must cease, or you will lose heavily in money some day and lose character as businessmen always.' And, soon after, he wrote to Henry

in St John's: 'Actively and soberly attend to your business. Don't stoop
to low ways and especially drinking with ship captains for as soon as
owners get this idea they will shy off you at once.'

To his second son, Charles, he wrote for the benefit of *his* son, also
Charles, now about twelve years of age:

> I do trust that you will look well after your son's education and training.
> Charlie is, I am sure, a very clever lad, and naturally good tempered, his
> habits and mind may at this time of life be moulded to anything. It is your
> place to set him a good example of sobriety and industry; don't let him
> fritter away his time in frivolity – but while he must have proper and
> rational amusement – teach him that such is not the main business of a
> man's life. Teach him the horror of idleness and intemperance, the latter
> too rife amongst young people.

The letter continues in a somewhat different vein:

> I see the *Ulster* was very badly rigged and the complaints that she was
> undersparred to sail with fish cargoes, and that the crew could not live in
> the house which we placed on her deck. You must try and remedy this
> defect as economically as possible. You cannot carry fish in a slow craft
> and you will never get a crew worth having to go in a vessel which is very
> uncomfortable.

Charles had purchased a horse in England, which he kept at a cottage he
had taken at Topsail, not far from St John's. The patriarch could not resist
introducing an admonitory note: 'I am glad to see your horse got out
without accident and that the animal has pleased you . . . You must take
care not to neglect your business, however, for the sake of riding out on
a handsome and good nag.'

The last two years of Charles Tricks' life were to be characterized by
the familiar amalgam of good news and bad, of success and failure, of
chirpiness and lamentation. In September 1883, he wrote to his fourth
son, George, thanking him for a box of partridges and, in his letter noted
that the news he was receiving from St John's was cheerful, not least
because the Newfoundland fishery was the best for many years. In
conclusion he wrote: 'Upon the whole I think the Bowring tribe should
have in business a fairly prosperous year and I trust they will not, like an
ill tempered cow, kick over the good pail of milk they have given.'

But his natural ebullience was, more and more, to be dampened by
the deterioration in his health. Early in 1884 he suffered yet another
violent attack of gout on which he dwelt broodingly in one of his letters:

I was more than fifty years of age before I got the gout but I have suffered since that time and I know full well that if I had not been so very careful and abstemious I should have had it long before I had. Who do we inherit it from? Some old scamp who years since drank his full of October brown ale. It was not my father, I know, for a more temperate man did not exist. Again I ask, who from?

This laudable abstinence was to be seriously challenged by future generations, many of whose members would experience considerable difficulty in satisfying their thirst; but more of that later.

Bowring ships were to be found among the world's wheat-carriers for many years to come. There were also several steamships built by the company during the 1880s for their Red Cross Line passenger service between Newfoundland, Halifax and New York, a service that would continue well into the twentieth century. Among these ships were *Romeo* (III), 2,279 tons in 1883, and in the following year, *Miranda* (II), 1,158 tons and *Portia* (III), 1,156 tons. (More will be heard of these two ships later). Also, in 1884, *Capulet*, 2,246 tons, joined the fleet, specifically for the company's transatlantic services.

At this time of a significant increase in the number of ships owned and operated by C. T. Bowring & Co. and Bowring Brothers, it is probable that Charles Tricks, though he had played a central role in building up the firm's involvement in shipowning, would have been less active. Although he had kept close contact, his health had in general been failing for some time.

C. T. Bowring, whose name would survive as the company's designation for more than the next hundred years, died peacefully on 23 September 1885, aged seventy-seven. No better tribute can be paid to his memory than the words of Arthur Wardle in his book, *Benjamin Bowring and his Descendants*:

> His life had been full and rich, not only from his own point of view, but that of other people. For nearly fifty years resident in Liverpool, he had been one of its most prominent citizens. At an early age ... he had secured a leading position as a shipowner and merchant; and when, by exertion, sound judgement, and business aptitude, he had placed himself in an opulent position, he devoted his leisure hours to public service. He was no orator, but essentially of practical and prudent action.

At a time when the Health Committee of the Liverpool Corporation was faced with serious problems concerning the unhygienic state of the poorer parts of the city, Charles Tricks was chosen to be its chairman. Under his influence and guidance sweeping measures were adopted to clear away unsanitary conditions and to abolish unsightly and dangerous alleyways and narrow streets, which were replaced by attractive new thoroughfares. Wardle continues:

> Had he not been a pronounced Liberal he would have become Mayor of Liverpool; as it was, party spirit prevented him from receiving so well merited an honour, and when, in 1877, he completed twenty-one years of service, the ratepayers (*of his ward*) held in his honour, at the Adelphi Hotel, Liverpool, a largely attended banquet.
>
> His business abilities can be gauged from the steady growth of the firm of which he was head for forty years, and also from the loyalty of the other senior partners, his brothers, a loyalty which speaks volumes for the sterling character of the eldest. He was of high intelligence, with the keenest sense of honour, a scholarly mind, and of impartial judgement, bringing all these qualities to bear in his relationships, whether public or commercial; and his forbearing and broad sympathies must have been highly esteemed by his contemporaries. In private life, Charles T. Bowring was greatly loved. Just to all, in his family relationships he was blessed.

Charles Tricks was buried at the Liverpool Necropolis where both his father, Benjamin and his mother, Charlotte, were also buried. Present at his funeral were his brothers, Henry Price and John, and his sons, William Benjamin, Henry and George Edward.

Chapter 5

A S THE BUSINESS BASED in Liverpool increased in size and influence under the leadership of Charles Tricks, so a clearer distinction between the activities of C. T. Bowring, Bowring Brothers in Newfoundland and Bowring and Archibald in New York, became apparent. Sadly, John Bowring, Benjamin's youngest son and successor to Charles Tricks as senior partner at Liverpool, died less than one year later at his home, Terra Nova, a mansion of some elegance, an indication, perhaps, of the increasing wealth and success of firm and family. Thus the next generation took up the reins and William Benjamin, Charles Tricks' eldest son, became senior partner. Towards the end of the 1880s, what was now developing into quite a 'group' of companies was dispersed between Liverpool, London, St John's and New York. The main activities comprised the growing fleet of sailing vessels and steamships; the Bowring-controlled English and American Shipping Company (founded in 1892), which carried freight between the United Kingdom, the Mediterranean and New York; the still young but developing petroleum trade and finally, insurance, which was managed in London by George Bowring and which would eventually become the major activity of a very much larger group in the future.

In Newfoundland, at this time, the fortunes of Bowring Brothers maintained their predictable ups and downs. The company had, however, developed a resilience and breadth of interests that would enable them to weather the worst of any economic squalls that might beset them. Towards the end of the 19th century, the firm had achieved predominance in the seal hunt, but if either this or the cod fishery were to fail, there were other successful operations, which would ensure some buoyancy if it seemed as though the tides of misfortune were rising. The coastal service was operating successfully and the company's fleet of small tramp ships was busily traversing the oceans carrying a variety of cargoes, by no means least among which was salt for the colony's staple industry, the cod fishery; and the store on Water Street continued to supply the needs of the people of the island. Meanwhile, the company's recently established Red Cross Line was operating regularly between St John's, Halifax and New York, carrying passengers and cargo.

In 1887 the partnership of Rothwell & Bowring was established in St John's by Edward Rothwell, an accountant with the local firm of J. Murray & Company, the other partner being Henry Bowring, third son of Charles Tricks. The company acted as agents for the contractors of the Newfoundland Railway and were much involved with arranging shipments of supplies and provisions for the workers on the railway. The company also acted eventually as agents for Fire, Accident, Motor Car and Plate Glass Insurance as well as their original business of flour, feed and provisions importers. After Henry Bowring's death, unmarried, in 1901 at the age of forty-two, his executors, Frederick, Edgar and Henry, sons of John Bowring bought the partnership as a going concern and in 1908 it was incorporated as a limited liability company under the management of Mr George Williams. This company continued to operate in St John's until the 1940s and was widely involved in various activities including trading in flour, cattle foods, provisions, leather, cigars, fertilizers and many other commodities. They were also agents for the Canada Accident & Fire Assurance Company. George Williams kept up a regular correspondence with Frederick, Edgar and Henry, of which there still exist many handwritten letters and, in the case of Edgar, judging by the variety of their origins, ample evidence of his penchant for globe-trotting!

All was going well on both sides of the Atlantic as the 1880s drew to a close when, early in 1890, great concern was felt for the safety of Captain Arthur Jackman and the crew of the coastal steamer, *Plover* which had recently left Sydney, Nova Scotia. News came on 14 January that she had been wrecked but that, fortunately, the master and crew had been rescued. But more bad news was to follow. It was in 1890 that Charles Tricks' second son, Charles, whilst senior partner in St John's, died or, as they say in Newfoundland, 'stepped aside'. He was only fifty years of age; but an equally tragic loss, only one year later, was the death of George Edward, fourth son of Charles Tricks, who succumbed to typhoid fever at the very young age of forty, shortly after returning to his family in Surbiton from a shooting holiday in Scotland. George, of whom there will be more to be said, was, by all accounts, energetic and far-sighted and his loss, so early in his career, was a serious blow to both his family and to the company. He had started his business life as a youth in Liverpool with Lamport & Holt but, in 1877, moved to London and joined Bowring, Jamieson & Company, shipping and insurance brokers, a partnership entered into in 1873 by his cousin, Henry Edward and John D. Jamieson.

To cover all the individual and increasingly varied activities of a growing group of enterprises chronologically at this stage in its development, might well be to miss some of the sequences of events leading to the progress of the main components. It seems logical, therefore, at this juncture to pick up the story of the original enterprise in Newfoundland from the last decade of the 19th century. The unhappy losses of two outstanding members of the family in 1890 and 1891, at ages when both had so much more to offer, was depressing enough news for the time being but, unfortunately, there was more to come.

At the beginning of 1892, Bowring Brothers' fleet of fish-carriers comprised the barquentines *Ulster, Dunure* and *Mary Cory*, the brigantine *Vidonia* and the schooner *Imogene* (III). These brave little ships, all of about 200 tons, *Ulster* being the largest at 290 tons gross, were capable of quite rapid passages and it was not unusual for them to complete the run from St John's to the Clyde, for instance, in ten to twelve days. On 22 January *Ulster* sailed from Newfoundland for Liverpool with a cargo of fish. As if to presage further reverses, she went missing en route and was never heard of again. At the end of February a fearsome storm hit Newfoundland at Trinity as a result of which many lives were lost. David Keir in *The Bowring Story* describes the disastrous circumstances of that day, 28 February:

> Early that day the weather had been so mild and clear and the sea so calm, that from Trinity itself and many neighbouring coves more than 200 fishermen rowed out to floating ice on which a large number of seals had been seen the night before. Most of the seals were gone by morning, but many of the fishermen pressed far out into the bay in the hope of meeting more. The older and more experienced hunters, having seen the early signs of storm, had started for home before it broke. Yet even some of these old hands reached land only after a desperate struggle; for the storm blew rapidly into a tempestuous and freezing blizzard. Others were too late. One party of 16 men managed to climb onto a high-standing ice pan and survived the night after breaking up their boat for firewood. Next day they were rescued by a volunteer crew from *Heart's Delight*. But it was also next day that 24 men were found to have perished.

But one of the worst disasters to visit the island was yet to come and its supposed origins whilst, perhaps, verging on the bizarre, serve nevertheless to this day as a grim warning. It is now generally believed that, during the late afternoon of 8 July 1892, a man pushing a cart into a barn at the east end of St John's stumbled and in so doing allowed some burning ash, which fell from his pipe, to set fire to a pile of hay. To add disaster to misfortune, the local water main was shut off pending repair and, worst of all and with sickening irony, the emergency water tank in the stable yard, where the trouble started, had not been refilled after a recent fire-fighting exercise!

The last serious fire in St John's, it will be remembered, was in 1846 when the Bowring Brothers premises were totally destroyed as on two previous occasions. In the intervening years many of the replaced buildings were of stone construction, as Benjamin had always so earnestly advocated. Furthermore, following the 1846 fire, the government imposed more rigorous planning regulations including broader streets and wider firebreaks in the more built-up areas. In addition, the businessmen of St John's promoted a scheme for a pipeline to be run from Windsor Lake, and they obtained the approval of the House of Assembly for fire hydrants to be installed at regular intervals throughout the city. Clearly the people of St John's had no wish ever again to see their city brought to ruin, and such minor outbreaks as occurred during the intervening years were successfully contained.

This new and most disastrous fire spread quickly, fanned by a strong wind. It soon engulfed nearby wooden buildings, which in their turn caused the blaze to leap from house to house, from one building to another with ever widening fury down towards the waterfront and in so doing, overwhelming the several commercial premises on Water Street, including those of Bowring Brothers. Members of the company made desperate efforts to move to safety as much of the firm's goods as they possibly could. The flames, having devoured some of the most substantial stone buildings in St John's, including the Anglican Cathedral, where many of the citizens had sought security for their furniture and other belongings, reached the waterfront at 2.00 a.m. on the morning of the 9th. The progress of the blaze was violent and unstoppable. Not only was the fate of the Bowring premises now sealed, but the onrush of the fire threatened the vessels moored alongside the wharves, which were also by now ablaze, and they had to be moved out into the harbour with watches sent aboard them to ensure that flying embers did not set them alight.

By dawn this, the most disastrous of the many fires that destroyed large parts of St John's, had laid waste some two-thirds of the city and left more than 11,000 people homeless. To add to their misery looters, as they had after previous fires, took advantage of the reigning chaos and stole whatever goods and property they could lay their hands on. It is almost impossible to imagine the utter despair with which the citizens must have viewed the smoking ruins of their homes and pondered the seemingly hopeless prospect of ever returning to a normal life. But the resilience of the people of St John's was once again in evidence and was to be rewarded by generous help in many forms from many sources.

Among the hundreds of buildings destroyed were the premises of all the newspapers including the *Royal Gazette*. However, someone remembered that the proprietors of this journal had purchased a small printing press, which had been given to Bishop Spencer by the Society for the Propagation of the Gospel for use in his diocese. It had been safely stowed away by the newspaper's owners and was quickly brought into service to produce, on 12 July, a single sheet, which carried a message of 'profound sympathy' from Queen Victoria and, from the Lord Mayor of London, the promise of a Mansion House Relief Fund. This sole publication also announced that pledges had been received from many cities and towns in England, Canada and America of money, clothing, blankets, food, tents and other essentials, all of which, the paper stated were already on their way. It was estimated that existing food supplies were available for only ten days.

There was, of course, a massive insurance exposure and the agents of British insurance companies in St John's assessed the cover underwritten by them at nearly $5,000,000. In their capacity as agents for the Liverpool & London & Globe, Bowring Brothers' involvement amounted to some $375,000. But the overall losses would eventually amount to a much higher figure, as will become apparent. The response of the insurance companies was, by and large, exemplary. They all let it be known that all claims would be met promptly and many of the companies' agents announced, from their temporary offices, that it was 'business as usual' and that Bowring Brothers, notwithstanding the fact that their business to all intents and purposes lay in ruins, managed to let the people of St John's know through an advertisement in the one-page *Royal Gazette*, couched in terms rather less than grammatically perfect, that they still had goods to offer:

> Though Bowring Brothers have lost a very large quantity of their goods by the fire they have still on hand three thousand brls. Flour, five hundred pounds Molasses, five hundred tubs Butter; also some sugar, Leather etc. For sale at their Store at Beck's Cove. And, 500 tons Anthracite and ordinary coals.
>
> July 13

If that was all the food that would be available, treacle tart was likely to be on the menu in many homes for some time to come. However, good fortune prevailed and several Bowring ships, in the ordinary course of their operations, were due to arrive shortly in St John's with the usual range of supplies. This meant that, as well as Bowring Brothers, other firms would soon be able to offer a variety of provisions and various necessary commodities. Aid was soon pouring in from Britain and Canada, and from a number of American cities, particularly Boston and Chicago.

In London £20,000 was raised as a result of the Lord Mayor's appeal, a considerable sum at the time, while at Liverpool, William Benjamin Bowring and Mr T. R. Job (a senior member of another family with long-standing Newfoundland connections) were made joint honorary secretaries of a committee which immediately set about raising funds. At a meeting in Liverpool on 13 July William Bowring said:

> We all felt glad that the Mayor had acted so promptly and generously in this matter as to call us together to show sympathy in what is the most terrible matter which has occurred in the Empire for many years. I hold in my hand a cablegram from Sir William Whiteway, premier of Newfoundland, and I can say that the accounts in the newspapers are not exaggerated. At four o'clock on the afternoon of the 8 July, in a small stable surrounded by little wooden tenements, there began a fire which was favoured by a furious gale, and it swept over two-thirds of the ancient city of St John's. It burned down many thousands of houses and between 7,000 and 10,000 people are rendered homeless, very large numbers escaping only with the clothes on them at the time. The estimated loss was 12,000,000 dollars. We are not pleading for the mercantile community, many of whom have been carrying on business there for two or three generations, because fortunately in a great many cases their losses have been provided for by insurance, but we plead for the unfortunate labourers and men whose only resources were in their immediate furniture and household effects, and whose means of livelihood have been taken away. These men are also destitute, and whatever is to be done for them must be done at once. The cathedral which has been burnt down was one of the finest structures in North America, and had taken some fifty or sixty years to complete and, unfortunately, a number of people had taken their effects into this building and all had been destroyed.

It was not, perhaps, an outstandingly eloquent performance, but it was certainly from the heart and successful in persuading the business community and citizens of Liverpool to support the appeal. On 20 July, Mr Job left Liverpool for St John's on the steamer *Barcelona* in which space had been made available for 300 tons of relief supplies, the distribution of which he personally supervised.

It would be difficult indeed to conjure up a more calamitous happening than the fire that had come so close to causing the complete destruction of St John's, but shortly before Christmas 1894 there occurred a financial crisis which very nearly sabotaged the whole of the colony's commercial system. In 1885, five years before Charles Bowring (Charles Tricks' son) died, he recognized, when he was senior partner of Bowring Brothers, the unsoundness of the loan policy of the Commercial Bank at St John's, of which he was a director. He was, indeed, so alarmed that he tendered his resignation, hoping that by so doing, his misgivings would be recognized and that the Bank would take note of his warnings and change their policy. However, when the Bank refused to accept his resignation he sold his shares, thus effectively disqualifying himself from holding a seat on the board. Had he been alive when the crisis broke, he would have been more than justified in saying 'I told you so'.

Arthur Wardle, in *Benjamin Bowring and his Descendants*, takes up the story:

> For forty years or so the Commercial Bank and the Union Bank had held the highest reputation in financial circles on both sides of the Atlantic, but large borrowings and indiscriminate loans in recent years had proved the rule rather than the exception, and such a policy was bound to end disastrously. On Monday, December 10, 1894, the two banks and the Savings Banks were compelled to suspend payments. The initial cause was the death of a partner in the firm of Prowse, Hall & Morris, London agents of those Newfoundland firms exporting fish to the European markets. This London firm declined to meet any further exchanges until their affairs had been investigated. Their bills were protested, and the banks made demands upon the Commercial Bank at St John's, the drawer of the bills. Unable to meet these demands, the Commercial Bank fell back upon its mercantile customers. Neither could these respond; hence the Commercial Bank had to suspend operations. Their customers were thereupon forced to make assignments; and so interwoven were the affairs of one establishment and another, nearly every business in the Colony found itself crippled. In fact, the crash was general, and the Bowring firm alone remained unscathed.

The results of this catastrophe were both financially and commercially far reaching and in some cases well nigh fatal. The effects were immediate; the Commercial Bank's debtors were unable to meet their obligations and the whole of the island's economy slid uncontrollably into deep distress. Both the Commercial and Union Banks failed. The Savings Bank put up the shutters for a while and the businesses of the colony's many merchants faced complete closure with the result that hundreds of employees found themselves without a job. Shopkeepers were ruined and the poorer elements of the population once again faced starvation as they had done so recently following the 1892 fire. Banknotes, which were circulating two days earlier at their face value, became completely worthless. Rioting and looting followed and the Prime Minister, A. F. Goodridge, approached the Imperial Government for a loan to save the economy, and the services of a man-of-war to quell further possible disturbances. He then resigned to be succeeded by D. J. Greene, who remained in office for seven weeks, during which a grant for relief of suffering was received from the Imperial Government; he, too, then resigned. It was now the turn of Sir William Whiteway, yet again, to take over as Prime Minister and discussions took place between representatives of Newfoundland and Canada with a view to Newfoundland becoming part of the Canadian Confederation, but these talks were not successful. Canada was not prepared to meet the colony's urgent need for money and appeals to New York for help in order to stave off complete financial collapse came to nought.

The first signs of hope of recovery can be attributed to the then Colonial Secretary at St John's, Robert (later Sir Robert) Bond who, with great courage and loyalty, pledged 100,000 dollars of his own personal credit in order to secure a temporary loan of 150,000 dollars from Montreal. Such was the significance of this generous gesture that, when he later went to England, he was able to arrange on the London market a long-term loan which was oversubscribed.

With the support of their sister companies in Great Britain and America, Bowring Brothers weathered the storm. While many of the other well-established merchant firms in St John's and other parts of the island were badly shaken, Bowring's continued to trade under the leadership, now, of Edgar Rennie Bowring. The company even went to the extent of issuing its own monetary notes in varying denominations to enable members of the staff to purchase life's necessities. The credit of the company was held in such high regard that these notes soon became acceptable at face value in shops and stores throughout the colony.

During these painful years for their shore based activities, Bowring's North American shipping ventures were progressing satisfactorily. The New York, Newfoundland and Halifax Steamship Company, which was registered in 1884, managed the affairs of what had become the well-known Red Cross Line, running its regular passenger and cargo service between St John's, Halifax and New York. This extended maritime programme had its origins in the runs between New York and Newcastle upon Tyne by *Portia* and *Titania* in the early 1880s, which had not been blessed with good fortune in the early 1880s. In 1884, two new vessels, *Miranda* (II) and *Portia* (III), were built on the Tyne for the Red Cross Line by Wigham Richardson & Co. These two ships were virtually identical in every respect. They were luxuriously furnished and provided cabin accommodation for sixty first class passengers. With a service speed of 12 knots and with the modern equipment of steam winches and power steering, they soon established a reputation for comfort and punctuality. There was no doubt, according to the ample coverage they received in the local press, that they made a useful contribution to the island's economy by developing business on the American run.

Let it not be thought, however, that the performance of these two popular ships always enhanced the Bowring reputation. In the winter of 1885 New York brokers chartered *Miranda* for a voyage to Constantinople. The cargo that she would normally have carried on her regular North American passages was offered to her sister ship *Portia*, but she, unfortunately, had insufficient hold-space to oblige. When this became known and the *Evening Telegram* revealed that *Miranda's* cargo was to be 60,000 rifles for the Turkish army, Bowring Brothers had to face criticism for neglecting the generally held view that their loyalty was to their Atlantic seaboard passenger and freight service rather than carrying arms to the Bosphorus. The firm and their agents were to face further reproach when, in June 1886, *Miranda* became stranded on her way to New York. Surprisingly, the company were reprimanded for failing to provide information regarding the condition of the ship and of her cargo.

One of the diversions from the regular North American coastal passages by *Miranda* and *Portia* was to convey, during the summer months, parties of American tourists on cruises. It was on one such a trip in 1894 that the popular and much admired *Miranda* came to the end of her 10 years of successful and enterprising service. With the usual complement of tourists and, on this occasion a group of scientists, she had completed two weeks without incident, visiting Greenland. But after leaving Sukkertoppen to cruise up the southwest coast to Disko, she hit a reef and had to be abandoned.

Portia enjoyed an equally eventful but longer career. In 1892 she was on passage from Pilley's Island to New York with her usual complement of passengers and a cargo of iron pyrites, when a magnificent iceberg came into view. Some of the passengers, unsurprisingly, asked the master if they might have a closer look. As *Portia* came near there was a mighty explosive roar and the iceberg disintegrated. A huge portion fell into the sea and came up under the ship, lifting her out of the water and putting her in danger of having her back broken. It was only a massive wave that saved *Portia* by sweeping her clear and, miraculously, depositing her on an even keel. David Keir, in *The Bowring Story* has this to say about the occurrence:

> Such incidents at sea can be exaggerated. But the passengers' account of the *Portia* affair gives the story authenticity. It is contained in a testimonial signed by them after their lucky escape. They said that a huge iceberg, which *Portia* was passing, suddenly "crumbled and turned in the water; striking and raising the ship from the sea and causing for the moment intense anxiety to all on board." The testimonial then warmly praised the captain's coolness, nautical skill and good judgement, though one is tempted to think that perhaps he might have shown still better judgement resisting his passengers' persuasions and giving the iceberg a wider berth.

To add to her list of adventures, *Portia* came close to complete destruction when, in April 1899, while she was discharging her cargo at New York, fire broke out in one of the holds. She was carrying several hundred barrels of kerosene which, had it been generally known, would have quickly dispersed the thousands of viewers who gathered to watch the blaze. Two steam tugs were summoned to pull the ship away from the wharf if necessary, but sustained efforts by firemen eventually brought the fire under control, confounding a local newspaper which had already published headlines reading, 'Destruction of Ship and Cargo Imminent'. The damage caused a delay of six weeks in a Brooklyn shipyard while extensive repairs were carried out, after which *Portia* set off again on her established run. But, sadly, her days were numbered; her refurbishment was to be of no avail. On the return journey to Newfoundland in July, she was wrecked on Big Fish Shoal in fog, just 10 miles off Halifax, with the loss, mercifully, of but one life.

In order to fulfil the need felt by the Liverpool office to establish closer links between the Red Cross Line and Liverpool, the steamship *Capulet* was built in 1884 at the yard of T. Richardson & Sons of Hartlepool especially, as mentioned earlier, for the transatlantic service. Registered under the recently created Canada and Newfoundland Steamship Line, she was described as having 'generous accommodation for saloon class passengers, space for upwards of 800 tons of cargo, and the capacity to average better than 11 knots on a normal crossing.' *Capulet* was certainly quite a fast ship at the time, frequently clipping a day off the steaming time of other vessels on the transatlantic run. Throughout almost all of her twelve years successful service, she sailed under the command of one master, Captain W. H. Ellis.

Very near the end of a voyage from Liverpool to St John's, in June 1896, *Capulet* reported that she was detained off the Newfoundland coast by fog and icebergs. Captain Ellis, groping his way through the thick fog, was suddenly confronted by an iceberg, with which he narrowly avoided collision by going full speed astern, and he safely made his landfall. Incidents such as this were not uncommon around the Newfoundland coastline, and in his thirty years of steamship command, Captain Ellis would certainly have experienced many.

However, his confidence, acquired over the years, would no doubt have been shattered some two weeks later when *Capulet*, having started her return journey on 22 June, and was on passage from Halifax to St John's, struck the cliff at Marine Cove, near St Shott's, St Mary's Bay, where many ships had met their end over the years in the strong, irregular currents, in waters which had become well known as a ship's graveyard. Bowring Brothers received a message early on the morning of 23 June, which simply said that the ship was aground, but that the passengers and crew had been landed safely. However, a later message from the local constable at St Mary's stated rather more graphically: 'ss *Capulet*, for St John's, a total wreck at Mariner's (*sic*) Cove. Passengers and crew saved.'

The stranded 67 passengers and crew were soon picked up by a coastal steamer, taken to Placentia railhead and put on a train to St John's. The ship's log, more than 50 mailbags and much personal property were lost, largely as a result of looting. The Governor ordered a court of enquiry, as a result of which Captain Ellis was held to blame for the loss of his ship. The court, however, recognizing the skill with which he brought all his passengers and crew to safety, decided that he should not be deprived of his master's certificate. The loss of *Miranda, Portia* and *Capulet* was a serious blow to the Red Cross Line, but the service continued, with the aid of ships of other owners until, in 1909, a brand new ship, *Florizel*, joined the fleet.

While the passenger and cargo services of Bowring ships continued to prosper notwithstanding these losses, the seal fishery, hazardous as ever, was being carried on with mixed fortunes. Bowring ships taking part regularly in the seal hunt during the 1880s and1890s were *Eagle, Falcon, Kite, Aurora, Algerine* and, towards the end of the century, the famous *Terra Nova*. This historic vessel was purchased by Bowring Brothers from the Dundee Seal & Whale Fishing Company in January 1898 and, during two separate periods of ownership by the company would experience a varied and, at times, precarious existence, in addition to her significant contribution to the seal fishery in the hands of her various owners.

On 19 March 1890 when at the ice, *Terra Nova*, owned and operated at the time by William Stephen & Co. of St John's, temporarily lost some of her men, who had left their ship at daylight in pursuit of seals. It wasn't until some six hours later that they came across a large patch, which kept them occupied until dusk. By this time *Terra Nova* was all of 20 miles distant; so the men made for *Kite*, lying only about six miles away. They hardly expected a particularly warm welcome, as there were over 200 of them. However, Captain William Knee, the master of *Kite*, in spite of having a ship's complement of nearly 150 men of his own, found himself acting as host to around 500 sealers who appeared from all directions.

Both *Kite* and *Falcon*, when not in the hunt for seals, frequently found employment with expeditions, as indeed did other sealing vessels. These two ships were both built in Germany, but neither of them joined the Bowring sealing fleet until some years after service with other owners. Barque-rigged with auxiliary power they both established a relationship with the explorer, Robert Peary and gave valuable service off Greenland and up into the Arctic on a number of occasions.

Kite first met up with Peary in June 1891 when he led an expedition sponsored by the Philadelphia Academy of Natural Sciences, the purpose of which was to carry out a study of the northern parts of Greenland. He was accompanied by his wife and five associates among whom was Dr F. A. Cook, who in later years was to become involved in a serious disagreement with Peary as to which of them reached the North Pole first.

The expedition left from New York and *Kite*, after leaving the Hudson River, set course for Whale Bay in Greenland. On 14 July the ship was forcing her way through broken ice when the wheel was torn from the hands of the two helmsmen. In going astern in order to give her space to build up speed and force her way through the next pack of ice, *Kite*'s rudder struck a submerged floe and the helm swung over violently, pinning Robert Peary against the bulkhead of the wheelhouse, breaking his right leg. Such a painful experience might well not only have ruined his expedition but could also have put him off using *Kite* again. But, a year later, she picked him up after he had crossed northern Greenland over the Humboldt Glacier to Independence Bay.

Falcon's participation in one of Peary's Arctic expeditions occurred two years later, in July 1893, when she sailed out of St John's with, not only the great explorer himself on board but, in addition on deck, according to David Keir in *The Bowring Story* . . . 'eight Mexican donkeys, two St Bernards, several teams of Eskimo dogs which Peary had brought back from his former expedition, and a number of homing pigeons'. Thanks to a voyage that was reasonably clear of ice, no damage was incurred either to man or beast and *Falcon* dropped anchor at the head of Bowdoin Bay on 3 August. As a demonstration of his satisfaction with the Bowring ship that had brought him safely and uninjured to his destination, he named the small harbour, in which the vessel lay, Falcon Bay and the cliff that rose above it, Mount Bartlett after her master, probably Henry Bartlett, one of a number of a family that served the company as sealing skippers between 1893 and 1929. This was one of *Falcon's* last voyages; she was reported missing in 1894 on a voyage from Philadelphia to St John's with a cargo of coal.

Before we leave Newfoundland for a while, and as the 20th century approaches, it is worth noting that the sealing trade would continue for many years with its habitual ups and downs. But a highly significant development was about to alter, for all time, the annual visit to the ice. This was the introduction of iron vessels to replace those of wood, which had served the industry so effectively for a hundred years or more. In 1906, Harvey's, a well-known Newfoundland family business, who also originally came from Devon and who had been involved in the sealing business for a number of years, sent, for the first time, an iron steamer to the ice. This, whilst clearly being a courageous move, was nevertheless dictated by a need to take advantage of an improving market and a desire to catch more seals. Prices for seal products were improving from a low point in the 1880s and larger vessels were needed. The wooden ships, whilst having served the industry well, could not penetrate deeply enough into the ice and the crews were subjected, as we have seen, to walking long distances and facing considerable dangers, sometimes without finding a single seal. The introduction of iron ships was by no means universally accepted; many of the older hands in the business believing that, whereas wood could withstand and absorb a battering by heavy ice, iron-hulled vessels would buckle under the impact. But they would soon be eating their words. Harvey's well-named *Adventure*, designed with a strongly plated bow and sturdy metal cross-bracing within her hull, could ride up on an ice-floe and crack it under her own weight. This very successful development soon had its adherents; a first season with a cargo of 30,000 pelts was enough to persuade others to adopt iron-hulled sealers and in 1909 Bowring Brothers launched the earlier mentioned *Florizel* (3,081 tons) to be followed a couple of years later by *Stephano* (3,449 tons). These two ships, of which there will be more to tell, were highly successful both as sealers and, when not at the ice, performing sterling service as comfortable passenger liners.

Finally, a word about an aspect of Bowring Brothers' business not yet touched upon, the fresh fish business as distinct from the cod fishery. In March 1898 Bowring Brothers wrote to the Liverpool office seeking information regarding the possibility of a market in England for fresh fish from Newfoundland. It appears that a Mr Reid (possibly of the same family as played a leading part in the construction of The Newfoundland Railway) had initiated the enquiry. The following letter provides an interesting aspect of this hitherto undisclosed activity, which would nevertheless be continued from time to time and in varying forms for many years.

18, Water Street
Liverpool April 5th 1898

Messrs. Bowring Bros.
St John's NF
Dear Sirs

Fresh Fish Business to Great Britain

Your interesting letter of 16th March has our attention, and we shall be very pleased to second the endeavours of Mr Reid. We have mentioned the matter to our London office, and we have no doubt they will be able to work in that market. In any case we could arrange the business satisfactorily through Liverpool. We have conferred with one of our largest distributors of fresh fish, who has already for some years been getting frozen salmon from Nova Scotia & Canada. In this class of fish and in lobster, the best prospect offers. There are times when codfish is so plentiful on these coasts and the quantity offering so much in excess of the demand & opportunities of distributing, that it is almost given away. It would only be at an occasional time when bad weather or other causes interfered with the catch of codfish, that there would be a chance of supplying the market, with frozen codfish from store, and getting a price to compensate for freight & storage expenses. There is ample cold storage on this side at Liverpool & London and the various distributing centres, the charge being for storage 20/- per ton for the first month, & 17/6 per month afterwards. There is no doubt a good opening for lobster, salmon, halibut, trout , fresh water eels, prawns, smelts and sparlings, and at times perhaps codfish. We would recommend a trial shipment. You will be alive to the necessity for care in handling, and seeing all arrangements for cold storage, during transit by rail, & to and from the steamers are complete. The great matter is to see that the fish are well frozen immediately after being taken from the water, while they are fresh. If the fish are allowed to lie about before being frozen, the condition will be very faulty on their arrival here. We have seen some frozen salmon styled chilled Canadian salmon, which sells in the shops at 10d to 1/- per lb. and which yields 7d to 8d per lb. to the importer. This should compensate for freight, storage and commission, which would be 5%, covering commission & guarantee. The salmon we saw comes in large cases about 6ft. by 2ft. by 3ft., carefully made of dried wood, the seams carefully dovetailed, and all lined with thick paper each fish being wrapped in paper. We have no doubt you could arrange for shipment by steamers with refrigerators across the Atlantic. We note your estimate with regard to lobsters. The average fresh lobster offered here during the season seems from 1lb. to 1 1/2 lbs., and an average price is 10d. to 1/- per lb. Whether you supply the quality to command this same figure remains to be seen. Some of the large lobsters run from 2/- to 3/- each. We shall be very pleased to take a trial shipment & do our best for you. We are making inquiries as to paper pulp, and understand there is a good opening for this article, the wood pulp being much preferred for certain purposes. As to investing in this or other enterprises of Mr Reid we shall be glad to consider the matter, when you can give us fuller details, as to the undertaking & the volume of business.

We are Dear Sirs
Yours very truly
C T Bowring & Co.

Chapter 6

AT THE END OF THE 19th century, the variety and locations of the growing number of different operations of Bowring branches called for a more structured organization and in 1899 C. T. Bowring & Company, Limited was registered with a capital of £600,000 to acquire and carry on the business of merchants, shipowners, insurance and general brokers etc.; at Liverpool, London, and Cardiff as C. T. Bowring & Company, at New York as Bowring & Archibald, and in Newfoundland as Bowring Brothers, each branch of the organization being incorporated in the country in which it was based. In addition to these three main constituents of the 'group', other companies had been registered to carry on specific activities, particularly with regard to the ownership and operation of the growing number of ships.

The first directors of the 'parent company' (C. T. Bowring & Company, Limited) were William Benjamin Bowring, Thomas Benjamin Bowring, Frederick Charles Bowring, Edgar Rennie Bowring, John Bowring Wimble, Lawrence Bowring Stoddart, Henry Alfred Bowring and Charles Warren Bowring. John Wimble and Lawrence Stoddart were married to Charles Tricks' daughters Harriet and Charlotte respectively.

While Bowring Brothers were wrestling with the vicissitudes of their business in Newfoundland, the companies in England were making rapid progress in relatively new and developing enterprises including, particularly, insurance broking and underwriting, about which there will be more to be said in due course. But it is now appropriate that we should follow the company's fortunes at sea.

As we have already seen, the New York, Newfoundland and Halifax Steamship Company was registered to conduct the affairs of the Red Cross Line; the English and American Shipping Company Limited, which was managed by the London branch of C. T. Bowring, was established to run the ships operated by that office, and the Red Cross Shipping Company Limited, registered at Liverpool, owned the larger sailing vessels and, later, the steamers *Benedick* and *Othello*.

In 1887 the shrewd and enlightened George Bowring, who was head of the London office and of whose untimely death in 1891 at the age of forty we are already aware, gave a considerable boost to the company's fortunes by purchasing a ship which was being built for other owners by John Redhead & Co. at South Shields. This vessel, *Tafna* (2,231 tons), was soon to be joined by the practically identical *Guy Colin*, completed in 1888 by T. Richardson & Sons at Hartlepool. Both ships were registered with the English and American Shipping Company, in which the ore-trading firm of Naylor Benzon & Company were minority shareholders. There was a strong relationship with this company, which was to last for many years, and which can be understood from the regular pattern of the voyages performed by these two ships. They were involved in a triangular trade between the United Kingdom, the Mediterranean and the USA. A typical voyage would include a cargo of coal from the Bristol Channel to a port in the Mediterranean, followed by a short passage in ballast to Huelva in Spain. Here ore, on behalf of Naylor Benzon, would be loaded for the USA. For the return voyage the ships would probably load grain and general cargo for the United Kingdom and, in some cases, the Continent.

The success of this operation so enthused the directors that later in 1888, they agreed to the purchase of *Avalon*, built by C. S. Swan & Hunter at Newcastle upon Tyne and the following year, *Elba* and *Benisaf* from the yards of T. Richardson at Hartlepool and Wm Doxford of Sunderland respectively. Now there was no stopping them. During the 1890s no fewer than 11 new ships were ordered involving heavy capital outlay and much sound judgement. All between 2,500 and 3,000 tons, these vessels were *Bona, Justin, Mokta, Huelva, Murcia, Adra, Vera, Roda, Pola, Inca* and *Mora*. But, as we know, the architect of these developments did not live to see the fruitfulness of his farsighted drive and entrepreneurial flare.

For all his commercial acumen, George could never be described as being of a wholly orthodox disposition. For example, the profit-sharing scheme he devised with his confidential clerk, though admirable in concept and no doubt well deserved by the fortunate participant, probably caused a certain amount of muttering among the elders in Liverpool, notwithstanding their broadly liberal outlook. But it was part of the family heritage to be non-conformist.

When George died there was no one immediately available in the London office with the ability to develop the ideas that had interested him so much during his short life. In *The Bowring Story*, David Keir throws some light on one interesting aspect of the conduct of the office:

> To see the workings of this liberal tradition we might well go to James Septimus Wellings, the confidential clerk . . . Wellings, who had come from the Liverpool office to London with his master, continued to keep a faithful eye on things. When Thomas Bowring returned from New York to take over the management of the London office, Mr Wellings, as he was called by everybody, was at his elbow with information and advice. Similarly, when George Bowring's second son Harvey joined the firm immediately on leaving school in 1904, Mr Wellings, as guardian and custodian of his old master's vision, welcomed the young man who was one day to succeed to the direction of the company's insurance affairs, and gave him all the proper words of advice.
>
> Tall, quietly spoken, dressed always in dark morning clothes with a short jacket, Mr Wellings was a dignified figure. Moreover, he gave an impression of thorough stability, so that both the younger and the older people in the office knew that they could take problems of any kind to him and be assured of sound, reliable, sympathetic advice, followed by an absolute respect of their confidences. He kept the personal accounts of many members of the family in his office, and he knew, but never disclosed, the financial affairs of everyone in the business from the senior members of the board room down to the newest apprentices. If an account went into the red, Mr Wellings would discreetly report the fact to the individual concerned; and such was the force of this honest personality that there was never any need for the matter to be raised again . . . In those days the office hours were nominally from 9.00 a.m. to 6.00 p.m; but if Walter Hargreaves, who became the company's leading insurance broker in 1897, stayed late the rest of the staff had to do the same. Yet although the only compensation for an unexpected day's work till 9.00 p.m. was a half-crown's tea money, Mr Wellings' calm example usually quelled any sense of resentment in the breasts of the other clerks. When the appropriate moment came, he would reach for his black bowler hat with the rest of them, and walk contentedly home to play the organ. This was a passion. In his last house he installed an instrument with an electric blower, and there as in the office devoted himself to harmonious pursuits.

Anyone who has been engaged in the shipping industry will aver that the ups and downs of its fortunes can be as varied and sometimes as menacing as the face of the sea itself. Over the years the Bowring maritime experience would prove to be no different from that of most other shipowners. Overall the English and American Shipping Company brought in considerable revenue in spite of occasional setbacks. The regularity of the Bristol Channel-Mediterranean-USA run could not always be maintained, however, and there were times when the ships would carry their cargoes of ore (invariably on behalf of Naylor Benzon) and coal to Sydney, Nova Scotia or to Montreal. The most besetting problems seemed to stem from delays in loading and discharging, and demurrage claims. Whether or not Thomas shared George's great enthusiasm for shipping I do not know, but he certainly had his work cut out in the early years of the twentieth century scouring the ports of Europe and the eastern Seaboard of North America for cargoes. One of his most persistent complaints concerned the length of time it took to discharge a cargo at Sydney, a much-visited port; if the delay were too long there would be no profit in the voyage. He was indeed constrained in 1901 to write: 'Things are very bad for ships now, and we find it difficult to make both ends meet'. By 1903, feeling in need of a rest, Thomas and his American wife, Annie, took a four month trip to Burma, Ceylon and India, and they attended the Durbar, the pageantry of which delighted them.

He found on his return that nothing much had changed and that the constant search for cargoes, the wrestling with delays and the dilatoriness of some of the companies with which he was dealing still persisted. But the many and frequently irksome problems of running a shipping company did not apparently seriously sap the energy of Thomas or the other directors nor, it seems, were they robbed of time needed to pursue other ventures. They started a duck farm.

In spite of, or maybe because of, the many years most members of the family had spent overseas, for some, the yearning to return to their roots was irresistible and both Thomas and his father, Edward, had bought houses in Moretonhampstead. It is reasonable to suppose therefore that Dartmoor Duck Farm Ltd was situated in or near the small Devon town at the eastern edge of Dartmoor, which was well known to and closely associated with some of Benjamin's successors and their families. Edward, on his retirement, purchased a large well-known house called Borohaye in Court Street, and Thomas, probably some years before he retired, acquired Pitt House in Ford Street. Not much is known about the duck farm and, in fact, it was not to enjoy a noticeably long or prosperous existence. However, there were times when it exercised Thomas's mind. In February 1906 he wrote, with some indignation, to the manager of the farm in connection with the local miller's intention to charge rent for Thomas's ducks' use of the millpond: 'I should not think of paying any rent, on principle,' he insisted. 'They cannot prevent your ducks taking a swim in the pond if they feel like it, and of course the land is mine . . . nor can they, I should think, charge you with trespass because your ducks swim on their water. We had the "first fruit" for dinner yesterday, and if all the rest are as good as that one, they are excellent . . .'

As chairman of this rustic enterprise, Thomas took the management of its affairs seriously, even to the extent of overseeing the stocktaking, a matter to which he gave as much consideration as if he were coping with loading delays at Huelva. In March 1908, on a visit to Moreton-hampstead, he noted that 127 duck, 794 hen and 72 goose eggs had been collected and that 336 eggs had been sold. Being reasonably satisfied with the conduct of the business, he left an order for a couple of dozen eggs and a chicken or a duck to be delivered each week to his London house at Palace Gate. It seems, however, that his fellow directors were somewhat less than satisfied with the brace of chickens they received at the end of the year in lieu of fees, and in April it was decided to wind up the company. Whether or not Thomas ever received any of the produce he had ordered for his household in London isn't known.

But, in contrast with the ill-fated poultry pursuits in Devon, the English and American Shipping Company was prospering. Their ships were operating profitably and were seldom in ballast. Such, indeed, was the success of the company that a number of new vessels were built during the first three years of the new century. *Mystic, Catalone, Mira,* and *Dominion* were all completed on the Tyne by C. S. Swan & Hunter Ltd who, in the years ahead, would be chosen to build other ships for various Bowring shipping interests. In the first ten years of the 1900s the fleet was further enlarged with the addition of *Zafra, Gafsa, Brica, Lorca, Tafna* (II), and in 1913, *Noya,* the last ship to be ordered before the outbreak of the First World War.

During these years of developing trade across the Atlantic, the New York office of Bowring and Archibald, with the co-operation of Thomas in London and his cousin William in Liverpool, turned their eyes towards the Pacific. At the end of the 19th century Laurence Stoddart was head of the New York office, having succeeded Thomas when he moved to London. He was assisted by Charles Warren Bowring, who had come to New York from St John's. In addition to his undoubted business skills, Laurence Stoddart was a golfer of some renown and in October 1894 won the first American Amateur Golf Championship. When not on the links, however, we can confidently assume that he was furthering the interests of Bowring and Archibald who, while still acting as shipbrokers and grain exporters, were New York managers of the Red Cross Line and helped to fix cargoes for the English and American Shipping Company.

Early in 1898, Bowring and Archibald and the Tweedie Trading Company were jointly approached by a Mr Butler, a prominent New York businessman, who had been informed that the Atchison, Topeka and Santa Fe Railway wanted a shipping company to operate in association with them out of San Diego to Japan and China. Butler wanted to know whether Bowring and Archibald and Tweedie Trading would consider joining him and a few others in a joint venture to start a shipping line to meet the railway company's wishes.

On 1 September 1898 Thomas wrote a letter to an old friend and business associate, whose name was Ascherson, in which he goes to some lengths to explain the positive thinking behind this proposal:

> A large cotton business is being rapidly developed between the Southern States of America and Japan and China, and during the cotton season I think I am correct in saying that almost full cargoes can be relied on. Again during the tea season from China and Japan full cargoes can be relied on. The tea season commences in the early part of the year and runs up to the middle of the year while the cotton season as you are aware commences in October and runs on into the Spring. Therefore speaking in a general way we are practically sure of full cargoes from California for six months of the year and full cargoes from China and Japan for six months of the year. At the same time of course there is plenty of other freight shipped all year round in both directions besides tea and cotton, and naturally as time goes on the business should develop materially. The other Railway Companies add continually to their fleets of steamers showing how rapidly the trade is being developed, and with a company such as the A. T. and S. F. Co. which has its own road all the way from San Diego to Chicago, they certainly should be in as good a position as any of the other lines. I should add that the arrangements between the other Railway Companies and their steamers are nothing like as favourable to the steamers as ours, inasmuch as some of the steamers get only 33 per cent of the through rate and the most that any of the others get is 40 per cent of the through rate, while we are to get 50 per cent.

Negotiations for the formation of a new steamship company were proceeding apace when Thomas wrote this letter; it was to be called the Californian and Oriental Line. The A. T. and S. F. Co. were to contribute a subsidy of $5,000 for each round trip, free wharfage would be provided at San Diego and the contract for running the service was to be for five years. It was intended that the new line would be fully operational in 1899 and to this end Thomas and William Bowring set about finding suitable tonnage. As a start they managed to charter a Furness Withy ship, *Carlisle City*, a vessel described by Thomas as being 'a boat of enormous cubical capacity', and capable of steaming at between 11 and 12 knots. They also succeeded in chartering *Belgian King* from Swan Hunter and spent much time and energy searching for additional suitable ships. When the various accountants had drawn up the shareholding agreements, the following was the apportionment of capital in the company:

	5% Mortgage or 6% Preferred as decided on	Common Stock
English and American Shipping Co.	$75,000	$150,000
Butler		$250,000
Parker	$10,000	$20,000
Bowring and Archibald	$32,500	$65,000
Harris & Dixon & Swift	$75,000	$150,000
T. B. Bowring	$5,000	$10,000
Jacobs	$2,500	$5,000
Tweedie Trading Company		$350,000
	$200,000	$1,000,000

It will be seen that the Bowring holding of stock amounted to 22.5 per cent divided between the English and American Shipping Company, Bowring and Archibald, and Thomas himself.

The management of the Californian and Oriental Line was in the hands of Bowring and Archibald who, in 1899, opened an office in San Diego, and early in the year the ships under their control were duly steaming between various Californian ports and Japan and China. Thomas was enormously enthusiastic about the future of this new shipping venture. He saw it as 'one of the opportunities that occur in a lifetime ...' and had visions of amalgamating the Californian and Oriental Line with the English and American Shipping Company thus creating a large enough company to be floated on the stock market which, as he saw it, would be to the mutual advantage of both. Sadly, however, his optimism was soon to be dashed. The life of the company was to be a short one and it went into liquidation in 1902, but in precisely what circumstances there is no record.

In 1900 Bowring and Archibald became a branch of C. T. Bowring & Co. taking on, for a short while, the name of the parent company, and the San Diego office was moved to San Francisco in order, it was hoped, to participate in a wider range of interests. Indeed, such were these hopes that a number of the more recently joined younger members of the parent company visited San Francisco during the next few years to participate in the branch's continuing business as shipbrokers, as traders in a variety of merchandise and in the exportation of lumber. As a branch of the New York office the name was changed to Bowring and Company and in 1903 Edward Skimming, the son of Edward Bowring's daughter Fanny Charlotte, was sent out to manage its affairs. 'Ted' Skimming was eventually to become chairman of the whole Bowring group of companies during part of and after the Second World War. Harvey Bowring, second son of the enterprising George, joined him in 1907. When Harvey arrived in San Francisco he found himself surrounded by the detritus from the previous year's appalling earthquake and subsequent devastating fire. The office had moved to temporary accommodation and a year later acquired new premises in Tacoma, where it hoped to have more success with the lumber trade. But the loss of records and the demoralizing effects of successive labour strikes following the earthquake led to a steady reduction in the prosperity of the business and it was sold in 1910 when Harvey came home to London. There he began his long and successful career as the first member of the Bowring family to devote his time and energy solely to the rapidly expanding insurance business and to develop the company's relationship with Lloyd's, so providentially initiated by his father.

In spite of a variety of interesting developments in numerous directions during the years that lay ahead, nearly all of them extensions of existing activities, it was the involvement in insurance that would eventually outstrip all other pursuits and, in due course, dictate the ultimate destiny of the Bowring companies. Such is the significance of this aspect of the growth of the business from the turn of the century onwards that it deserves to be considered separately. In the meantime, however, developments in trading and shipping, and even excursions into the worlds of industry, chemical manufacture and engineering, would add to the prestige and worldwide recognition of Benjamin Bowring's commercial heritage in the years ahead.

While Harvey Bowring in London was engaged in developing the company's status in the insurance business generally and at Lloyd's in particular, his kinsmen in Liverpool were faced, in 1911, with a serious strike which brought the city's commerce to a virtual standstill. Dockers, seamen, firemen, railway and electricity workers, and street cleaners all withdrew their labour. The streets became clogged with stinking rubbish and deliveries of coal to hospitals were paralysed. Some 3,000 special constables were enrolled to help the hard-pressed police force when rioting and arson followed the dock-workers being kept out of the docks. After more than two weeks settlement was achieved, but not easily. Although in a number of cases agreement was reached with the strike leaders, sympathetic strike action caused many men to remain out of work. In all some 80,000 members of Liverpool's labour force took part in the strike including, in addition to those already mentioned, stewards, carters and warehouse workers.

At this stage in the firm's development the closest association with industrial labour was with ships' crews, and the welfare of those employed by the various Bowring shipping interests was a matter of profound concern to the directors. This became a matter for special consideration after the appalling winter weather at the beginning of 1912. The severity of the conditions is well described by David Keir in *The Bowring Story*:

> For months passages were delayed as ships ran for shelter or were driven far off course in the gales and hurricanes unleashed on the North Atlantic. In the company's offices both at St John's and in Liverpool the movements of the fleet were anxiously watched as ship after ship limped home with deck-houses battered by green seas, top hamper and boats torn away, and cargoes often damaged by shifting or by salt water.

Possibly a little shaken by the discomforts endured by some of their crews during the previous winter, the directors felt that all members of the ships' companies should be aware of their responsibilities towards them. At the end of October 1912, maybe as much with thoughts in mind of the morale of their crews in general as anything else, Thomas Bowring wrote to a senior ships' manager regarding one particular aspect of concern:

The question of the housing of the crews on Merchant ships is one that should receive very much more attention than we fear it is getting . . . We feel, however, that you yourself are in sympathy with the movement to improve conditions and we believe that most of our masters are imbued with the same spirit.

The present letter is to say that we wish you to impress upon each of the Masters as well as Officers employed in ships which carry Apprentices that we require them to see that our Apprentices are treated in a manner befitting young men who before long will be fellow officers of theirs.

We do not in any way mean to infer from this that the treatment they already give these young men is anything which it should not be, but it is merely to let them all know that it is a question we intend to watch very carefully.

We wish you to give instructions to each Master carrying Apprentices that they have their meals in the cabin, and to any objection which might be made in regard to their being 'dirty' etc., we would say that this is no real objection at all, and it will be a discipline for the young men, inasmuch that they will have to wash and brush up before going into the cabin for their meals.

Office staff were also treated with similar consideration, of which I give a rather whimsical example. At Christmas in the Liverpool office they were subjected to a slightly bizarre ritual when everyone, managers, clerks, office boys and all levels of employees, took part in a procession past the desks of the directors, (except for the chairman they all sat in the same room), who would dispense largesse in the shape of a shiny half-sovereign, (the same for all, regardless of rank), convey seasonal greetings and generally express appreciation of each individual's efforts during the past year. It was on one such occasion, some twenty years on, that Frederick Charles Bowring, who had become chairman of the company, and who might well be remembered for his supervision at New York of the loading of Molasses over a cargo of bacon aboard *Juliet*, was confronted by a quite senior departmental manager:

'Now let me see, you are?' he asked
'Jack Baxter,' came the reply.
'Ah yes, Baxter, and how long have you been with us now?'
'Nine years, sir,' answered Baxter with some pride and satisfaction.
'Oh good, Baxter,' said Fred, 'are you settling down alright?'

Fred Bowring, a bachelor, was a most generous supporter of numerous charities, a staunch Liberal, as indeed were virtually all his kinsmen, and, as the above incident shows, inclined on occasions to behave with a modicum of eccentricity. Like them he devoted much of his time to civic matters, about which there will be more to be said anon; suffice it to say at this stage, the pace of business life at the turn of the century was so much gentler, that there was more time to take an interest in public affairs – and there was far greater willingness to do so among businessmen than there is today.

Chapter 7

IT WILL BE RECALLED that back in 1862, shortly after the establishment of Bowring and Archibald at New York, this new company became involved in the transport of petroleum products, as well as its more usual activity of purchasing a wide range of commodities for shipment to Great Britain. This was a bold entry into an industry which was in its earliest stages of development, oil only having been struck three years previously near Titusville in Pennsylvania by a one-time railroad conductor named Edwin Drake, whose well produced oil from a depth of under 70 feet. Although the existence of oil had been known since before 3,000 BC in Mesopotamia, Drake's discovery marks the introduction of *drilled* oil to the Western world.

It would be interesting to know precisely what persuaded William Bowring, who was in charge of the New York office, to become involved in the transport of the products of the oil well – and when. The internal combustion engine was still some way off and the main uses for mineral oil were for lubrication and as lamp oil – not, one would have thought, a particularly exciting commercial prospect. Nevertheless, the industry did develop with great speed and oil wells soon sprang up in many parts of the world, particularly the USA and Russia; and there were those farsighted enough to see that vast fortunes would be made in the future from the refining and marketing of 'black gold' as it soon became known. No doubt William and his colleagues soon became fully aware of the current 'buzz' in United States commercial circles, and of the progress being made by John D. Rockefeller, who in 1870 established the Standard Oil Company of Ohio, creating at the time a virtual monopoly until the Swedish Nobel brothers made their discovery of huge supplies of oil at Baku in Russia. In his history of The 'Shell' Transport and Trading Company 1897-1997, *A Century of Oil*, (Weidenfeld & Nicholson, 1997) Stephen Howarth observes:

> The Baku fields had been hand-dug since before Marco Polo's time. In 1872, in order that they could be more thoroughly exploited, they were released from their limiting status as a state monopoly. In 1874, the region's annual production was 600,000 barrels. Ten years later, that figure

had multiplied 18 times over, to 10.8 million barrels, or nearly one-third of contemporary American production.

But in the meantime American production dominated, and Charles Tricks noted on 9 January 1873, (by which time William had been succeeded at New York by Thomas Benjamin as head of Bowring and Archibald) that he sold 200 barrels of imported petroleum and four days later he recorded the sale of a further 750 barrels. By March Bowring and Archibald, now well established in the business, authorized him by cable to sell 10,000 barrels. Between 1873 and 1875 they made a number of shipments of naphtha and petroleum, each of around 2,000 barrels. But barrels were not a satisfactory method of transporting oil. They stowed badly because of their shape, and they leaked. There was, in these early days, an alternative method of shipment in packaged pairs of five-gallon tins; this was known as 'Case Oil' and was popular with the transatlantic trade because of its ease of handling both by crews and customers. The highly inflammable nature of oil, especially in leaking barrels, was anathema to sailors, for whom fire at sea was a much dreaded hazard. It is recorded that the first shipment of oil across the Atlantic in barrels was aboard a sailing vessel named *Elizabeth Watts*. When her crew became aware of the nature of the cargo they took to their heels, and a scratch crew was enrolled by taking on heavily inebriated 'volunteers' from nearby dockside hostelries.

As a result of the destruction of records during the Second World War, there is a dearth of information about Bowring's early days in the transport and trading of petroleum products, but there is a reference in the *Petroleum and Mining News* of 9 April 1904 to the effect that the company was one of the pioneers in the importation and distribution of oil in Great Britain, and when the Bowring Petroleum Company Limited was formed in 1900 to consolidate the various oil interests, they confidently stated in their advertisements that they were the 'Oldest Importers of Petroleum into Great Britain', a claim that was never openly disputed.

It might be helpful at this juncture to revert to members of the family of whom, though they played their part in the development of the company, little has been heard. Benjamin Bowring's fourth son, Edward who, it will be recalled, incurred paternal displeasure when he played fast and loose with the girls of St John's, came back to England in the mid 1850s after some twenty years as a partner in Bowring Brothers. He retired to Moretonhampstead for a while before moving to East Molesey in Surrey where he died in 1873 aged fifty-four, by which time his elder son, Thomas Benjamin, had succeeded to the management of Bowring and Archibald at New York. Edward's younger son, Henry Edward, elected to remain in England and in 1873 entered into partnership with John D. Jamieson. By establishing the firm of Bowring and Jamieson in 1873 as ship and insurance brokers with offices at 17, Fenchurch Street, they had effectively created the first Bowring office in the City of London.

Four years later, Henry Edward was relieved of his duties by the arrival in London of Charles Tricks' son George who, without a moment's delay instilled into the partnership the growing importance of oil. Thus a strong and effective relationship between Bowring and Archibald at New York and Bowring and Jamieson in London was established. This soon resulted in sizeable quantities of oil and petroleum products being imported into Thames Haven. By the end of 1880 the trade had expanded to such an extent that Thomas in his New York office was in serious negotiation with the Standard Oil Company for increased supplies. During the following year the exports of petroleum products from America to England were greatly increased.

But, as my father often advised me, 'the band doesn't play all the time'. Notwithstanding the growing success of the oil operation, there would be uncertainties and setbacks, as can be discerned from a letter written in July 1881 by Charles Tricks to Thomas:

> I must own to disappointment at the result from New York – for looking at the enormous business done by Bowring and Archibald in Petroleum and their commissions and brokerages on ships and goods, I looked for much more. There must have been some large losses which we know nothing about here, and only surmise it must have been on joint interest in sugar or some other article.

Whatever the cause of Charles Tricks' vexation, the overall picture was rosy enough. In 1882 he wrote to his son Charles, who was still managing the affairs of Bowring Brothers in Newfoundland, reporting that the petroleum business in London was proving to be so successful that Bowring, Jamieson and Company (as they were now designated) had purchased their own wharf. This was the St Leonard's Wharf on the Thames where the quantity of oil from America, landed and sold, impressed Charles Tricks so much that he wrote in good humour to St John's:

We have just heard from George the result of the first 6 months' working of his wharf which looks very well, and George himself is very sanguine of making a real good thing of it. If the petroleum trade continues on the same scale as it has for some years assumed, I have no doubt but it will be a very good thing ... We have advanced a large sum of money to Bowring, Jamieson and Company to carry it on and it certainly promises well, but it is young times.

In the early part of 1883 Charles Tricks was happily experiencing some relief from the gout that had become such a burden to him in recent years, but he was beginning to feel his age. He was surely cheered, however, by the progress being made by his son in London and on 4th January he wrote again to St John's:

No doubt George has developed a wonderful business in London and the wharf appears to look as if it was a very good thing. His general account shows a credit balance of £9,309.16.5. of which George's share is £6,271.10.1 and Jamieson's £3,038.6.4 ... They appear to hold a large quantity of petroleum, which William says has been taken at prices which will pay. So on the whole our London partner may well congratulate himself. He has indeed done very well for himself and us.

So successful was George during the next year that the parent company were persuaded to acquire the 815-ton barque *Slieve Bloom* to carry increasing cargoes of paraffin in barrels from the United States to the United Kingdom. These petroleum products now enjoyed the brand name Royal Daylight. It seems, however, that *Slieve Bloom* may not have been entirely satisfactory as she was sold in 1886. Nevertheless, even after the later introduction of oil transport in bulk, the New York office continued to export great quantities of their petroleum products in barrels to the United Kingdom and the Continent on a variety of ships including the White Star liner *Cufic* and the Rank, Gilmour steamers *St Regulus* and *St Ronans*.

During the 1870s and 1880s there was much experimentation in the development of oil tank steamers. The earliest vessels were designed to have a number of separate tanks with space between them and the outer skin of the ship. But there was great difficulty in creating leak proof connections in the pipes and valves joining the tanks and this presented a serious risk of explosions. There were, in fact, a number of serious such disasters at several ports including Hamburg and Rouen.

However, these discouraging incidents did not prevent George, and his relatives in the Liverpool office, from taking part in the development of safe and practical methods of transporting oil by sea in bulk, and towards the end of the 1880s they were discussing with shipbuilders and naval architects possible designs for the tanker of the future. It is probable that their growing interest was stimulated by the existence of the vessel *Gluckauf*, completed in 1886 for Standards's German subsidiary company at the yard of Armstrong, Mitchell and Company, and generally considered to be the forerunner of the present day ocean-going oil tanker.

Whilst by no means lacking in interest in George's fervent support for the burgeoning oil trade, it wasn't until 1887 that William in Liverpool, having become a member of the Petroleum Committee of the Mersey Docks and Harbour Board, began to show keen enthusiasm for this aspect of the business. He engaged the services of the firm of consulting marine engineers Jacobs and Barringer, (who later became Jacobs, Barringer and Garratt and continued advising the company for three generations) to assist in the design of the oil tankers which the firm hoped to build in order to transport the products of Rockefeller's Standard Oil Company from New York and Philadelphia to Liverpool and London.

But these plans and consultations were postponed within a year for reasons that have never been fully explained. There is record of a tentative arrangement made in 1888 by which Bowring, Jamieson and Company would become agents in the United Kingdom for the Standard Oil Company. However, there seems to have been a misunderstanding. What in fact actually happened was that Jamieson made a separate and independent deal from which emerged the Anglo-American Oil Company who became the agents for Standard and, of course, he left the company. The name of the company was then changed to C. T. Bowring and Company, the same as the head office at Liverpool, under which it continued to operate as ship and insurance brokers, marine underwriters and oil importers, and within a year George moved to larger London offices at 51–52 Lime Street.

Such was the enthusiasm for and belief in the oil industry that, as a result of a sudden joining of forces between Bowring's and the well-known Mellon family interests in Pittsburgh, the Bearcreek Oil and Shipping Company was formed to own and manage the first oil tanker to fly the Bowring flag. The steam tanker *Bear Creek*, with a deadweight of 3,500 tons, was built in 1890 by Sir W. G. Armstrong, Whitworth & Co., successors to the company that built *Gluckauf*. Shipping of oil in bulk was now becoming a matter of growing interest to a number of shipowners among whom 'tankers' were a regularly discussed topic. A current issue of *The Shipping World* described the use of the word 'tanker' as being 'ingenious if not elegant'.

The rather complex issues following the company's further involvement in oil are described in some detail by David Keir in *The Bowring Story*:

> Events were obviously taking on a new tempo, for both the Rockefeller-controlled Standard Oil and the Mellons, who had maintained their independence against the full competitive fury of the Rockefeller 'ring', must have known that Bowring's were planning a tanker fleet. Consequently, when the Bowring connection with Standard ceased the powerful Mellon interests moved in. *Bear Creek* was built with the least possible delay. And on 29th July 1890 the Bearcreek Oil and Shipping Company was duly registered, with various Bowring and Mellon nominees (from Pittsburgh) as the chief shareholders. To Bowring's the Mellon interests at the time seemed suitable allies. In common with Marcus Samuel, young William L. Mellon had gone into the oil industry in the late eighties. At first he was a producer only, and Standard Oil was his best customer. But in 1889, when Standard bought up a company outside its ring, which sold a lot of its oil to foreign refiners, Mellon persuaded one of Standard's leading French customers to buy from him instead, and at the same time greatly enlarged his own production. He also stepped up his purchases of crude oil from other independent producers, laid plans to increase his pipelines to the coast, and concluded his arrangements with Bowring's to launch the Bearcreek Oil and Shipping Company.

But it was not long before disaster befell the new partnership. *Bear Creek* seemed so admirably suited in every way to the work she was to carry out and had been built to the highest specification, but she was soon to meet her end. Whilst on passage from Amsterdam to Philadelphia in ballast on 26 December 1892, she began to ship water in very heavy seas. Notwithstanding the presumed excellence of her construction, her riveted plates began to open up and she had to be abandoned in the North Atlantic.

This loss came when the company was still recovering from the untimely death the previous year of George Bowring whose commercial wisdom and foresight would have been at a premium in the developments that were to follow. The most significant event both in terms of Bowring's involvement in the oil business and their progressive ties with international commerce on a much wider scale than hitherto would soon manifest itself. There was about to be a skirmish with Marcus Samuel, the founder of Shell, concerning the use of the Suez Canal.

By the second half of the 1880s Bowring's were playing an increasingly significant part in trans-oceanic general trading. By 1890 there were some 70 ships belonging to various owners carrying oil in bulk, *Bear Creek* being one of them until she was abandoned. There was a steady and growing traffic in bulk oil between North America and Europe, as there was also from southern Russian ports. However, no oil in bulk was reaching Middle or Far Eastern countries. Middle East oil was yet to be discovered, and it was not until 1908 that oil was found in Iran and much later, in 1927, in Iraq. Up until the beginning of the second decade of the twentieth century, the United States was producing between 60 and 70 per cent of the world's oil supplies. In subsequent years discoveries were made in areas dominated by Britain and the Netherlands and by 1919 Britain controlled 50 per cent of the world's proven oil reserves.

The fact that no oil in bulk was reaching the Middle and Far East during the 1880s can be attributed largely to the strong resistance felt towards shipping such inflammable cargoes through the Suez Canal, where a collision in such confined surroundings might prove to be catastrophic.

Over a comparatively short space of time the oil industry had become one of the most competitive in the world, and the enormous savings to be derived from reducing the amount of time spent in unnecessarily long voyages by using the Suez Canal were only too obvious. It is not surprising, therefore, that by the spring of 1891 there were rumours in London and New York that permission was being sought by certain oil interests to take tankers through the Canal. The Bearcreek Oil and Shipping Company were at this time shipping case-oil and oil in barrels in considerable quantities to the Orient. At the same time the Mellon interests were planning their Crescent Pipe Line to bring oil direct from Pittsburgh to the coast. Whereas the Standard Oil Company's particular strength was in the Western hemisphere, Mellon's were more especially concerned with their trade with Eastern countries. If permission were to be granted for oil tankers to pass through the Suez Canal there would be implications of undercutting not only for the Mellon interests, but

Bowring's as well, since they managed much of the Mellon's European and Eastern trade. And, furthermore, Standard would be similarly vulnerable. It will come as no surprise, therefore, in view of the context in which he has been mentioned earlier, that the cause of the discomfort being felt by these members of the industry was none other than Marcus Samuel.

In 1960 Robert Henriques wrote a biography of Marcus Samuel. In his book, (*Marcus Samuel*, Barrie and Rockliff, 1960), he writes:

> Thus it was C. T. Bowring & Co., in defence of their case-oil trade to the Far East, who opened the opposition to Marcus with a letter sent to the Board of Trade, 'on behalf of a group of British shipowners', protesting against any contemplated change by the Suez Canal Company in the regulations prohibiting the passage of tankers. Here the matter rested for nearly three months; and it was not until the end of October that the eminent firm of solicitors, Messrs. Russell and Arnholz, acting for unknown clients, launched a much more serious attack not only through the Board of Trade, but also through the Foreign Office.

The Russell and Arnholz letter, dated 30 October 1891, was written to Lord Salisbury, then Prime Minister. In the meantime the Bowring letter was passed successively at weekly intervals to Lloyd's, the Board of Trade, The Foreign Office and the Directors of the Suez Canal Company. According to Robert Henriques, Bowring's had written:

> Clients of ours inform us that they hear with apprehension it is contemplated that steamers carrying petroleum in bulk will be sent through the Canal . . . which on the assumption that they are constructed to carry the oil next to the outside plates in large chambers would, in the event of hole being made in their side (by collision or similar mishap), discharge the oil into the Canal.

Bowring's attitude in these circumstances, bearing in mind the fact that they were overtly enthusiastic about the development of the tanker, smacks a little of the 'dog in the manger'. Russell and Arnholz's letter clearly represents the view of a client whose business would be adversely affected if the Canal were to be opened to tanker traffic. Whilst the identity of their client continued to be something of a mystery it was generally assumed, in view of the fact that Bowring's had already represented their views and those of the Mellon interests, that the solicitors were probably acting on behalf of Standard Oil as well. Whoever their clients were, Russell and Arnholz maintained a vigorous campaign on their behalf in a series of letters, and even invoked the intervention of the Foreign Office to concede that there were special dangers to be considered in transporting oil in bulk through the Canal. They also drew attention to the fact that there was considerable doubt as to the efficacy of the prevailing marine insurance laws.

Bowring's continued staunchly to press home their strongly held misgivings and, through their English and American Shipping Company, obtained the support of a number of shipowners for a petition, which was published in *The Times* on 28 December 1891, and which expressed serious objections to recently issued draft regulations governing the passage of oil in bulk through the Canal.

Notwithstanding these strongly held and vigorously expressed views, which attracted much support in shipping circles, they were not to find sympathy either among the Suez Canal Company's directors nor the Foreign Office. And, on 26 July 1892, Marcus Samuel's new 5,010 ton tanker *Murex* sailed from West Hartlepool, where she had been built, to Batum to load a cargo of 4,000 tons of Caucasian oil. On 24 August she passed through the Canal, albeit under tow as a precaution, and sailed on to Bangkok, an historic voyage which, in the fullness of time, would prove to be of enormous benefit not only to Marcus Samuel himself and eventually The Shell Transport and Trading Company, but to the oil industry and oil users everywhere.

Although it would seem that, throughout the protestations against the outcome of the Suez Canal conflict, it was Mellon exports from Philadelphia that were most directly affected, Bowring's, having been importers and distributors of petroleum products for a long time and having a substantial holding in the Bearcreek Company, clearly had a vested interest of their own. Some of the loudest objections came from shipowners who had little or no interest in petroleum but who recognized the dangers of possible leakage and explosions in the scorching conditions of the Canal. Henceforth, however, there would be significant improvements to the Canal Company's safety regulations and in the construction standards of the increasing number of tanker hulls being laid down.

Early in the 1890s Bowring's had opened an office in Cardiff where, apparently, there was a growing demand for imported petroleum products; they also invested in storage tanks. As the demand increased so did tough competition between the main contenders, Standard Oil's Anglo-American Company, the Bearcreek Oil and Shipping Company (representing Mellon's production and Bowring's distribution interests) and a local organization somewhat ponderously named The Bristol and West of England and South Wales Petroleum and Storage Association Ltd.

The management of the Cardiff operation, conducted from the London office, was in the capable hands of Thomas Benjamin Bowring, whose considerable experience in the oil business was gained from his time spent with Bowring and Archibald at New York. His skilful handling of the rapid increase in the volume of exports from America can be attributed to this experience and his exceptional commercial acumen. The development of the tanker was clearly the most significant factor in the substantial development of the petroleum business as the following American export figures show. In 1885 the exports from the USA in barrels and tins amounted to some 2,000,000 gallons compared with 1,750,000 gallons in bulk. In a little more than ten years the quantity in barrels had dropped to 1,700,000 gallons while the amount shipped in bulk had soared to 484,000,000. From their storage and distribution points at Cardiff and at Thames Haven and St Leonard's wharves in London the company profited handsomely from both methods of shipment.

This rapid growth in the petroleum trade was to have a profound influence on Bowring's relationships with the big players in the industry. In 1895 Standard Oil bought the plants in America of Mellon's Bearcreek Refining Company and thereby its shares in the Bearcreek Oil and Shipping Company. It appears that the purpose of this seemingly successful takeover was, primarily to reduce Mellon's productive capacity and therefore the Bowring competition in distribution in Great Britain, and secondly to eliminate Mellon's supply of crude oil to French refiners. Thereafter, Standard acquired two refineries in France, which would handle only Standard products.

As a result of these complex manoeuvres Bowring's found that, by 1896, the Mellon controlling interest in the Bearcreek Oil and Shipping Company had been transferred to Standard Oil's Anglo-American Oil Company in London. Thus Bowring's found themselves, of necessity, once again allied to Standard and its Anglo-American agency, which, it will be recalled, had been created as a result of the 'misunderstanding' between George Bowring, J. D. Jamieson and Standard Oil some years before. The company continued to manage the Bearcreek Oil and Shipping Company's vessels.

The demand for petroleum products throughout the developed world continued to grow apace and it became evident to Thomas in London and to William and Fred (John Bowring's eldest son, who had returned from New York) in Liverpool that they must give serious thought to investing in more tankers.

The ill-fated *Bear Creek* had been replaced by the 2,710 ton (gross) *Snowflake*, built in 1893 at Newcastle upon Tyne for the Bearcreek Oil and Shipping Company. (*Snowflake*, in the hands of many subsequent owners and under a number of different names, survived until 1952 when, believed to be the oldest tanker afloat, she was broken up at Rosyth.) In this ship and those of other companies, large quantities of petroleum were being imported regularly by the Bearcreek company, but much more tonnage was needed, especially as they were on the threshold, by arrangement with Standard's Anglo-American company, of importing increasing quantities of Russian oil. There is little doubt, however, that the most compelling reason for wishing to build more tankers was quite simply the growing worldwide demand for petroleum products.

There were other developments, which fired the company's enthusiasm to become more deeply involved in the transport of petroleum products. Early in 1899 there were two American companies, The Pure Oil Company and The Columbia Oil Company, described by Thomas as 'outsiders' because they were not included in the Standard ring, who were keen that Bowring's should become their British agents. Because of the deterioration in the relationship with Standard, following the acquisition by that company of the Mellon holding in the Bearcreek Oil and Shipping Company, Bowring's were far from being opposed to such an arrangement. Furthermore they were anxious to increase their involvement with the Nobel brothers' Russian oil interests, especially as they had been their agents for some years. Among other concerns that were exercising their minds at the time was a strong desire to have more control over prices. As will become evident from a letter written by Thomas to the Anglo-American Oil Company on 7 April, there was another element in the transportation of oil in bulk of which we have heard nothing hitherto: 'I take this opportunity of mentioning,' he wrote:

> that the present arrangement with regard to our selling prices for oil in railway tank wagons will have to be altered. When the agreements were first made this particular branch of the trade was with us a steadily

increasing one but owing to the prohibitive prices which you ask us to
quote, the trade in railway tank wagons has steadily declined until we have
practically lost it all.

In successive letters Thomas gives us an idea of the complex nature of
the oil industry, which he and his colleagues now have to contend with.
On 3 May in a letter to the New York office he wrote:

> The situation remains unchanged here and it will be several days yet
> before I can tell whether the Anglo mean business. They want to renew
> . . . It is true that we would renew our arrangements with the Anglo under
> certain conditions, but these preliminary negotiations with the outsiders
> have no bearing whatever on the issue between the Anglo and ourselves.

In a letter a month later Thomas told his New York colleagues that the
position was still open and he added:

> We have the Anglo offer in our possession, but our desire is to make a
> permanent arrangement with the outside refiners provided it can be come
> to on a satisfactory basis.

As things turned out the relationship with Anglo was about to come to
an end, as a result of which a clearer picture would emerge. On 25 July
1899 Thomas wrote again to the New York office:

> I have just cabled you that our agreement with the Anglo terminates in
> October, and that we should consequently require the 100,000 barrels
> between October this year and July 1900.

After further reference in the same letter to the proposed deal with the
'outsiders' Thomas continues:

> It is a little early yet to say when we should require the first cargo (*from
> the 'outsider's, in this case The Pure Oil Company*) and all will depend on the
> arrangements we can make with the Anglo for supplying us with some
> spot oil at the termination of the agreement on 20th October. If they will
> supply us on reasonable terms with spot supply, we should not require the
> first cargo shipped until about the middle of November, but if they
> decline to supply us on reasonable conditions with spot oil at the
> termination of the agreement, we should probably want the first cargo
> about the 1st October and I shall probably know how this will be before
> you receive this. Our idea would then be to keep the *Snowflake* running
> regularly, and she would just about carry the 100,000 barrels between
> November and July.

(Reference to barrels when referring to the tanker *Snowflake* may seem a little odd; 100,000 barrels presumably indicates the quantity of bulk oil that they would contain and which the ship could accommodate in her tanks over several voyages.)

In the summer of 1899 the company had acquired the tanker *Beacon Light* from a Liverpool owner and were about to take delivery of a new ship, *Lucifer* from the yard of Swan Hunter on the Tyne; and further additions to the tanker fleet were planned. Neither Bowring's nor Standard really wanted divorce. On 4 August, in yet another letter to his colleagues in New York on the subject of the relationship with Standard, he reminded them of the complications inherent in the company's oil interests and that they might well be facing further problems in the future: 'I may mention', he wrote, 'that our friends the enemy the Standard Oil Company are stockholders (*in the Bearcreek Oil and Shipping Company*) to the extent of £15,000, and we do not know for example whether they would sell and at what price.'

In consideration of the various issues at stake Thomas and William, towards the end of 1900, boldly and with wisdom formed The Bowring Petroleum Company with a view to bringing the family's various interests in the oil business into one corporate unit. This significant move was followed at the end of November by a new and apparently harmonious compact with Standard's Anglo-American Company. The New York office was advised of these developments in a letter dated 4 December to Charles Tricks' grandson, Charles Warren Bowring, (later to become known by the American branch of the family as 'The Boss'):

> We are amalgamating our various interests in the oil trade under one Company which will purchase the St Leonard's Wharf Company, our London business, the Imperial Oil Co., James Barringer and Sons Limited, the Cardiff business, and all the shares that C. T. Bowring & Co. hold in the Bearcreek Oil and Shipping Company. This will consolidate all our interests, and make a very strong combination. We shall have four Directors; the Imperial Oil Company two; and Barringer one, and I think you will say the movement is a good one.

Apart from the Cardiff business and the Bearcreek company, the constituent members of The Bowring Petroleum Company are new to us. The St Leonard's Wharf Company had been formed in London in 1893 for the temporary storage and distribution of petroleum products and was managed by C. T. Bowring & Co. Of James Barringer and

Sons I have been unable to find any reference; one can only assume that they, too, were involved in some capacity or other in the oil trade. And the presence of The Imperial Oil Company is puzzling. A company of this name was formed in southwest Ontario in 1888 and soon became Canada's largest producer. It is unlikely that this is the same company unless it was a British subsidiary operation of Imperial in which Bowring's had a majority shareholding, but that seems unlikely; we would surely have heard much more about it had that been the case.

At the turn of the century The Bowring Petroleum Company was importing annually from America an estimated 310,000 barrels of which 175,000 came from producers not within the Standard ring. Thomas had entered into fresh negotiations with the Nobel interests for supplies of Russian oil and the business, notwithstanding the occasional irksome complications, seemed to be forging ahead. In 1899 no fewer than five tankers were regularly bringing cargoes of petroleum products from New York, Philadelphia and Batum to London and Cardiff. They were the company's own *Snowflake* and four chartered vessels, *Astrakan, Tinra, Rion* and *Suram*.

In May 1901 a letter was received from the Union Petroleum Company of Philadelphia inviting Bowring's to take on the selling agency for their petrol in Britain. From Thomas's reply it isn't difficult to understand the troublesome restrictions imposed by some of the internal arrangements that had become a feature of the industry.

'You are aware possibly,' Thomas wrote:

> ... that we are sellers in this country of both American and Russian Refined Petroleum having acted as the selling agents in London for Nobels' Russian Petroleum for some years. The Agreements we have with the Russians preclude our dealing in Gas Oil of any description either American or Russian, and I regret to say therefore that personally we shall be unable to take up the proposition for which I have to thank you.

During the next few years the company's involvement in the oil trade continued to grow. Between them, in 1899, the five ships mentioned above imported more than 8,000,000 gallons, mostly of paraffin for lighting purposes, but also small quantities of refined and lubricating oils. In the following year Bowring's own three tankers, *Snowflake, Beacon Light* and the new *Lucifer* with another ship, *Prudentia*, were continuously and heavily engaged. *Beacon Light* alone on two voyages – from Philadelphia and Novorossisk respectively – brought in over 1,000,000 gallons. The new *Lucifer* was a steel steamer with a capacity of 5,000 tons and a service speed of 10 knots.

The steady burgeoning of Bowring's engagement in the petroleum business prompted Thomas, on 13 September 1901, to write to Charles in New York reporting enthusiastically that:

> The Bowring Petroleum Co. is now thoroughly established, and doing a very good trade, in fact selling more oil than we have hitherto done. Everything seems to be working satisfactorily, and I think that we shall find that the formation of the Co. to have been a very wise move. Clive, George's eldest son, is taking hold of that branch of the business with great energy and ability. We have lately made a further agreement with the Anglo to store and deliver all their Southampton oil at our wharf, at least 20,000 tons per annum, and are now building a 25,000 barrel tank there for the purpose. There is practically no tankage to be had in London.

The increase of activity in the oil market called for further tonnage and two new ships joined the Bearcreek Oil and Shipping Company's fleet in 1901 and in 1902. *Kinsman* (4,534 tons gross) was built at the Newcastle upon Tyne yard of Armstrong Whitworth & Co. Ltd. It is quite likely that, when the ship was launched in November 1901, she was named by Thomas's wife whom, as Annie Kinsman, he married in 1877. The second new tanker, *Cymbeline* (II), of similar size, was launched at the same yard in October 1902. In spite of an inauspicious start, being involved in three minor accidents during her first two years at sea, she survived for thirteen years before being sunk by a German U-Boat off Fastnet in 1915.

As the fleet grew over the next few years so did the scope of its activities. The now virtually global nature of the business resulted in the company's ships visiting an ever-increasing number of ports including, at home Hull, Cardiff, Liverpool, Newport, Devonport, Avonmouth, Gravesend, Sheerness, Penarth, Port Talbot, and overseas New York, Port Arthur (Texas), San Francisco, Port San Luis, Venice, Flushing, Lisbon, Oporto, Rouen, Calais, Rangoon, Yokohama, Trinidad, Algiers, Guatemala, Constantinople, Ancona, Bilbao, Antwerp, Hamburg, Bergen and many others.

In one of its issues in 1904 the *Petroleum Review* noted:

> The Bowring Petroleum Co. is now fully equipped for carrying a very large trade under the new conditions of bulk distribution, for not only do

they possess their own storage depots and their own road wagons, but they own five tankers for the transportation of petroleum in bulk. Two of the largest of these ocean oil carriers are the *Cymbeline* and the *Kinsman*.

It was by now abundantly clear that the market for petroleum products was developing steadily throughout the world as the extensive list of ports visited by the company's ships shows, and there was beginning to be a demand, albeit still relatively small, for motor spirit. In 1906 Thomas Bowring sought to secure a deal with Sir Weetman Pearson Bt, later to become Viscount Cowdray, for the marketing in Britain of the oil and petrol from his Mexican refineries. Although by far the greater part of oil produced generally was for illuminating purposes, the motor car with its petrol engine had come to stay and the demand for motor spirit would inevitably increase. In correspondence with Sir Weetman, Thomas noted:

> I have discussed the question of spirit very thoroughly with our people. They say it is of course a very much smaller trade and is dealt with in very much smaller quantities, and consequently the cost per gallon of selling, of cartage, and of handling is of necessity increased. I may say that we shall make no money whatever on spirit sold in country districts at the price named, but will hope to make it up by larger sales in town.

Intense competition was beginning to manifest itself in all aspects of the industry and, as an illustration of the acquisitive nature of an entrepreneur with the bit between his teeth, at the same time as he was negotiating with Sir Weetman Pearson, Thomas was exercising his powers of persuasion on a London distributor to whom he endeavoured to point out the virtues of his transferring the handling of his business to The Bowring Petroleum Company. He wrote:

> I believe the business of distributing petroleum spirit is greatly curtailed by reason of its non-paying character, and your position will not be improved when The Bowring Petroleum Company become Messrs Pearson's agents . . . In fact I would go so far as to suggest that as the advent of The Bowring Petroleum Company into the spirit trade will doubtless cause disturbance, the business of distributors such as yourself must of necessity suffer, not of course from any deliberate action of The Bowring Petroleum Co . . .

He even went to the extent of suggesting that Messrs. Tilling, a company in some way or other connected with his correspondent, should obtain its supplies of lubricating oil from him because Bowring's used Tilling horses to pull their tank wagons!

That Thomas Bowring was possessed of unusual flair and energy, a class act in current parlance, is clearly demonstrated by David Keir in *The Bowring Story*:

> At such a confused stage in the petroleum industry's development Thomas must sometimes have had his work cut out keeping his right hand informed of what his left hand was doing. The oil industry had rapidly wrapped around itself a vast web of protective and restrictive agreements – with producers, refiners, carriers and distributors playing for very high stakes. In addition to his Mexican negotiations, Thomas in 1906 found himself trying to find a new set of agreements in order to release a supply of oil he had previously ordered from a Philadelphia company. He was also coming to terms with other suppliers on mutual boundaries for trading territories in India, and seeking to consolidate the market in fuel oil with the Admiralty. Conferences in London, confidential meetings in Rotterdam, prices calculated to the last half-penny, and even gratuitous advice on improved soldering as a remedy for leaking tins: all these were part of his normal round.

And so, the relentless upsurge in the demand for oil continued throughout the world, a demand that far exceeded the available tonnage. It was inevitable, therefore, that Thomas and his fellow directors should seize the opportunity to participate in the increasing need for tankers, and in 1907 they created the Oil Tank Steamship Company which acquired the tanker *Oberon* currently being completed at Newcastle-upon-Tyne. She was followed by the third vessel to be named *Hermione* in 1908, and later that year *El Lobo*, which the new company managed for Lobitos Oilfields Ltd, was added.

The shortage of tankers wasn't helped by the persistently hazardous nature of the trade. In 1905 *Beacon Light* ran aground off the north coast of Denmark and incurred severe damage. After it had taken no less than six months to refloat her she was towed to the Tyne for extensive repairs; and in 1907 the company lost their *Lucifer* while on passage from New York to Ireland. These and other mishaps to the company's ships and those of other owners prompted them to become associated in the following years with research into safety which was to influence the design and development of tankers in the future.

As the natural outcome of the laws of supply and demand, the rush to build tankers soon created yet keener competition and, inevitably, freight rates tumbled. Temporarily, at any rate, what had been a highly profitable trade experienced a serious downturn. Freight rates were slashed and owners found themselves facing a period of recession. However, such was the continuing increase in the use of oil products, especially motor spirit as the development of the motor car took hold, by 1911 freight rates began to improve again. In these more encouraging conditions the directors of the Oil Tank Steamship Company were persuaded to place an order with the Tyneside shipbuilder, Swan, Hunter & Wigham Richardson Ltd for the second *Cordelia*, a tanker of 6,533 tons gross, the eleventh ship to be built for the company at this yard, bonding a relationship which would continue for the next sixty-seven years with very few breaks. Soon to be added were *Elsinore*, *Silvia* and *Rosalind*, all much the same in size and capacity as *Cordelia*.

Mention earlier of Lobitos Oilfields marks the beginning of another close and durable relationship. Bowring's London office was appointed their fleet managers in 1908 and, following *El Lobo, El Toro* built in 1913 and *El Zorro* in 1914 were added, to be succeeded in later years by seven further Lobitos tankers the last of which, another *El Lobo* (whose predecessor had been sold) joined the fleet in 1959.

The high point of the Bowring involvement in the marketing and distribution of petroleum products was probably reached around 1913. In 1911 the association with the expanding Cowdray domain was greatly enhanced by the appointment of Thomas and Clive Bowring to the board of The Eagle Oil Transport Company, a recently established shipping subsidiary operating tankers for the transportation of Mexican Eagle Oil products. Notwithstanding the apparent strengthening of the relationship with Lord Cowdray by these appointments, Fred Bowring in Liverpool was less than wholly supportive of the association with Eagle Oil Transport and made it known that he considered the profits derived therefrom to be inadequate and he felt that the services of Thomas and Clive on the board of this new company were poorly recognized. He insisted, furthermore, that Bowring's should be receiving a commission in respect of the company's first tanker, *San Fraterno*, launched by Lady Bowring in March 1913. (Thomas was knighted earlier that year). The reasoning behind this contention seems, to say the least, obscure. Thomas, however, after dealing with the matter of the questionable commission, strove earnestly to justify his arrangements with Lord Cowdray and pointed out that the relationship would provide substantial insurance business on Eagle Oil ships. 'I only wish,' he added, 'that you or I could pick up another such commission for one of our branches as that which I obtained from Pearson's.'

Scott's Antarctic expedition, January 16 1911. The Terra Nova *and a berg at the Icefoot*

The Aurora *and* Vanguard, *sealing steamers, at Harbour Grace, 1885, known as the 'Wooden Walls'*

13th June 1901.

To the Directors of
Bowring Brothers Limited.

Gentlemen.

We hereby severally nominate C.T.Bowring & Co
Limited as our nominees to whom are to be allotted the number of
fully paid up shares of 50 Dollars each in Bowring Brothers Limited
mentioned opposite to our respective names to which we are respectively entitled under the Agreement dated the 27th day of April
1901 and made between ourselves of the one part and Bowring Brothers
Limited of the other part and we authorise and request you to allot
the same fully paid shares to C.T.Bowring & Co Limited accordingly.

Name.	Number of fully paid shares.
[signature]	2492.
[signature]	3292.
[signature]	1972.
[signature]	411.
[signature]	555.
L B Stoddart	565.
Henry A. Bowring	216.
Charles Bowring	461.
	9964.

List of shareholdings in Bowring Brothers Limited transferred to C. T. Bowring & Co. Limited as nominees in 1901

Bowring vessels in St John's Harbour in the early 1900s. Left to right: SS Kite, SS Algerine, one of the firm's barquentines ready to sail for Brazil, SS Terra Nova, SS Aurora, and steam launch Eagle

Edward Bowring's grave at the Unitarian Chapel in Moretonhampstead,
where other members of the family and relations are also buried

Sir William Benjamin Bowring Bt, JP, 1837–1916, Chairman 1899–1916

The Bowring Library in Moretonhampstead, Devon, presented to the town by Sir Thomas Bowring

Sir Thomas Benjamin Bowring, 1847–1918

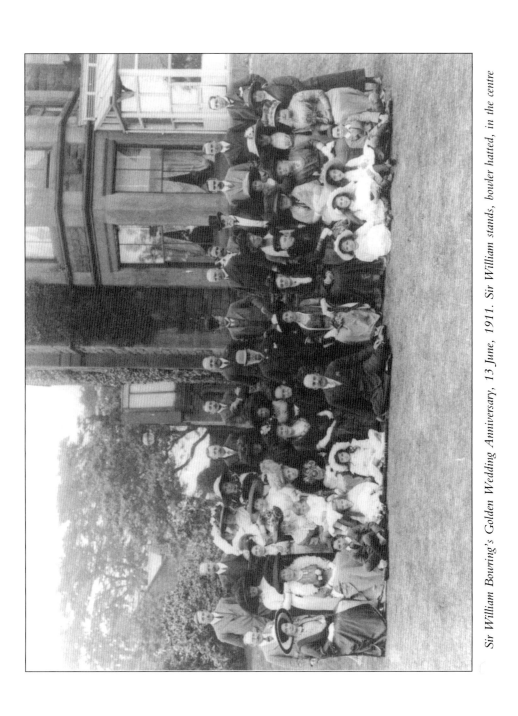

Sir William Bowring's Golden Wedding Anniversary, 13 June, 1911. Sir William stands, bowler hatted, in the centre

Bowring Brothers' ship SS Florizel, built in Glasgow in 1909, seen here in occasional use as a sealer

*An Anglo-Mexican horse-drawn tanker delivering Bowring's petroleum products
in the early 1920s*

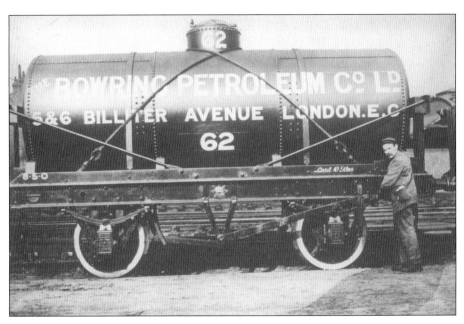

An early petroleum rail tanker of the Bowring Petroleum Company

In 1912 the complicated network of Bowring interests in the petroleum business underwent significant changes. In that year Anglo-Mexican Petroleum Products Co. Ltd acquired a substantial holding in The Bowring Petroleum Company, and thus they absorbed the greater part of Bowring's petroleum business. Two years later Anglo-Mexican took over the whole of Bowring's fuel oil activities. By 1919 The Bowring Petroleum Company were making it known that their kerosene and motor spirit business had been subsumed by Anglo-Mexican. It was emphasized at the time however that, though Bowring's by the end of the First World War were virtually out of the business they had done so much to nurture from its earliest days, they retained their interest in the supply and distribution of lubricating and other oils. This and their ownership and management of tankers were to continue for many years.

Chapter 8

IN 1911 THE FIRM celebrated its centenary, and at St John's the occasion was marked with a commemorative dinner for the entire staff. At this event, which was attended by every employee, they were informed by Edgar Rennie Bowring, who had taken over management of Bowring Brothers in 1890 on the death of his cousin Charles, that each of them would receive an additional month's salary. He also announced that, as a centenary gift to the community generally, the company, both in Newfoundland and throughout the world, were to present a park, which would be laid out and landscaped in the vicinity of St John's. Plans were drawn up by a well-known landscape architect from Montreal and work was started later in the year. Although not completely finished, Bowring Park was opened by the Duke of Connaught in 1914 and to this day is greatly enjoyed by the people of St John's and many visitors from overseas.

A further event in the same year was the presentation by various members of the family to the International Grenfell Association of the site at St John's for the King George the Fifth Institute for Fishermen and Sailors.

It says much for the sons and grandsons of Benjamin that, having surely inherited in some measure – in some cases evidently more than in others – his business acumen, courage and perseverance, they had built up during the past century a shipping and trading operation of international standing. No doubt his stern, sometimes harsh remonstrances delivered from Liverpool to his sons in St John's when their efforts or intentions worried or displeased him, had paid off. They and their sons' enthusiasm for the development of the business he had founded and their determination to honour the heritage that he passed on to them were beyond doubt. No 'clogs-to-clogs-in-three-generations' here.

In Newfoundland, while impressive progress was being made on the opposite side of the Atlantic, the business continued to grow in much the same manner and at a similar pace as it had during the previous decade. Bowring Brothers were still leaders in sealing activities, though sending a rather smaller fleet to the ice each year than previously. This

116

was because much larger iron ships had replaced the 'wooden walls' of the past. Two of these early 'dual-purpose' vessels were *Silvia*, 1,704 tons gross and *Rosalind*, 2,568 tons gross. Each led a perfectly respectable double life performing a popular passenger service for the New York, Newfoundland & Halifax S.S. Co. Ltd when not up at the ice catching seals. One cannot but wonder, nevertheless, whether a lingering odour of pelts, blubber and oil might not have detracted somewhat from the reported luxury of these vessels during the times when they performed their passenger-carrying duties, which were managed from the New York office. They were followed in 1909 by *Florizel*, 3,081 tons, the first sealing vessel to be equipped with wireless, and in 1911 by *Stephano*, 3,449 tons. Both these ships would at one time or another have been under the command of the redoubtable Captain Kean, one of the most famous of all sealing skippers.

While to most of us the slaughtering of seals for any reason, except perhaps for controlled culling purposes, is abhorrent, it needs to be remembered that nearly a century ago prevailing attitudes were very different. In the first place, in an area where regular employment was at a premium, the seal fishery provided jobs each year for several thousand men, albeit for a brief part of the year. The pelts and oil, whilst not necessarily being unique among the purposes for which they were used, were nevertheless required for clothing and lighting, and the flesh, for a population whose diet was rather limited, was a source, though of questionable appeal, of nourishment. Bearing this in mind and accepting the fact that we are considering what at the time was considered to be a reasonable commercial activity, the relevant statistics make impressive reading. Another fact mentioned earlier and worth recalling, is that the seal hunt was extremely hazardous, during the history of which many lives have been lost.

Florizel first went to the ice in 1909. In that year Bowring Brothers sent twice as many ships as any other company; eight ships in a fleet of 231, ranging between the little 280 ton *Kite* with 90 men on board, and others including the 677 ton *Eagle* (lll), the 764 ton *Terra Nova* and *Florizel*, each with up to 200 men aboard. *Eagle* returned having caught 20,423 seals, Terra Nova with 15,468 and Florizel with no fewer than 30,488.

Proof, if it were ever needed, of the superiority of the iron-hulled ships was provided the following year when on 1 April *Florizel*, dressed overall and sitting low in the water, entered St John's harbour with an all-time record-breaking catch of 49,000 pelts.

Captain Kean received a formidable welcome as described by David Keir in *The Bowring Story*:

> As the ship came through the Narrows the crew, assembled on the forecastle, burst into cheers which were rapidly echoed by the crowds who flocked down to the wharves on hearing the news of *Florizel's* good fortune. The triumphant ship fired off rockets, *Viking* and *Algerine* sounded their sirens, and a wild *feu de joie* was fired from rifles by a band of excited employees from a neighbouring firm. A fleet of steam-launches, motor-boats and rowing boats escorted *Florizel* to her berth; and before she had finally moored the first members of Bowring Brothers had climbed on board to offer their congratulations.

The St John's newspaper, *Evening Telegram*, gave generous coverage to the occasion. Under the headline 'A Record Trip', more than five columns were accompanied by a photograph of a bearded and smiling Captain Kean standing on his bridge after berthing at Bowring Brothers' wharf.

In his own report of this memorable voyage Abram Kean records that *Florizel* left St John's on 12 March at the head of the fleet. On the following day she was locked in ice off Fogo Island but was freed on the 14th, to continue her north easterly course in rain and fog. On the 15th the fog cleared, but the ship encountered more heavy ice from which she wasn't free until 9.30 that night. *Eagle*, also now equipped with wireless, reported on the night of the 16th that she was near a large patch of seals and by 11.30 a.m. on St Patrick's Day, to the particular delight of the many Irishmen among the crew, *Florizel* was within reach of thousands of whitecoats.

With this beginning to the start of the 1910 seal fishery the score simply went on mounting and for the next several days the slaughter continued relentlessly. By Sunday 20 March *Florizel's* sealing crew had caught 29,000 seals to which were added a further 12,000 the following day. By the 24th over 20,000 had been loaded and there were thousands more to be picked up in the strengthening north westerly wind. But in the worsening bad weather and thickening ice the ship was unable to make more than about one mile a day. During the next several days other members of the Bowring fleet arrived on the scene and were themselves hard at work. By 28 March *Florizel* had more than 35,000 seal pelts stowed below decks, another 2,500 on deck and many thousands still to be collected from the ice. Early on the 29th Abram Kean signalled by radio to his son Joseph, who was in command of *Eagle*: 'All records broken, 42,420 stowed, 1,000 on deck and 40 flags on ice.' *Florizel*, having collected the last of her kill, turned for home during the afternoon of 29 March. She had not been underway for much more than two and a half hours forcing her way through the ice when she deviated from her course to run to the assistance of the small steamer *Iceland*, also out of St John's. The ice had crushed her wooden hull and she was on fire. Captain Kean took her crew on board shortly before she sank. *Florizel's* contribution and of the other vessels of the Bowring sealing fleet to the Newfoundland seal hunt in 1910 amounted to 141,098 out of a total of 333,349. In 1912 *Stephano* joined the Bowring sealing fleet and Abram Kean was promoted to command her while his son Joseph took over *Florizel*.

Captain Abram Kean is known to most Newfoundlanders as the island's most famous ship's captain. The son of Joseph and Joan Kean, he was born on Flower's Island, Bonavista Bay on 8 July 1855. His brief attendance at school ended at the age of thirteen when he persuaded his father that he was old enough to start fishing and he first went to sea with his uncle, William Kean.

By the time he was twenty-three he was commanding a fishing schooner. This early experience qualified him later to command ships engaged in the Labrador coastal, mail and passenger services. But it was at the seal hunt that he gained such fame as to become the colony's most distinguished seafarer. His exploits at the 1910 seal hunt are described above and there were many other occasions when, through his skill and experience, his catches exceeded those of his competitors at the ice, and he is reputed to have brought home more than one million pelts during his forty-eight years at sea. But Abram Kean will also be remembered for other less deserving reasons.

On 30 March 1914 both Abram, as skipper of *Stephano* and his son Westbury in command of *Newfoundland* (not a Bowring ship) were at the seal hunt, their ships being a few miles apart. Westbury Kean sent a crew of something over 100 to *Stephano* to obtain from his father directions to a patch of seals. (The Kean family, regardless of the company for which they were working, would invariably assist each other in locating seals.) Abram indicated to the crew where to find the patch and, in spite of the fact that a storm was expected, told them to return to their own ship after they had dealt with their catch. The expected storm became a reality – and with a vengeance. Both father and son assumed, as the conditions deteriorated, that the men were safe aboard the other's ship, an assumption that might have been avoided if *Newfoundland* had been equipped with a radio. Of the 115 who left the ship 78 died of exposure or drowning as a result of being stranded for 53 hours without shelter or adequately protective clothing. There seems little doubt that within a very short time of the men leaving *Stephano* the storm increased in violence and Abram Kean has been considered irresponsible for not having conducted a search for *Newfoundland*'s men.

In the eyes of many Captain Abram Kean is still considered to have been at fault for sending over 100 men back to their ship some miles away when he might well have been aware that there was the possibility of the storm becoming more severe. However, at a government inquiry Abram Kean, whilst being found partially guilty, was not suspended and, indeed, continued to hunt seals until his retirement twenty-two years later, much of his time being with Bowring Brothers.

Before we leave *Florizel* and *Stephano* and consider the other activities being pursued in St John's and New York since the turn of the century, we should not forget that these two handsome state-of-the-art vessels, which spent the months of March and April at the ice hunting for seals, were designed primarily as passenger carriers and in this capacity earned themselves a reputation for comfort and excellence. One must assume that, before they could undertake these duties and deserve such enthusiastic approval, platoons of cleaners would have boarded with mops and pails, and adequate quantities of deodorant, to remove any noisome remnants of their earlier pursuits.

Their owners, Bowring's Red Cross Line, recognizing the need to establish a service between St John's, Halifax and New York for business men and freight, saw that there was also a 'cruise' element to be exploited and that there were Americans in search of relaxation, comfort and entertainment on board in addition to exploration, fishing and hunting in Newfoundland. To this end the company took advertising space in American magazines extolling the virtues of a brief spell at sea to ease the stress of business life before a relaxing camp life ashore. *Stephano*, for instance had accommodation for 180 first class passengers in de luxe and two-berth cabins, and for 60 second class passengers. There was a luxurious dining saloon amidships, which extended the full width of the ship and a spacious lounge area in the forward part where music by the ship's orchestra and other recreational activities were provided. The advertisements made much of the ships' splendid cuisine, some justifica-tion for which can be gleaned from a newspaper article appearing many years later in 1960, long after The Red Cross Line had been sold following the First World War. Under the heading 'Off the Beeton Track' an Edinburgh writer with a keen appreciation of food wrote the following in the gastronomic column of *The Scotsman*:

The passengers on board the *Stephano*, a steamship of the old Red Cross Line, which plied from Newfoundland to New York by way of Nova Scotia, did pretty well in the dining saloon ... On 27th January (1913) the passengers in the first-class started with a choice Bluepoint oysters, Queen Olives (whatever they may have been), and caviare sur croutes.

There was a choice of soups, a small dish of fried snapper with a béchamel sauce, and then salmi of venison, epigrammes of mutton, or, for ichthyophils, squab lobster, and hominy.

By this time the edge of appetite, whetted by the keen winds whipped across the drifting floes and shrilled in the rigging overhead, had been gently blunted. It was now time to serve the main course of the meal. Roast ribs of beef au jus (I can almost see the blood-red gravy); or roast pork if you prefer; or duck; and since there is a limit to the amount of fresh meat that can be carried, corned ox tongue, which is probably better from the tin than in its slightly fibrous fresh state. Plenty of vegetables of course, including asparagus.

Four puddings, fruits, raisins, nuts, figs and preserved ginger; Roquefort for the gentlemen, Edam or Young American cheese for the ladies; and no doubt one would enjoy a cigar with the coffee. And then something like a twelve-hour wait till breakfast time.

Two days later they enjoyed a richer meal, for this was the Captain's dinner and something of an occasion. You could start with either a Martini or a Bronx cocktail – both perhaps if you were lucky and sitting next to a conspiring but teetotal lady. Oysters, caviare (a little monotonous perhaps? Then why not try the salted almonds, nibble an olive, or take some fresh celery?)

Mis-spelt Amontillado with the soups; salmon; a choice of five made-up dishes ranging from pheasant to shrimps, with a glass or two of Chateau Batailley; Vermont Turkey with all the trimmings, or beef, venison, ham with a champagne sauce, and a Haute Sauterne; an exciting variety of sweets and, of course, fruit, nuts, and cheese. I don't know if any of Captain Clark's guests were pre-occupied with the expanding universe, but I bet they worried about their expanding waist-lines.

And with the Chateau Batailley available at one dollar a quart, Mumm champagne at two dollars a pint, and the *Stephano's* barman willing to dispense gin, whisky and rum at one dollar and twenty-five cents a quart or fifteen cents a glass, the services of Alcoholics Anonymous might well have been urgently sought on returning to New York.

These summer and autumn cruises became so popular that the Bowring offices in New York and Liverpool were led to give consideration to winter cruises to warmer destinations. These soon became a reality. In 1913 *Stephano* was offering twenty-one day cruises for $100, which included visits to Bermuda, Jamaica, Colon at the entrance to the newly constructed Panama Canal and back to New York by way of Cuba. In order to ensure maximum comfort only 150 passengers were accepted on these excursions. The relevant brochure boasted 'A swimming pool, numerous baths, showers, electric fires in all rooms, and forced ventilation from deck will assure coolness and comfort.' There would be carriages and 'autos' to meet passengers at all ports of call and time would be passed pleasantly with sports, dancing to the ship's orchestra – and, of course, the gastronomic wizardry of the ship's cook.

In the years following the turn of the century, before *Florizel* and *Stephano* became engaged in the Red Cross Line cruises and their participation in the seal fishery, the port of St John's was a constant and colourful scene of maritime activity. The affairs of Bowring Brothers were in the capable hands of Edgar Rennie Bowring and his younger brother Henry Alfred (my grandfather), both sons of John, the youngest of Benjamin's sons. One of their vessels, the 434 ton *Algerine*, originally built by Laird Brothers of Birkenhead as a gunboat for the Admiralty, was purchased by Edgar Bowring in 1893, and served at various times both as a sealer and a collier. (It was not unusual for ships owned by family businesses to be registered in the names of individual directors.) To add to the varied nature of *Algerine's* service, she spent all of the summer of 1901 accommodating a group of American scientists who were trying to locate mineral deposits along the Labrador coast and in Hudson's Bay. Meanwhile the company's sailing ships continued to carry cargoes of dried salt cod to the Mediterranean and South America.

While he was writing *The Bowring Story*, David Keir met Mr Fred Ellis who had been a shipping clerk with Bowring Brothers, and who was able to recall the bustle of activity in the harbour at St John's in the days when sailing vessels were still the main feature. Mr Ellis remembered a sea-shanty he used to hear when vessels, laden with their cargoes of dried cod were about to depart:

Oh, we'll heave up our anchor and away we will go
Hurray, me bully boys, out we're bound
We're bound to the West Indies, where the sugar does grow
Hurray, me bully boys, out we're bound.

Not perhaps destined for 'top of the pops' but, as Fred Ellis explains:

It didn't matter if the ship was outward bound south from St John's either
to Barbados, Jamaica, Brazilian ports or elsewhere, the melody and words
helped the men on the fo'c's'le head as they laboured to break the anchor
out and hoist it into the catheads. The pleasant noise of the pawls clanking
over the windlass drum added to the effect. What beautiful ships they
were! The majority of them with white painted hulls had enough
coloured trimmings to make a contrast. This, with their shining spars and
black painted standing rigging, helped to complete the picture. On
Sundays all the foreign-going ships in port were made shipshape to
produce a pleasing sight for the owners or their representatives and the
general public, who frequently went down to the wharves after lunch.

Bowring's *Dunure*, the last of their square-rigged barquentines, was often
singled out for special attention whether she was departing for Brazil with
a cargo of dried cod in barrels, or returning from Barbados some three
or four months later laden with casks of molasses. Her crew, well tanned
after three months in the tropics, having ensured that her gleaming white
hull and freshly painted spars would gladden the hearts of the citizens of
St John's who eagerly awaited her return, would no doubt be on the
lookout for the familiar landfall of Cape Race and hoping that the
weather, as they approached Newfoundland, would not be too boisterous.

But, as Fred Ellis's recollections attest, the return of *Dunure*, or for that
matter any ship returning to St John's was not always an occasion for
spontaneous rejoicing. Fred Ellis continues:

I remember opening a telegram one morning, which read something like
this:

'*Dunure* off Cape requires a tug'

and which was signed by the senior light-house keeper, as Cape Race was
a Lloyd's signalling station. The telegram brought results, as either Mr Eric
Bowring (a grandson of Charles Tricks) or Mr J. S. Munn (a director of
the firm with family connections) ordered a tug to be despatched
immediately, but before she had gone very far a sudden change of wind

blew up and the tug returned. The skipper knew *Dunure* could not 'hold the land' and would have to run for searoom away from the treacherous coast. Sixteen days later Dunure arrived in St John's still looking in good condition, but everyone tired and fed up. And no wonder – 14 days from Barbados to Cape Race, a distance of about 2,000 miles, and 16 days from Cape Race to St John's, a mere 60.

Mr Ellis was never short of stories about the fortunes, good and bad, of Bowring ships. The 600 ton *Cordelia*, a long, lean vessel built with fast passages in mind, was one of the last of the Bowring Brothers' Atlantic barques. Built at Port Glasgow in 1867 she had a long adventurous life until being sunk by a German U-Boat in 1917, after having been sold to unknown Glasgow interests in 1911. There was one occasion when *Cordelia*, homeward bound to Newfoundland in midwinter with a cargo of coal, ran into a severe south-westerly gale in mid-Atlantic. 'The Captain,' related Fred Ellis, 'lying in his bunk, felt her make a terrific lurch, accompanied by a heavy rumbling noise, and the ship lay on her beam-ends. The worst had happened, the cargo had shifted, and she was lying helpless in an Atlantic gale.

It was a desperate situation of which the Captain gave a full account to Mr Ellis.

> The Captain told me, that he knew all hands would be gathered on the poop awaiting his orders. An essential was morale at the top, so he dressed, put on his hard pot hat, which he always wore at sea, and scrambled on deck. What a sight met him! A disabled ship, lying on her side, with heavy seas breaking over her – it looked hopeless. He turned to the crew, 'Only one chance, boys, all hands but me and the cook down through the lazarette hatch and shovel for your lives; if you can get her back on her feet she can live.'
>
> 'The Captain told me that almost every man went into that pitch-black hold and shovelled. They put her back on her feet and they drove her home to Newfoundland . . .'

Early in 1904 Bowring Brothers were once again invited by the Newfoundland Government to run the Coastal Mail Service. The terms of the agreement were encapsulated in a contract:

> . . . made and entered into this fifth day of February Anno Domino [sic], nineteen hundred and four, between the Right Hon. Sir Robert Bond,

as Colonial Secretary for the Island of Newfoundland, for himself and his successors in office, acting for and on behalf of the Government of the said Island, hereinafter called the Government, of the one part, and BOWRING BROTHERS, LIMITED, of St John's, Merchants, hereinafter called the Contractor, of the other part; whereby the Contractor covenants and agrees to and with the said Government, for the consideration hereinafter mentioned, to provide and furnish two steamers, to ply and run between St John's and the several other ports, to be appointed as hereinafter provided in the Postal Service, and in any other Public Service, as the Government may from time to time direct, in manner and under and subject to the terms and conditions hereinafter set forth . . .

There follow general specification requirements of the vessels to be provided. The ship for the Northern Service, for instance, was to be of about 1,000 tons gross and about 300 feet long, and have suitable accommodation for 60 cabin and 90 steerage passengers. For the Southern Service the ship was to be smaller at 800 tons gross and about 185 feet in length, but with accommodation for the same number of passengers. They were both required to achieve a speed of 12 knots on their trials and, not unnaturally, to be classed 100 A1 at Lloyd's. Notwithstanding the specific requirements laid down in the contract, it seems that Bowring Brothers had two identical ships built in 1904 for the Coastal Mail Service, *Portia* (IV) and *Prospero* (III), each complying with the larger specification. They were launched at Glasgow and named respectively by Mrs Thomas Bowring and Mrs William Bowring.

The Northern Service involved thirty-three calls, the final one being Griguet at the tip of the northwest peninsula. Some of the small harbours and settlements visited en route bore a variety of esoteric names including Seldom-Come-By, Exploits, Leading Tickles, Nippers Harbour and Jackson's Arm. The service called for nineteen fortnightly trips each year beginning on or about 1 May. The ship providing the Southern Service was required to make twenty-six fortnightly trips, also starting at the beginning of May, making some twenty-nine calls. Some of the small fishing outports visited by this service also enjoyed intriguing names such as Placentia, Lamaline, Hermitage and Pushthrough. This service terminated at Bonne Bay, at the southern end of the northwest peninsula.

To give some idea of the modest scale of the operation, the terms of the contract required that:

The said boats shall stay at each intermediate port of call not less than one half hour and at each terminal port not less than six hours; provided that the Captain of the boat and the Mail Officer on board agree that they may increase or lessen the time of such stay.

The contract was signed by Sir Robert Bond and Edgar R. Bowring and had a life of fifteen years. But in his book, *Benjamin Bowring and His Descendants*, Arthur Wardle records . . . 'without a single loss of life, Bowring Brothers' coastal steamers plied regularly for thirty seven years . . .' It is unclear, however, which of their vessels were employed during the later years of the service. Both *Portia* and *Prospero* were sold to the Newfoundland Government in 1919.

Chapter 9

AT THE OUTBREAK of the First World War the company were probably best known as shipowners with a fleet of forty-two vessels, ranging in size from the auxiliary barque-rigged sealer, *Kite*, of 280 tons gross to the tanker, *Lompoc*, of 7,270 tons.

An early casualty was the 6,542 ton tanker, *Elsinore*, built in 1913 at Swan, Hunter's Wallsend shipyard for Bearcreek Oil & Shipping Company. Within a few weeks of the commencement of hostilities in 1914, the Master, Captain John Roberts, wrote in the ship's log:

Sept. 6. At noon left Corinto (Nicaragua) for Port San Luis, California, in ballast.

Sept. 10. Manzanillo abeam at noon about 23 miles. Set course to pass 10 miles of Cape San Luis.

Sept. 11. At 2.15 a.m. 2nd Officer reported to me that he saw smoke on the Port and I at once went to the Bridge. At 2.30 a.m. the weather was overcast with a fresh wind from the S. W. and heavy rain, when I was covered by a search light from a vessel unknown, and taking precaution I put my vessel at the 'Stand By,' and after a lapse of about 20 minutes the vessel in question 'Morsed' me in a foreign language which I failed to understand, when I was immediately fired upon, the shot passing across my bows, upon which I stopped my ship and hove to.

At 3.15 a.m. a boat fully armed with 25 officers and men came alongside, and proved to be from the fast German cruiser *Leipzig* (I may mention that I had been navigating with reduced lights, my main mast head and stern lights being out and a careful lookout had been kept throughout). The officers and half of the crew of the boat came on board (fully armed) and the leading officer informed me that his Commander had sent him to inform me that my steamer was seized and that I and the rest of my crew were prisoners. He then demanded all the ship's papers including the ship's register, official log-book, crew's agreement and scrap log. He then required a full statement regarding all stores and bunker load, and seemed very disappointed when I told him I was burning oil fuel and had only about 35 tons of coal on board for cooking purposes. I was then ordered into the boat and conveyed on board the Cruiser and was informed by the Commander that I was his prisoner, and that I was to steer N.62E.Mag. for 70 miles and to have all my boats provisioned. Myself and the crew were to leave the ship, as he was going to destroy her. I asked for what reason he was going to destroy a fine new steamer that had no contraband on board and only in water ballast, and he replied that British men-of-war were doing the same thing on the Atlantic side. He then ordered me to return to my vessel and steer the course abovementioned.

At 4.10 a.m. I arrived on board my own vessel and set the engines at full speed, and course was set N.62E. At 5.30 a.m. I was signalled by 'Morse' to alter my course to S.15E. and again at 9.25 a.m. was signalled to steer S.65. Then I began to get anxious wondering when we had to leave, as I was at this time 50 miles from land. At 10.10 a.m. I was signalled to make the best speed possible and at 10.30 a.m. we sighted a cargo steamer which proved to be a German ship named *Marie* but which at first I thought to be a poor unfortunate like myself owing to his manoeuvres, but I afterwards found that he was only obeying orders from the *Leipzig* and that the meeting was pre-arranged, and that the *Marie* was in company with the *Leipzig* supplying her with coal and stores.

At 11.15 a.m. I was again signalled to heave to and proceed on board *Marie*, taking sufficient stores for eight days, and they allowed us two hours to be out of our ship, so I immediately proceeded to obey these orders. In the meantime, a number of armed officers and men from the *Leipzig* came on board and commenced ransacking the ship, taking all stores and articles of any use to them. They also took our boats and hoisted them up in the davits of the *Marie*. Our position at that time was latitude 19.31, longitude 105.56. west. At 12.30 p.m. myself and crew boarded the *Marie* and at 10.10 p.m. the Cruiser commenced firing upon the *Elsinore* at about a mile distant. The sight was too heart-breaking for me to witness, so I kept to my room, but my officers afterwards informed me that they put 12 shots into her, and she became ablaze, and she sank stern first. Before my vessel sank, the captain of the *Marie* was ordered to go full speed on a course, and so came the end of one of the finest Oil steamers on the Pacific Coast.

When first taken prisoner by the Germans, the Commander promised to put me off a few miles from Cape Corrientes, which he afterwards failed to do and I think the reason was that he was rather anxious for his own safety.

Sept. 12. The *Marie* proceeding on the same course S. by E. and during the day the Cruiser would lead ahead at about 3 miles distant, and by night about the same distance astern. There was an armed crew of 14 men placed on board the *Marie* from the Cruiser to guard my men and myself.

The Commander of the Cruiser signalled to the officer in charge to treat my men as well as possible.

Sept. 13. Ordered to stop by the Cruiser, when they passed several hundred coal bags on board to be filled by my crew who they would pay their usual rate of wages . . .

Sept. 14. Again stopped by Cruiser, and more coal bags passed on board to be filled by my crew.

Sept. 15. and 16. We are steering for the Galapagos Islands.

Sept. 17. Sighted Galapagos Islands 7.00 a.m. came to anchor in Tagus Cove, Albemarle Island, and at 11.30 a.m. the Cruiser came alongside and commenced to bunker. 7.00 p.m. owing to the cove being so small the Cruiser cast off and went to safer anchorage. Previous to her going away, the Commander sent for me to come aboard. He then told me that he would faithfully land us all safe and how sorry he felt for me in such a position, and being a sailor himself he was sorry he had been obliged to sink such a fine ship. Then I informed him that I had a bag of mail on board from the American cruiser Denver for San Francisco, which he promised he would safely deliver.

Sept. 18. The Cruiser came alongside at 6.00 a.m. and again commenced to bunker; 9.00 a.m. completed 500 tons. At 11.30 a.m. both ships got under way and proceeded out of the cove at full speed, and course was set South.

Sept. 19. Came to anchor off Hood Island, Galapagos Islands, at 8.30 a.m. and the Cruiser left and proceeded for Chatham Island for fresh provisions, which I believe was not necessary, as he had more important business in view.

Sept. 20. Ship still at anchor off Hood Island, and 6.00 a.m. I am positive I saw two distinct smokes from steamers in the direction of Chatham Island, and this proved to be correct, as the Cruiser had another steamer awaiting her with stores etc. and equipped with wireless. At 6.00 p.m. the Cruiser returned and anchored close to and signalled that the Commander would send his boat to take me on board as he wished to speak to me. On arrival on board the Cruiser, he informed me that owing to information he had just received he was unable to fulfil his promise to land me at Callao, but he had made arrangements at Chatham Island for our board etc. and that after 14 days a vessel would take us off for Guayaquil, and I was to be prepared to land at 8.30 the following morning. The Commander seemed now to be working in some mysterious way as if he was anxious to get clear of us. He invited me to take dinner with him, but I was obliged to refuse owing to being so depressed to find the precarious position that fate had placed both my crew and myself in, so I came back on board and called my Officers together and told them the exact words the Commander of the *Leipzig* had said, but when the crew were informed they became very dissatisfied which caused the Cruiser's people to double up the armed guard, but however the night passed quietly.

Sept. 21. At 8.00 a.m. we embarked in the Cruiser's boats with our remaining effects and a small amount of provisions, and at 9.00 a.m. we landed on Chatham Island, with only two houses in sight and a large store shed in which the crew were lodged. This island belongs to Ecuador and is used as a convict station. I arranged with two Officers to remain with the crew to keep order, and taking the Chief Officer, Chief Engineer and Second Engineer, we rode on horseback to the settlement 6 miles inland (a sugar and coffee plantation) and even here we fared badly regarding food and beds, but the crew fared very hard, as the provisions were very scarce and had to be carefully watched.

Sept. 22. This day passed after many troubles regarding sleeping accommodation etc. but my crew seemed to be getting very dissatisfied, for up to the present they had borne their hardships bravely.

Sept. 24. To-day I made arrangement with the Governor of the Island, a Mr Aray, to take me and half the crew to Ecuador as this was the only means of getting into communication and reporting the loss of the ship, and he arranged to send us away in a small sloop of 50 tons, the distance to Guayaquil being about 670 miles, so he provisioned her accordingly, she being about half loaded with dried fish and hides and ordinarily would not have sailed for another ten days. The Commander of the *Leipzig's* sole intention was to detain me on the island as long as possible to prevent me from communicating with the authorities and spoiling his chance of sinking other merchant vessels, for when the Governor of the island offered to assist me one of the German officers remaining on the island strongly objected. But the Governor insisted on our leaving owing to the scarcity of food, there being not sufficient to keep all the crew for any length of time and also owing to his feeling towards us. So after some considerable time, I picked out half the crew that was to accompany me on what turned out to be one of the most monotonous and hardest few days at sea I ever experienced. The accommodation of the crew was in the hold, where they slept on the hides and dried fish, and the smell at times was really terrible. So at 3.00 p.m. after saying good-bye to the remaining crew, we boarded our small craft, lifted anchor and set sail for Guayaquil. I may mention that this is the most isolated and unfrequented stretch of water in the world. Mr Aray, the Governor, accompanied us, and we occupied the cabin together, and he was most kind and considerate to us right through the trip and did all possible for our comfort.

Oct. 1. This day we arrived at Guayaquil after a most eventful trip in many ways. The total number of persons on the small craft was 29, so our comfort and living can be better imagined than described. I may add that this report was duly reported to H.B.M. Consul who immediately cabled to Lloyd's the loss of my vessel also asking them to inform my owners.

After several weeks on Chatham Island under conditions of extreme hardship, the crew were eventually repatriated. During their time on the island they were employed filling bags of coal for the *Leipzig* at their normal rates of pay. *Elsinore* was one of the first British ships to be sunk through enemy action and was the first of some eighteen Bowring ships to be lost during the war, most of them operating under Admiralty orders.

Nevertheless, during the early part of the war the company, in its varied activities on both sides of the Atlantic was, in general, thriving. The Newfoundland sealing fleet, though reduced in size since the decline in numbers of the smaller wooden vessels, continued to make its significant contribution to the island's economy with *Stephano* and *Florizel* playing a major part when not fulfilling their much sought after passenger and cargo services between St John's, Halifax and New York where, from the office of Bowring & Company, they were still managed. As well as the export of dried salt cod being satisfactorily maintained, *Prospero* and *Portia* continued to implement their profitable mail contract for the Newfoundland Government.

But as the war pursued its relentless course there would be serious and irreparable damage to the hitherto well-ordered progress of the company's activities and its established trading routine. To add to the loss of ships and of members of staff being called up for military service, the company and family lost two of their most dedicated and public-spirited members. Sir Thomas Benjamin Bowring died on 18 October 1915, aged sixty-eight, and his cousin, Sir William Benjamin Bowring Bt, on 20 October 1916 at the riper age of seventy-nine. Both might well today have been described as 'movers and shakers'.

Thomas Bowring, as we have already learnt, was a pivotal figure in the development of the company's oil interests. The journal *Syren and Shipping* once observed that no one knew more than he did about the intricate business of shipping oil in bulk across the oceans. Although, after his return from New York in 1891, he was frequently at Pitt House, Ford Street, Moretonhampstead, he kept what sounds as though it may well have been a substantial residence at 7, Palace Gate in London, which was regularly supplied with plump poultry from his Devon Duck Farm. He had joined Bowring & Archibald at New York in 1870 and, as well as energetically pursuing his commercial career, was a leading figure in the Society of St George of which, in 1888, he became treasurer. As already mentioned he took over the management of Bowring's London office in 1891 following the untimely death of George Edward Bowring. But he is probably best remembered today at the little Devon town of Moretonhampstead. He took a great interest in the affairs of the county and was an enthusiastic member of the Mid-Devon Liberal Association. He was appointed a Justice of the Peace in 1906 and received a knighthood in 1913. As a benefactor to the small town where he spent much of his time he will be remembered especially for the library he gave and endowed, and for the twenty-five cottages, which he built and named Kinsman's Dale after his wife, Annie Kinsman. All these are still to be seen today as is his grave and those of other members of the family at the Unitarian Chapel in Cross Street, which he generously endowed, and for whose resident minister he built a substantial manse, Hornhills House, overlooking Kinsmans Dale. He also set up a scholarship fund for local schoolchildren, available for three years for a boy or girl to attend the secondary school at Newton Abbot.

William Benjamin or, as he later became known throughout the family, 'Billy the Bart', was probably even more industrious and generous than his cousin Thomas. He was born in Newfoundland and followed the now well-established family career pattern. Having received his education at Liverpool and Birmingham, he started his business life at the age of sixteen back in St John's learning from and helping his uncles Henry, Edward and John. In 1861, at the age of twenty-four, he married Isabel Maclean, the daughter of Edward Lutwich Jarvis and a few years later, as we have already learnt, went to New York where he established the firm of Bowring and Archibald. In 1868 he came back to Liverpool and was soon to become a distinguished figure in commercial and municipal circles. He lived at Beechwood, Grassendale, then a leafy suburb of Liverpool. Although it took him a little time to share Thomas's enthusiasm for the petroleum business, his growing knowledge of it and his experience as a shipowner and merchant were suitably acceptable qualifications for his appointment to the Mersey Docks and Harbour

Board on which he served for eight years. In 1884 he was elected to the Liverpool Town Council representing the St Peter's Ward in succession to his father, Charles Tricks. A member of the Bowring family represented this Ward for over forty years without a break. 'Billy the Bart' was no mean benefactor to Merseyside and to public life in general. He gave much of his time and energy to many local and national institutions and was, at various times, Chairman of the Liverpool Reform Club, a member of the Liverpool University Council, chairman of the Liverpool Peace Society and President of the United Temperance Society, the latter manifesting a degree of abstinence not evident in succeeding generations. Among his commercial appointments were a number of directorships including the Alliance Marine Assurance Company, the North-Western Bank, and he was appointed chairman of Cearns & Brown, Limited, a well-known purveyor of provisions with its origins in Liverpool and run by several generations of Stoddarts to whom, through marriage, the Bowring family are related.

In 1893 he was elevated to the chief magistracy and became Liverpool's first Lord Mayor, later to be created a baronet. During his year as Lord Mayor the potato crop in Ireland failed, which caused much distress not only to the inhabitants but also to the growing Irish population in Liverpool. Much in keeping with his philanthropic nature, Sir William created a relief fund and decided to go to Ireland in order to dispense the proceeds himself. One of the Town Hall footmen went with him in full gold-braided livery, complete with knee breeches and cocked hat. This, in contrast to Sir William's sober apparel, caused the inhabitants of one small village, as they greeted his train, to misdirect their vociferous welcome and the Lord Mayor of Liverpool was totally disregarded, seeming to be of no great importance.

Of his many benefactions, he will probably be longest remembered for his gift of Bowring Park to the people of Liverpool. On 11 January 1906 he wrote to the Town Clerk:

> Having signed a Contract for the purchase of Roby Hall Estate, consisting of about 100 acres, and a mansion with some cottages, beautifully situated just outside the City Boundaries, and feeling strongly the advantage to the citizens of securing such a property in that position, I hereby offer to the Corporation the said Estate for the use of the inhabitants of Liverpool for all time. I do so to commemorate the fact that my father and I have been members of the Liverpool Council for nearly half a century. I make no condition as to the use of the Estate except that it shall be utilised for the

benefit of the inhabitants of the City but I shall be glad if the Corporation will allow me a voice in any suggestion which may be made as to its ultimate use.'

The Estate was named Bowring Park and remains open to the public to this day. The presentation and official opening took place on 12 June 1907.

Soon after the start of the First World War Bowring ships were requisitioned for Government service and among those to fly the Royal Fleet Auxiliary Flag, either as tankers or colliers, were *Hermione*, *Silvia*, *Rosalind*, *Trinculo*, *Cordelia*, *Beacon Light*, *Lompoc*, *Zafra*, *Pola and Huelva*. The tanker *Hermione* was the Admiralty's first regular oil transport.

On the other side of the Atlantic a relatively unreal situation prevailed. A couple of weeks after the outbreak of war the New York office was busily encouraging travel agents to draw to the attention of their customers the virtues of holiday cruises to Newfoundland. Taking advantage of the fact that it was no longer possible for Americans to arrange trips to Britain and the Continent, their persuasive letter read:

> It is thought that as the situation in Europe is so uncertain, not to say unsafe, considerable passenger traffic will be diverted to the different coastwise lines. Naturally this line wishes to secure its share of this business and with its two modern steamers *Stephano* and *Florizel* is well prepared to take care of any additional traffic which will result from the trouble abroad.

Furthermore, attention was drawn to the fact that, as Halifax had been chosen by the British Government as its main naval and military base on the East coast of North America, it would be of special interest to tourists.

Shortly after this letter, advertisements for the 1915 season began to appear. One of them ran:

> No Europe this year. Visit foreign America. Excellent fishing and shooting. This most healthful and desirable vacation cruise from New York combines novelty, grandeur, delightful climate and a charming voyage with absolute comfort and remarkable economy. New tourist steamships . . . fitted with every device for comfort and safety – full boat equipment for passengers and crew, wireless, bilge keels, submarine bells, etc.

And the ultimate enticement 'magnificent climate – hay fever unknown.'

The two ships continued to lead their double lives as cruising vessels and sealers and, as these tempting advertisements were appearing in the American press, they were, in fact at the ice front. But the 1915 seal fishery was little short of disastrous, owing to a dense wall of ice that impeded even the iron-hulled vessels and prevented them from reaching the larger patches of seals. The total catch amounted to only just over 47,000 among thirteen ships of which four belonged to Bowring Brothers. It will be remembered that in 1910 *Florizel* alone brought in no fewer than 49,000 seals. However, catches of cod were unusually good and fish prices rose. Notwithstanding the hardships of war, Newfoundland was to enjoy a period of unusual prosperity and a spirit of optimism prevailed. There was high employment and business turnover was buoyant.

However, immediately after the outbreak of war Newfoundland set about recruiting men for military service. It was natural that the expert qualities of seamanship, born of their experiences with the hunt for seals and fishing for cod, would bring many young Newfoundlanders to the Royal Naval Reserve depot, HMS *Briton*, to sign on for service with the Royal Navy. In the wider context of the conduct of the war and in recognition of the island's strategic importance, a powerful radio station was set up by the Admiralty at Mount Pearl in order to enhance North Atlantic communications.

In the rather less familiar garb of a soldier's uniform and marching boots, the First Newfoundland Regiment had soon recruited some 540 men of the 7,000 who would eventually be enrolled. Known as 'The Blue Puttees' – for this was the colour of the leg-wear hastily provided for them by a local manufacturer – this small initial contingent embarked in *Florizel* on 3 October 1914, destined for Devonport and, almost immediately after their arrival, for training on Salisbury Plain. The Regiment gave a praiseworthy account of itself both at Gallipoli and in the mud of Flanders. Their most distinguished action was at Beaumont-Hamel during the Battle of the Somme, where they suffered grievous losses. Of the 763 brave Newfoundlanders who went into action on 1 July 1916 there were only 68 who answered roll call the following day. On land and at sea the loss of human life was heavy and Newfoundland was deprived of many of the cream of its younger men. Of approximately 8,500 enrolled in the two services, The Royal Newfoundland Regiment, as it was later named, suffered about 1,300 killed and over 2,300 wounded; of those who joined the Royal Navy, some 180 lost their lives and 125 were invalided home.

★ ★ ★

In April 1915 Edgar Bowring was awarded a knighthood, and no doubt his colleagues and members of the company in St John's would have recognized this honour with some admiration and pleasure. However, such euphoric sentiments as may well have been expressed were inevitably subdued, if only temporarily, by the sensational news of a narrow escape experienced by Charles Warren Bowring, who at the time was part of the management team at the New York office. A grandson of Charles Tricks, it will be recalled that he had for a number of years been head of Bowring Brothers in Newfoundland, where he also became a leading politician.

On 1 May 1915 the British ship *Lusitania* sailed from New York for England carrying nearly 2,000 passengers, of whom Charles Warren was one, and 173 tons of ammunition. She was an extremely popular transatlantic vessel. One of the largest, she was well known for her speed and luxurious accommodation. Her departure was believed to have been in the face of warnings by the German authorities that she would be sunk. However, the owners, Cunard, were confident that their 25-knot, 32,500-ton liner could outpace any likely assailant, especially a relatively slow submarine.

On 7 May, after six uneventful days of the crossing, when the ship was practically within sight of the Irish coast, the Master, Captain Turner, ignoring the recommendation that ships should alter course every few minutes, held his ship in such a position as to present a perfect target to a lurking German submarine whose periscope neither he nor any member of his crew had noticed.

What followed is taken up by David Keir in *The Bowring Story*:

> With most of the other passengers he was lunching happily when the liner was attacked 15 miles off the south coast of Ireland by a German U-Boat. In his own words, he heard 'a damnable concentrated thud'. Portholes in the dining saloon were shattered, and an enormous column of water exploded up the ship's side where he was sitting.
>
> Realizing the ship had been torpedoed Charles rushed up to the boat deck and helped with lifebelts while the crew packed women and children into the boats. When finally he abandoned ship the deck rail was less than 10 feet from the water, and as he struggled clear he narrowly missed being carried under by the funnels when the ship capsized and settled. After more than three hours spent in a boat which, with a lifeboat in tow, picked up survivors from bits of floating wreckage, he and his companions were rescued by a naval auxiliary, and landed at Cobh in County Cork.

In view of the fact that *Lusitania* was carrying 128 US citizens, and that the sinking aroused a great wave of indignation in the United States and elsewhere, it was surprising that the American Government decided to maintain its neutrality.

Misfortune at sea was no stranger to the family. It will be recalled that Benjamin's eldest son, William, lost his life at sea when, in 1829, he was returning from St John's to Devon with marriage to Harriet Harvey in mind. Nearly sixty years later, George Edward Bowring came close to perishing when, as a passenger on the company's ship *Romeo*, which was headed for Rouen, he faced being drowned in the Seine. Apparently the ship ran aground at night and before a tug could reach her she was hit by a massive tidal bore. George, who was on the bridge, was thrown into the swirling torrent and, as he was wearing several layers of heavy clothing, came close to being dragged under. He was an exceptionally strong swimmer, however, and after struggling for an hour and a half, managed to free himself of his clothes and to swim to the riverbank on the side opposite to where *Romeo* had capsized and become a total loss. He eventually found refuge with a farmer and his wife, who gave him dry clothes, which, in his own words, he thought gave him the appearance of a 'Normandy yachtsman of a low class'. Had George not survived this ordeal, although he was in fact to die prematurely only four years later, one cannot but wonder whether his efforts up to the time of this incident would have been sufficient to develop the company's insurance business, about which he was particularly enthusiastic, to the prominence it eventually achieved. Forty years after Charles's escape, George's grandson, another Benjamin, survived many hours in the English Channel in circumstances about which we shall learn more later.

In both Liverpool and London, wartime conditions were having their effect and, inevitably, staff numbers were reduced by enlistment for military service. At Liverpool the Port Authority was of the opinion that recruiting campaigns had been too successful, leaving the docks and shipping companies badly understaffed. Indeed, the Docks Board had provided no less than three battalions for the army and altogether some 5,000 dockers were lost to the forces. This gave rise to severe labour shortages and caused industrial unrest and higher wage demands. As shipping was being diverted to Liverpool from other ports, congestion and delays developed, and dock facilities came under severe strain. To make matters worse and to add to the general mood of depression, the winter of 1914/1915 was one of the wettest on record.

In London conditions were no better, but for different reasons. Here again the demands of the armed forces had reduced staff levels, and for the first time ladies were enrolled to take on the clerical duties of those who were called up. Necessary and unfamiliar wartime regulations, relating to insurance and shipping, kept staff at all levels fully occupied from 9.00 a.m. to 6.00 p.m. every day, and frequently until much later. But those who experienced those dark days aver that, generally speaking, morale remained high, notwithstanding the anxieties naturally arising from concern for those at sea whose lives were at risk, especially from the worsening U–Boat menace. German naval activity was already taking a huge toll of British shipping and Bowring ships, being mainly tankers, were from the very beginning especially vulnerable. German strategy was designed to prevent supplies of all kinds from reaching Britain and, as many Royal Navy ships at the beginning of the war had become partly, and in some cases, totally oil burning, the significance of the German determination to destroy as many British tankers as possible is only too clear.

Within a period of two weeks two further Bowring tankers (*Elsinore*, it will be recalled, having been sunk on 11 September 1914 in the Pacific) fell victim to German U–Boat supremacy. On 23 August 1915 *Silvia*, with 7,750 tons of valuable fuel oil on passage from Halifax, Nova Scotia to Queenstown, was sunk by gunfire from the German submarine U–38 forty-seven miles west of Fastnet. Some twelve days later, at midnight on 3 September, the 4,500 ton *Cymbeline* was captured and torpedoed by U–Boat U–33, in much the same sea area, on a voyage from Port Arthur, Texas, to Dartmouth with another vital cargo of oil. Six members of the crew were lost, but had it not been for the skill of the Master in getting the ship's boats away quickly, many more would have lost their lives. Again, within a few more days, the 3,000 ton cargo vessel, *Mora*, while on passage from Santander to Newport with iron ore, was sunk by gunfire from the German submarine U–20.

There might well have been fewer ship losses had there not been an incomprehensible lack of security, which persisted during the first two years of the war. Trade journals continued, with alarming lack of responsibility, to publish regularly the movements of tankers. It is astonishing that there had been no guidance from the Government in this respect and it must be assumed that this inexplicable dereliction almost certainly contributed to the early losses. The proposed voyages of several Bowring ships were mentioned and in an issue of *The Petroleum Review* of 2 January 1915, *Beacon Light* was reported to be headed for Marseilles from New York, *Cordelia* was on her way from San Francisco to Vancouver and *Trinculo* from San Luis to Port Arthur. It was not until October 1916, after disclosing the names of tankers, their destinations and quantities of oil they discharged and, in addition, details of the losses due to enemy action, that this journal, and others, published the following notice.

THE MOVEMENT OF OIL TANKERS

We much regret to inform our readers that for the time being we shall have to suspend the publication of the specially prepared list of the movements of the world's fleet of oil-tankers, which list, compiled by Lloyd's, has been a feature of the *Review* since its inception. In future all oil-carrying vessels, so we understand from the Press Bureau, will have to be treated in the same way as on Government charter, that is to say they are all added to the list of vessels whose movements are not to be published either in the trade press or in any shape or form whatsoever. Until the above mentioned instruction is withdrawn, the *Review* will, therefore, be minus this long-standing feature.

The U-Boat was by far the most effective naval weapon used for the German blockade of Britain, which began on 18 February 1915, and any vessel of any kind approaching the 'war-zone', which was taken to mean, roughly, all approaches to the British Isles, would be torpedoed without warning. However, following the sinking of the *Lusitania*, the *Arabic* and, in the spring of 1916, a cross-Channel steamer, *Sussex*, President Wilson prevailed upon Germany to promise that no more merchant ships would be attacked without warning and that it would confine its aggressions to the 'fighting forces of the belligerents'. This undertaking was not to last long, though. Expecting that by resuming unrestricted attacks on allied shipping Britain would be isolated and starving within a few months, before the likelihood of there being any American participation in the war, attacks without warning were authorized again from 1 February 1917. From this time shipping losses began to rise alarmingly.

British shipyards were hard put to it to catch up with these losses. But replacements were coming along and during the course of the war four new Bowring ships were launched; *Huelva* (II), 4,867 tons gross in July 1915, *Murcia* (II), 4,871 tons gross, also launched in 1915, *Adra* (II), 4,860 tons gross in 1917 and *Merida*, 5,951 tons gross in 1918. *Huelva* and *Murcia* were both sunk by enemy action. *Adra* survived only to be torpedoed and sunk in the Second World War. *Merida*, though torpedoed in July 1918, managed to reach port, but was wrecked off Le Touquet later that year on a voyage from Baltimore to Le Havre and Dunkirk with a cargo of wheat.

Shortly before the end of the war Bowring Brothers acquired the auxiliary schooner, *Bianca*. Towards the end of August 1918 she encountered a U-Boat in the Western Atlantic, which tried unsuccessfully to sink her by gunfire. She was towed into port but was eventually abandoned in the North Atlantic on 31 October 1919 while on a voyage from Labrador to Gibraltar with a cargo of fish.

Certainly the loss of two leading members of the family during the vicissitudes of war was upsetting enough, but the loss of a large part of the company's fleet must have been heartbreaking. Between September 1914 and July 1918 eighteen Bowring ships, cargo vessels and tankers were, as already mentioned, destroyed by enemy action.

In Newfoundland there had been an upturn in the fortunes of the seal-hunt. In contrast to the previous year's lamentable result, 1916 was generally considered to have been a successful year, with a total catch of 242,302 seals. *Florizel* came close to matching her all time record of 49,069 in 1910 by coming home with 46,481 pelts. But the good news was not to last. Later that year, on 8 October, when the Red Cross Line's regular passenger service between New York, Halifax and St John's was in full swing, *Florizel's* sister ship, *Stephano*, with many Americans on board, was sunk by a torpedo from the German U-Boat U-53, two and a half miles from the Nantucket light-vessel while still in neutral waters. Fortunately, the passengers and crew were rescued by United States destroyers. The loss of *Stephano* was a serious blow. She was a popular ship with American tourists and had served the company well, both as a cruise vessel and as a sealer, for ten years. Unfortunately, because she was operating only in neutral waters, it had not been thought necessary to insure her against war risks.

But tragic though so many losses through enemy action most certainly were, the wreck of *Florizel* was probably the most heart-rending catastrophe to be experienced during the long history of Bowring shipowning, especially because, although it occurred during wartime, it was not the result of enemy action; and it was the cause of close personal loss.

As we already know, *Florizel* was as successful as a cruise liner as she was in the seal-hunt. Not only did she, from time to time, leave the ice and fog of Newfoundland for the warmth and blue skies of the Caribbean with sun-seeking holiday makers, she was also performing the duties of a troopship taking gallant volunteer Newfoundlanders to the European bloodbath.

At 7.30 p.m. on Saturday, 23 February 1918, on a black forbidding night of strong winds, rain, sleet and snow, *Florizel* slipped out of the comparative calm of St John's harbour through the Narrows into the turbulent ice-strewn Atlantic beyond. She carried 138 passengers and crew, among them John Munn, managing director of The Red Cross Line and a director of Bowring Brothers, his three and a half year old daughter, Betty, and her nurse. They were on their way to New York to be with his wife who had been there in hospital for some weeks. The ship was under command of 43-year-old Captain William Martin, who had been with her as Master for four years, and for two years previously as mate. He was an experienced skipper and had the reputation of being a sound and reliable navigator. In her book, *A Winter's Tale* (published by Doubleday Canada, 1976), Cassie Brown gives a sensational and convincing account of the events leading up to and following the tragedy of *Florizel's* running aground with the loss of 94 lives at Horn Head Point, at about 4.30 a.m., in the darkness and foul weather of the morning of 24 February.

It wasn't until the morning of Monday 25 February that the citizens of St John's became fully aware of the disaster when *The Newfoundland Daily News* headlines confirmed the rumours that had been bandied about since the middle of the previous day:

> Big Marine Tragedy near Cappahayden: s.s. *Florizel* Goes Ashore in Snow Storm, and is a Total Wreck.

As a result of this disaster, the reasons for which remained unexplained for a long time, John Munn and his daughter lost their lives. The loss of John Munn, who was very well known in Newfoundland's business circles and who had such a promising future with the company, together with the sinking of their most prestigious vessel, was a double tragedy for Bowring Brothers. The drowning of little Betty Munn added further to the sadness and utter desolation of the population of St John's who were at a loss as to understand how and why such a catastrophe could have occurred where it did.

At the time of the wreck Sir Edgar Bowring was on holiday in Florida and the responsibility for handling the situation for the owners, in whatever way possible, devolved upon his twenty-four-year-old nephew, Eric Bowring, brother of Charles Warren. Although an SOS signal had been transmitted from the sinking vessel shortly after grounding, no further contact was forthcoming except for agonized messages from dumbfounded observers on land who, without any hope of being able to help, were watching a devastating tragedy unfolding before their eyes barely 250 yards away as *Florizel* began to break up in the heavy swell. The possibilities of an early rescue operation were remote. There were ships at St John's in various states of readiness to go about their normal business, and it became a matter of organizing as many of them as possible to proceed to the scene of the wreck and to save as many lives as they could. Eric is reliably reported to have been, quite understandably, badly shaken, but with the help of the Honourable John Crosbie (later to be Sir John Crosbie), Minister of Shipping, Harry Reid of The Reid Newfoundland Company, the Newfoundland Shipping Company, owners of the whaler *Hawk*, the Dominion Coal Company, whose ship *Cape Breton* was in port, *Terra Nova*, *Hawk*, *Home* and *Cape Breton*, were as hastily as possible dispatched to the scene of the wreck, to be followed soon after by *Prospero*.

Although these efforts to carry out a rescue operation were performed as expeditiously as possible, there was little that could be done until the weather moderated. Those passengers who were unable to escape from the flooding of the lower decks, many of whom were trapped in their cabins, drowned in what must have been terrifying circumstances.

In St John's rumours abounded. *Florizel's* time was up said some, rats had been seen leaving the ship before she sailed; she had succumbed to submarine attack, said others; and Captain Martin and his crew were all drunk; *Florizel's* engines had been sabotaged and her compass had been tampered with, and so on. It was clearly essential that immediate steps should be taken to establish, if at all possible, where blame for the tragedy lay, and a Marine Court of Enquiry, under the jurisdiction of Mr James P. Blackwell, K. C. began its investigation on 5th March, 1918. Captain Martin and members of his crew were grilled by a powerful Court of distinguished lawyers. Although their deliberations failed to establish exactly what happened during the night of 23/24 February, the blame for the wreckage of the *Florizel* was ultimately laid fairly and squarely at the door of the Master, whose certificate was suspended for twenty-one months; but the Court considered that, in view of his past good record and general care and attention to duty, Captain Martin should be allowed to hold a Chief Mate's Interim Certificate during his suspension. He soon left Newfoundland and settled in New York where, in view of his previous generally good record, he found employment with Munson Lines.

But the *Florizel* disaster and the loss of many distinguished citizens will never be forgotten in St John's.

Chapter 10

ALTHOUGH FINANCIAL COMPENSATION for the wartime ship losses was received, Bowring's fleet was seriously weakened. The petroleum importing and distributing business had almost disappeared and, soon after the end of hostilities, in 1920 and 1921, there was an economic slump which had its effect on trade generally. In these disappointing circumstances it was encouraging to see that the insurance business, in the development of which George Bowring had played such an outstanding part before his untimely death in 1891, was beginning to show signs of great promise. There had been considerable growth in marine insurance before the war in which the company had been involved and, notwithstanding the inevitable interruptions to building up business during wartime, useful contacts and cordial relations had been developed with American clients and friends. In the years ahead these connections would prove to be of tremendous value, as the growing significance of insurance in its great diversity became the mainstay of the rapidly growing group of Bowring companies.

The essence of insurance is well defined as follows:

The loss lighteth rather easily on many than heavily upon few.

From the principle, so succinctly summed up in this ancient precept, a massive global business has developed, which provides protection against the financial risks inherent in virtually any aspect of our existence including life, health, accident, legal liability, property and countless other potential hazards to which anyone or any organization might be subject.

When addressing the Brighton Insurance Institute on 7 November 1961, Mr A. F. O'Shea cleverly gave an illustration of the all-embracing nature of the insurance business:

'Insurance,' he said, 'is inextricably woven into the pattern of our lives. It is not just something we provide for ourselves, it enters into the make-up of everything we own, use or eat. Take the humble loaf of bread. It was insured from the time the corn was in the ear until the finished product emerged. Moreover the combine that reaped the corn, the silo that stored it, the vessel that transported it and the mill that ground it were all insured and had been, in various guises from the time they too were in the raw material stage. So, too, were the liabilities of the various operators to their employees and to the public. The baker who sold the loaf was probably insured, *inter alia*, against liability in respect of poisoning risks, and the consumer, if a prudent man, would be protected against the same contingency by a sickness policy and by life insurance . . . As with the loaf, so it is with other things, whether it be a motor car, the Zambesi Dam, a parish fete or an atomic reactor in Brazil, the stabilizing thread of insurance runs through them all.

Probably the most significant events in the development of Bowring's involvement in the insurance business were the appointment in 1849 of Bowring Brothers as the Newfoundland agents of the Liverpool & London & Globe Insurance Company, and the early association with Lloyd's of various members of the family, the first being Edward who, in 1866 after his return to England in the mid 1850s, became a subscriber to Lloyd's, and George, who became a member in 1876. It was the latter who, during his all too short life, did so much to ensure that the company's entry into insurance, an activity that would eventually eclipse all others, would continue to be pursued energetically, by encouraging his kinsmen and colleagues of its long-term virtues. And it was his son, Harvey, born in 1885, who was largely responsible for maintaining this enthusiasm. However, as will later become apparent and has often been stated, it was in spite of most members of the Bowring family rather than because of them, with a few notable exceptions, that the company made such outstanding progress in this field of endeavour. What they *were* good at was recognizing and employing experts, some of whom we shall hear more of in due course.

At the risk of stating what, for many readers, may be the obvious, a brief explanation of the principles of insurance may not be altogether out of place. An individual or organization wishing to obtain insurance cover makes payments called 'premiums' to an insurer who accepts the risk of paying the insured in the event of specified types of losses being suffered. The terms of agreement between the two parties are drawn up in a legal document called a 'policy'. In both theory and almost invariably in practice the amount of money collected by the insurer in premiums outweighs whatever may have to be paid out against claims. But, it is possible to imagine a situation where a loss might potentially be too large for one insurer to accept, such as the sinking of a ship. It was such

circumstances that gave rise to the 'pooling' of risks through organizations such as Lloyd's, which, unlike the many well-known insurance
companies, is composed of a number of syndicates, which individually
accept agreed fractions of risks, thus spreading the overall cost of meeting
any particular casualty.

Because the Bowring involvement in the insurance business has been
to a very large extent with Lloyd's, it might be helpful to know something
of that organization's origins. In 1688 Edward Lloyd was operating a
coffee house at Tower Street in London. His customers consisted largely
of merchants and shipowners, who would drop in for a gossip and a
beverage. They found the experience so agreeable that their numbers
increased to the extent that Lloyd was forced in 1691 to acquire larger
premises in Lombard Street. Soon the coffee house became a whirlpool of
commercial transactions including ship auctions, placing of cargoes,
arranging travel and a general sharing of ventures. Furthermore, Edward
Lloyd became quite an authority on a wide range of marine matters,
thereby increasing the attraction of his premises as a maritime intelligence
exchange. It isn't difficult to see how, from these beginnings and in the
prevailing 'sharing' atmosphere, the principles of marine insurance
became topical and the broker/underwriter relationship manifested itself.
When Edward Lloyd died in 1713 the coffee house was still expanding,
and from 1720 to 1750 it became a centre of shipping information and an
insurance market. Regrettably, in the years that followed, more of a
speculative and gambling climate developed, and a number of its regular
customers decided to create a new Lloyd's House of their own in Pope's
Head Alley off Lombard Street, where their underwriting activities were
conducted in a more appropriate and controlled manner. So successful
and generally accepted was this move that in 1771 a large number of these
underwriters moved into yet larger premises, elected a committee and
created a subscription membership, thus giving birth to the Lloyd's as we
know it, operating today as a market of some sixty-six syndicates.

Many commercial enterprises with interesting historical backgrounds lost
records of their early years as a result of bombing during the Second
World War and this was the case when air raids destroyed the Bowring
offices in Liverpool. Unfortunately, because of enemy action, there is
little evidence of the company's early experiences in insurance. But we
do know that the founder, Benjamin, before sailing with his family for
Newfoundland in 1816, insured his life with the Provident Life Office,

and that when his business was virtually destroyed in the 1833 St John's fire, he was covered by a policy with the Phoenix Assurance Company with whom he lost no time in lodging a claim. No doubt, as we have noted earlier, the appointment of Benjamin Bowring in 1849 by the Liverpool & London & Globe as their Newfoundland agent, heightened the company's interest in insurance generally. And, of course, from the earliest days of shipowning, Benjamin and his successors made sure that all their vessels were at all times fully covered.

It was in the middle 1850s that Charles Tricks is known to have sown the seeds of what would eventually become the respectable double life of broker and underwriter. He opened his own private marine underwriting account in Liverpool. At that time a number of private companies were underwriting risks for their own account in Liverpool as well as placing business for their clients in the London market.

But underwriting, at a time when communications were painfully slow and unreliable, was no bonanza. In 1864 Calcutta was struck by a devastating cyclone of such destructive violence that over 60,000 people lost their lives, more than 160 ships – steamers and sailing vessels – were sunk or cast ashore and 17 ships of differing sizes were never seen or heard of again. According to the records of The Thames and Mersey Marine Insurance Company:

> It was probably the biggest single disaster which fell upon British shipping and underwriters; Liverpool as the centre of sailing ship operations received a crippling blow. Many shipowners went out of business; a considerable number of private underwriters were bankrupt and, as a result of their losses, two marine companies in Liverpool – the 'Albion' and the 'Empire Marine' – together with the Mercantile Insurance Co. of London had to go into liquidation ... All the Liverpool marine companies sustained heavy losses, one having to pay out over £60,000 after only twenty months of existence – a sum equal to nearly one-third of its paid-up capital.

However, despite the many large marine disasters that occurred during the latter years of the 19th century, insurance premiums eased because of the increasing use of steam power and the belief, not altogether unrealistic, that a steamship would be better able to overcome the risks of bad weather than a sailing vessel.

A few years after George became a member of Lloyd's there occurred another event which, quite fortuitously, played a significant role in the development of the company's insurance activities in general and particularly its business with the United States. David Keir describes in *The Bowring Story* what occurred:

> An American broker called Albert Wilcox, finding it necessary to insure a certain shipowner's Lake Fleet on competitive terms, referred to *Lloyd's Register of Shipping*, the only book he connected with Lloyd's as a name. At the time he was in Cleveland, and on finding the name Bowring and Archibald listed in the *Register* as Lloyd's agents, he wrote out a telegram addressed to Bowring and Archibald in New York, added the style 'Bowring of Lloyd's', and requested a clerk in the shipowner's office to send it off. The telegram asked whether the fleet could be insured on terms equal with those quoted by a competitor; it was at this point that chance stepped in. By a remarkable coincidence – so the story goes – the clerk, an emigrant from England, had worked in an office near Bowring's London office, and he knew that Bowring's were members of Lloyd's. Presumably, too, he knew that if the telegram was sent to New York it might bring a reply that though the office there acted as agents it took no part in actual insurance dealings at Lloyd's. Accordingly, this wise clerk redirected the cable to the London office; George Bowring promptly took it to his underwriting friends; and in due course the transaction was completed so satisfactorily that other business followed, not only from Wilcox but from Chubb and Sons, the Fireman's Fund and many other old and trusted friends.

This chance introduction to a burgeoning relationship with American insurance interests was pursued and developed by W. W. Puttick, the chief executive of the insurance department, who made a number of visits to the United States. It is, perhaps, worth noting that, in these early days of the company's development of its insurance activities, no member of the Bowring family had actually become directly involved in the day-to-day running of the insurance 'branch'. Whilst the main area of growth was marine insurance, progress was being made, albeit slowly, in the non-marine sector through the long-standing involvement with commodities such as oil, sealskins and the widening range of merchandise being handled by the company.

Events and developments throughout the world, as the 19th century was coming to a close, were fuelling the boundless prospects for a rapid increase in the demand for insurance. In North America and elsewhere the proliferation of industrial activity, the increase in the movement of ships carrying goods and commodities of every kind between the industrialized nations, and the demands imposed by the Spanish-American and Boer wars, added to the importance of insurance in all its many and increasing diversities.

The year 1897, during which Newfoundland was celebrating its four-hundredth anniversary as Britain's oldest colony, seems to have been something of a landmark year for the Bowring family and their commercial progress. Edgar Bowring, the leading light in Bowring Brothers in St John's, was made a member of Newfoundland's Legislative Council. It was also the year in which my father, Frederick Clive Bowring, who in due course became chairman, was born in St John's. Back in London Walter Hargreaves joined Edward Stevinson (who had entered the company the previous year) to establish a formidable team that would introduce a period of substantial growth in the company's marine insurance broking. This powerful and able combination took advantage of the fact that the marine insurance market in the United States was insufficiently developed to handle the demands made upon it, whether in the form of insurance or reinsurance. Harvey Bowring, who was the first member of the family to become totally involved in insurance to the virtual exclusion of any other activity within the company, gives an authentic account of how the firm reacted to the shortcomings of the American market:

> The Pacific Coast, with its centre in San Francisco, was also expanding its commerce. It is probable that San Francisco was almost as foreign to the Eastern States of America as it was to Europe, and from that fact another development occurred, to our own good fortune. A pool of the most important Eastern underwriters was formed, to take care of and, in fact, monopolize the grain export business. In forming this pool they ignored the quite large interest of the Fireman's Fund Insurance Company. This company had been established in San Francisco, the stockholders being many of the most influential banking concerns on the 'Coast'. The Fireman's Fund had a number of grain accounts on their books, which, owing to this pooling arrangement, they were unable to reinsure. Mr J. B. Levison, the Marine Secretary of the company, having failed to obtain satisfaction from the Eastern companies, was advised that Lloyd's would probably be glad to accept the necessary reinsurances. He therefore boarded the first available liner from New York, with the intention of contacting the London market. Fortunately, on board the same steamer, he met another insurance man who was on his way to visit our office and

to whom he explained his company's predicament. 'Go and see Hargreaves of Bowring's' was the advice given him. Levison called on Hargreaves, who was successful in meeting his requirements. The connection – of which we are extremely proud – was formed in consequence and there developed many personal friendships, not only between Levison and Hargreaves, but between many other members of the two organizations.

Such was the progress made shortly after the turn of the century, especially as a result of the efforts of Hargreaves and Stevinson in strengthening the company's American contacts, that it was decided in 1903 to form a separate company to handle all the London insurance broking activities, and a new wholly owned subsidiary, C. T. Bowring & Co. (Insurance) Ltd, with John Bowring Wimble (a grandson of Charles Tricks, whose daughter, Harriet Jane, was married to his father John Wimble) as Chairman, and Walter Hargreaves as Managing Director.

A couple of years before this historic manifestation of Bowring's determination to pursue energetically their highly promising progress in the world of insurance broking, Thomas had displayed considerable enthusiasm for inaugurating a marine underwriting syndicate at Lloyd's and in the summer of 1901, Walter Hargreaves' brother, Percy, was chosen to be the active underwriter of a syndicate whose members, or 'names', were John Wimble, Thomas himself and G. B. Hunter of Swan, Hunter and Wigham Richardson Ltd, the shipbuilders whose supremacy in their industry was well known to Bowring's, their fleet owning several of their vessels. The financial arrangements, modest enough by today's standards, involved their risk being limited to £200 each. They paid Lloyd's a membership fee of £400 each, and a joint guarantee of £5,000 in securities. Percy Hargreaves received the princely sum of £250 by way of annual salary, but was entitled to ten per cent of the syndicate's profits, and it is noted, happily, that his underwriting skill provided unbroken profits for many years.

Until the early years of the 20th century Lloyd's underwriters had concentrated mainly on marine insurance, but it was not long before they were accepting non-marine risks, as a result of which it took but a few years for premium income, in this aspect of insurance at Lloyd's, to become predominant. The early days in this promising field saw steady progress rather than rapid development, and Bowring's were not slow in becoming involved. According to Edward Stevinson – who with Walter

Hargreaves, it will be recalled, masterminded the first serious ventures into marine broking – the company's first major placing in the non-marine market was the insurance of the legendary Calouste Gulbenkian's oil interests in Borneo and Celebes against the possibility of earthquakes and tidal waves, or tsunami as we now know these potentially devastating catastrophes.

Bowring's had moved into new London offices at Winchester House, Old Broad Street, when perhaps the most significant event in the development of their progress in the non-marine business, and indeed in the growing trust placed by America in the British insurance market generally, was the terrible San Francisco fire of 1906. The demands made by this disaster on the insurance market everywhere were enormous. The fire, as it is almost always referred to was, in fact, caused by a severe earthquake. But the cost of the damage caused by buildings and other possessions being destroyed by fire far exceeded destruction attributable simply to seismic shock. Some insurance companies were ruined. But in the final analysis practically all the British insurance companies met their claims promptly and, in some cases, even generously; and this un-doubtedly went a long way towards cementing the growing confidence felt by America in the British insurance market.

At Liverpool, still the head office of the parent company, C. T. Bowring & Co. Ltd, as it would be so for many years to come, enthusiasm for marine underwriting was equally evident. In the early 1900s, as an extension, as it were, of Charles Tricks' personal entry into underwriting some fifty years earlier, the members of the parent Board formed themselves into a private marine underwriting syndicate, handling hull and cargo risks. This innovative operation would continue well into the middle years of the twentieth century, long after the company headquarters had moved to London.

And so it can now be seen that the company and, inescapably, individual members of the family, were embarked upon what, at the time was considered to be, and would continue to be, the perfectly respectable double life of broker and underwriter.

In his book, *Lloyd's of London* (Allen Lane, London 1984), Godfrey Hodgson gives an interesting account of Bowring's early days in the business of insurance:

> Bowring were badly hit by shipping losses in the First World War. They
> continued to be involved in shipping, though on a reduced scale . . .

Meanwhile the firm's involvement in insurance grew steadily. Individual Bowrings had written marine insurance in Liverpool early in the nineteenth century, but it was not until 1876 that the first of them became a member of Lloyd's. By the end of the century, as brokers, Bowring were expanding into the growing non-marine market. As early as 1897, they placed the reinsurance for the Fireman's Fund in San Francisco. In 1912 a young Bowring broker succeeded in insuring the *Titanic* in the overdue market after Lloyd's was closed and *after* the first news of the disaster.

The story is a classic example of the doctrine of 'utmost good faith', the fundamental principle traditionally underlying all business transacted at Lloyd's, whether verbal or written.

Godfrey Hodgson then quotes an extract from Bowring's own archives:

> A cable was received in our office at 5.30 p.m. requesting us to place what was in those days a large line on the Titanic against total loss at 'best possible'. A young broker was dispatched to Lloyd's to see whether anything could be done. After searching the Room, the Captain's Room and elsewhere with no result he met on the stairway of the old Lloyd's in the Royal Exchange Mr John Povah, a well-respected leader in the overdue market. On being offered the risk he remarked, 'The rate at the moment is 25 guineas per cent, but if you want me to write so large an amount as that, I must have 30 guineas.' Having an order at 'best possible' this offer was accepted and Mr Povah said, 'Bring the slip round to me tomorrow and I will put it down–I am in a hurry now.' By next morning there was no doubt about the total loss of the *Titanic*; there was likewise no doubt in any one's mind that the verbal acceptance was binding.

In the early days of the First World War the insurance market seems to have been somewhat bewildered and underwriters were either refusing to accept business or quoting outrageous rates of £20 per cent or even higher. However, the market began gradually to settle down and, as David Keir writes in *The Bowring Story*:

> . . . and rates fell by the end of 1914 to two guineas and early in 1915 to one. As we shall see they were to rise again when it appeared that if such ships as Bowring's *Elsinore* could be sunk in the Pacific by a fast German Cruiser, so too their *Cymbeline* and many other ships could be torpedoed by U-boats off the west coast of Ireland and in the Bay of Biscay. All waters were dangerous. In the meantime steadying influences had been at work, and at the end of the war not only Lloyd's but its leading members were more firmly entrenched than ever, and as a reward for their courage

and tenacity many Lloyd's syndicates came out of the struggle with considerable rewards.

Among the countless changes that the war would bring was the inevitability of many of the younger men working in brokers' offices being called to the colours and their jobs being taken on by women to the undisguised chagrin of their reactionary elders. Some of the more successful ladies got as far as visiting insurance companies on behalf of their employers to obtain initials to brokers' 'slips' and agreements; some even penetrated the merely clerical realms of Lloyd's. At no time did they manage to enter the male sanctum of the 'Room' at Lloyd's, nor, indeed would they be able to do so for very many years.

There had been a marked degree of nervousness among underwriters during the months leading up to the outbreak of hostilities, about the possible effects of a global war in which shipping might become the target of submarine attack. In the event that the major navies of the world became locked in conflict, it seemed likely that merchant shipping would become a prime target in a prolonged war at sea, and the possibility of crippling losses filled underwriters with deep anxiety. Foreseeing and understanding their natural reluctance to committing themselves to immense war risks, the British Government in 1913 appointed a committee to consider and inaugurate a scheme for the insurance of merchant ships and their cargoes in the event of a war breaking out. Thus a Government War Risks office was established which, by August 1914, was committed to shouldering the risks to British hulls. Bowring's noteworthy contribution to the formation of this office was in the shape of Walter Hargreaves who devoted a great deal of his time to its work.

During and for many years after the First World War there were few names, if any, more resounding in the London insurance market than that of Mr (later to become Sir) Walter Hargreaves. He will be remembered for his energy and initiative in many aspects of the insurance business. As the work of Lloyd's expanded, the matter of policy-signing became complex and tedious and was seriously in need of reform. It was Walter Hargreaves who came up with the definitive solution, the circumstances of which are best described by Harvey Bowring, who writes:

> The signing of Lloyd's policies was a complicated affair, entailing a great deal of unnecessary detail work and, in view of the condition of many of

the completed documents, it is surprising that they were accepted by the insuring public. After preparation in a brokers' office the policy was put in charge of a junior, known by some as a 'policy shover' and by others as a 'policy pusher' – an envied position, as this meant that his foot was on the first rung of the ladder that led to becoming a broker. It was his duty to 'shove' the policy from one underwriter to another for signature and collect it as and when signed. Each syndicate signed the policy individually and when signed it was placed in a wire basket attached to the end of the syndicate's box. From there it was collected by the 'shover', who grabbed all policies in the basket, selecting those belonging to his firm, with little regard for those belonging to others. As a result a policy underwritten by a large number of syndicates was, in its final stages, in a state of dilapidation, tattered and dirty. The young men concerned in this work were no respecters of persons and 'shovers' (or 'pushers') was a very apt description of their manners and activities.

The final outcome of one particular policy negotiated by our firm gives the extreme result of the methods employed. We insured for a large sum a famous picture by Millet, 'The Man with a Hoe', and, in consequence, many syndicates at Lloyd's were interested. After signature the policy was torn and dirty – but worse was to follow! The picture was sent on a trip from San Francisco to Chicago on exhibition, for which an additional premium was charged, and therefore the policy had to go through the mill again. After very few syndicates had initialled the additional premium endorsement the policy completely disintegrated, and all that the then 'shovers' could find were one or two small pieces, of very little value to the Accounts Department with the result that many of the underwriters never received their additional premium, their portion finally being subscribed to Lloyd's Benevolent Fund.

For some time Hargreaves was the leader of a crusade to do away with this archaic method of signing policies. Lloyd's underwriters are always ultra-conservative and his efforts met with great opposition. After the outbreak of the 1914–1918 war the situation became far more acute and in 1915 Hargreaves prevailed upon several of the leading brokers and the leading underwriters to set up a bureau for signing policies, the cost of which, in its primary stage, was borne by those taking part.

Hargreaves had intended that his proposals should be only a wartime measure, but so successful were they that his Policy Signing Office at 53, Cornhill, was subsumed by the Corporation of Lloyd's of which it became a department.

The company continued to be attracted by the virtually unlimited range of non-marine business, the development of which Hargreaves and

Stevinson had nurtured since before the outbreak of war, and the increase of the American catastrophe and reinsurance business, which followed the San Francisco Fire, was showing healthy profits. These post-war developments came at a good time. In other areas of endeavour the company's fortunes had suffered. Shipping losses had taken their toll. The future of the Red Cross Line, whose two chief vessels, *Stephano* and *Florizel*, had been lost, was in doubt, and the company's fleet of cargo ships operating out of London, Liverpool and Bristol, had dwindled, mainly as a result of enemy action. If the company was to maintain its standing as a growing commercial enterprise it would be necessary in the years ahead to rebuild the fleet of cargo vessels and tankers, and to take advantage of the good reputation reached in the insurance market; and, maybe in the longer term, consider new trading ventures. But of all the options available it was clear that development of insurance broking, both marine and non-marine – especially the latter – would offer the most immediate and promising likelihood of success.

To this end Bowring's, in order to strengthen their ranks in this field, engaged the services of a broker named Crawley who, for reasons explained by David Keir in *The Bowring Story*, seemed, on the face of it, to be an improbable candidate. 'That Crawley should have been an insurance broker at all appears surprising.' writes Keir:

> He was preternaturally absent-minded, which made it seem unlikely that clients would rest their confidence in a man who was often seen to dash out of his office, only to return a little later with a plaintive request for someone to find the umbrella already dangling from his arm. They might also have been a little shaken, as he himself was, to be told that he once set off with a large wreath to represent his family at a funeral, got himself immersed in several antique shops on the way and returned a few hours later with the wreath still perched on top of his car. At a last glance they might even have wondered if a product of the old and leisurely county life of Hertfordshire was really fitted for Gracechurch Street where his office lay. If so, their worries were needless. Ernest Crawley had so many friends and business contacts that he proved a valuable ally when his own firm was merged with C. T. Bowring & Co. (Insurance) Ltd, soon after the war.

Crawley, in spite of his apparent absent-mindedness, was an extremely persuasive non-marine broker. He hadn't made up his mind to enter the City until he was thirty-three, having previously, it would appear, led the comfortable life of a country gentleman and, after coming down from

Cambridge, maintaining his reputation as a distinguished cricketer and Real Tennis player. At about the turn of the century, he made up his mind to find some kind of work and formed a small insurance broking firm, which was known as Crawley, Dixon and Company. He also became an underwriting member of the first non-marine syndicate at Lloyd's, which was started by his friend, Cuthbert Heath.

While on the subject of underwriting at Lloyd's and to bring us up to date on Bowring's involvement, it is relevant to confirm their position. At about this time the company were managing two marine syndicates, the oldest established in 1901 and a second in 1912. While these two wrote a small amount of 'incidental non-marine' business, which included small risks on docks or ships laid-up for repairs, it wasn't until 1921 that Bowring's were managing a fully non-marine syndicate. In the same year a third marine syndicate was added to be followed by a fourth the following year and a fifth in 1927.

In 1919 a crisis arose that seemed likely to have a serious dampening effect on the company's steadily growing business with America. For very many years before the war insurance policies for American clients were issued in sterling, generally recognized as the staple currency of the world, at the fixed rate of $4.86 to the pound sterling. However, the value of sterling had depreciated to such an extent that American clients made it quite clear that business with them was unlikely to prosper unless some method could be developed to provide policies issued in dollars. The reality of this situation became only too significant when one of the major American merchant fleet's insurances came up for renewal in September. The owners refused to accept sterling policies. Harvey Bowring explains how the difficulty was resolved to the apparent satisfaction of all concerned:

> . . . something had to be done and our firm therefore drew up a scheme based on a monthly settlement to bring about the desired effect. Although considered revolutionary, the method suggested by us was accepted by all the London companies and Lloyd's underwriters, who fully realized that times had changed and that it was necessary to move with them if London was to continue as the central marine insurance market . . . We therefore had the satisfaction of being the promoters of a scheme which resulted in policies for American assureds, issued in London, being expressed in United States currency. In the meantime the company had benefited from a substantial increase in the business it did in the USA, particularly in the field of reinsurance.

Again, for the benefit of those not well-versed in the complexities of insurance, an explanation of the practice of reinsurance might be helpful. It is the procedure which enables insurers to spread the risks they carry by insuring part of them with other insurers.

The development in London of the reinsurance of risks underwritten in the United States was, to some considerable extent, due to the intervention and energy of one Guy Carpenter, whose involvement in insurance had been as manager of the Cotton Insurance Association. As something of a visionary and with the experience gained in this role, he set up, in due course, as a reinsurance broker. In this capacity he secured the interest of several American fire insurance companies. Following a series of disastrous fires and floods experienced by the cotton industry in America, as a result of which underwriters' rates had fluctuated nervously, he devised what became known as the Carpenter Plan. Realizing that underwriters might expect a reasonable profit, his scheme involved a method by means of which annual premiums would be arrived at through use of a formula, which took account of the ratio of losses to premium income over a period of time. The Carpenter Plan became a standard for the cotton industry and, in the fullness of time, for most other insurance risks.

Such was the rate of expansion of Bowring's London business following the merger with Crawley, Dixon and Company (which became Crawley, Dixon and Bowring Ltd in 1919), that larger premises were required. In 1921 occupation of Winchester House came to an end and C. T. Bowring & Co. (Insurance) Ltd moved to more spacious offices at 52 Leadenhall Street. In the following year, Sir Frederick Bowring, head of the parent company, C. T. Bowring & Co. Ltd in Liverpool, and his fellow directors, as a demonstration of their confidence in the merger, decided to make an offer for all the outstanding Crawley Dixon shares. The offer being accepted, the staffs of both companies came under one roof. Ernest Crawley was appointed Vice-Chairman of C. T. Bowring & Co. (Insurance) Ltd, and several of his directors were elected to the Board including Clive and Theo Uzielli.

But the euphoria engendered by visions of future successes at the house of Bowring was by no means general. Whilst the years 1919–20 were a period of increased prosperity, by 1921 ships were being laid up and the post-war boom was shrinking. Bowring's trading activities on both sides of the Atlantic were in decline and in the field of insurance, both marine and non-marine, unprecedented problems arose. An epidemic of theft and pilfering broke out, and certain foreign shipowners were indulging in deliberate scuttling of their vessels. To quote an article appearing in the *Shipping World* (12 January 1921): 'The war seems to have bred a moral laxity among the men engaged in it and there has grown up an indifference to the rights of property.' The article continued:

> Where it is located in particular has not been discovered, whether it is that goods in transmission disappear on the railways, from the warehouses, from the docks, or from on board ship, or from all of these, is inscrutable, but when goods are despatched from a trader to his customer their safe arrival is very problematical. In every country it is the same. Here perhaps the risk is less than in other countries. French underwriters in 1919 refused to insure against the risk of pilferage in ordinary marine policies, and drew up a tariff of insurance against such risk. The rate differed for various countries, and the British Isles was as low as 2s *(two shillings)* per cent, while goods shipped to the interior of Central and South America by the Pacific Coast could only be insured against pilferage at 80s per cent. Lloyd's underwriters adopted a similar scheme, with the proviso that only 75 per cent of the value of the goods stolen could be recovered under the policy. By this measure it was thought that extra care would be exercised by shippers in packing their merchandise, and that the liability would not be altogether cast on the underwriter. But the evil still prevails, and has grown to such dimensions that it is a serious menace to the commerce of the world.

As it was now clear that the future success of Bowring's would, to an increasing extent, depend on insurance, it seems logical to follow the fortunes of that side of the business, and to revert to the growth of the company's trading and shipping activities at a later stage.

During the war a number of companies were set up to engage in marine underwriting, several of them inspired by gambling instincts rather than a serious assessment of the commercial risks involved. By 1922 many of these companies, together with several with more substantial credentials, were faced with bankruptcy, some leaving the market altogether. A few sought to limit their losses by indulging in reckless undercutting of rates. In these unpromising conditions it is, to say the least, surprising that a new marine syndicate at Lloyd's should be set up. However, in 1922 the company created the FCB Syndicate – the initials being those of Sir Frederick Bowring – of which the leading underwriter was Edward Bowring Toms. 'Eddie' Toms was a grandson of Edward Bowring, whose daughter, Emmeline Susan was his mother. In the early days he divided the business of the syndicate between 75 per cent of cargo risks and 25 per cent hulls. He had a catholic taste in the sort of risks he was prepared to take on, including cargoes and commodities of an almost unlimited range, and, notwithstanding the very gloomy prevailing economic climate, managed to make modest profits. The following years saw no improvement in the insurance of hulls, the shipping industry continuing to slump.

Insurance generally was further adversely affected by the onset of the world depression which first manifested itself in the stock market crash in the United States in October 1929, and which persisted well into the 1930s. All forms of commercial activity were badly afflicted for many years to come and in 1931 the British Government decided to leave the gold standard. For the benefit of those readers who, like me, have but a hazy idea of the significance of the 'gold standard', a dictionary explanation defines it as a 'monetary standard under which the basic unit of currency is equal in value to and exchangeable for a specified amount of gold'. Once again the *Shipping World* throws light on the effects experienced by underwriters:

> The suspension by Great Britain of the gold standard has created a special problem for everyone engaged, or interested in foreign trade, and for marine underwriters it presents difficulties which have no parallel in other branches of commerce.
>
> In respect of their foreign business, the depreciation of the pound in terms of foreign currencies imposes upon underwriters the necessity of immediately formulating and adopting a basis of settlement which will protect them as far as possible against loss by exchange fluctuations, either in premium or claims payments.

In spite of the fact that the depression persisted relentlessly for some years, the worldwide good reputation enjoyed by Lloyd's was enough to ensure that the London insurance market generally, and Bowring's part in it, prospered. In these circumstances, therefore, it was not such a paradox as it might have seemed, for the company, in 1935, to start yet another marine underwriting syndicate.

Edward Stevinson, since 1920, had been making regular visits to the United States, which certainly did much to maintain the company's steady development as brokers during the bad times, as indeed did a build-up of business with other countries including, significantly, Japan.

The growth of business with Japan may well have resulted from the amicable settlement of problems arising from the devastating Yokohama earthquake in 1923, one of the most terrible ever recorded. Once again the *Shipping World* throws some light on the matter. The following article appeared on 8 October 1924:

> But in view of the vastness of the catastrophe there was much popular discontent, and to deal with the situation in a sympathetic manner the Japanese insurance companies with the aid of the Government agreed to make ex gratia payments up to 10 per cent of the amounts insured. The foreign companies doing business in Japan, on their part, decided to return one year's gross premiums ex gratia. The next stage was a request from the Japanese companies who had reinsured their risks with British and foreign companies that they might receive similar treatment as individual clients of these companies. At a recent meeting of representatives of British insurance companies it was decided that in all cases where a Japanese company had made a payment to its policy-holders and obtained a quittance the insurers should return the reinsurance premium. The prompt and ready way in which the request of the Japanese companies had been responded to should be conducive to the smooth working of reinsurance business in the future.

There is no doubt that the earthquake had an intense effect on the market, and underwriters remained cautious for some time. Bowring's meanwhile took the opportunity to develop further their involvement in the Japanese reinsurance market but, as an extract from the records of the company shows, this was not always easy.

> Soon after the very severe earthquake in 1923 we were asked to insure £200,000 on a risk in Yokohama against earthquake, at a rate of 1 per cent. Unfortunately the cable was deciphered as Yen 200,000 rather than £200,000. The exchange rate at the time was Yen 10 to £1. We placed Yen 200,000, equivalent to £20.000, at a rate of 1 per cent. We duly sent our cover note to Japan but, as in those days this went by steamer, well over a month elapsed before we received a cable asking us to amend our cover note to read £200,000 instead of Yen 200,000. Naturally this error, when it came to the notice of our insurance company's Chairman, Walter Hargreaves, caused reverberation throughout the office from the most junior broker upwards. The placing of the shortage of £180,000 (a very large sum in those days) presented an extremely difficult task due to the fact that the market had been very heavily interested on earthquake risks

in Yokohama and because the market rate had increased from 1 per cent to 3 per cent in the interim.

During the twenties and early thirties the problems facing the shipping industry persisted and the prosperity of the company continued to rely very much on the expansion and success of its insurance activities. These now started to became somewhat more diversified, one area of development being the provision of Protection and Indemnity insurance to American Pacific Coast shipowners, many of whom did not carry this type of cover. A brief explanation of P&I insurance might not be out of place.

As far back as the early 18th century shipowners had organized themselves, usually on a local basis, into unincorporated cooperative associations, known as 'Clubs', or more literally as Mutual Hull Underwriting Associations, the purpose of which was to provide insurance cover for risks not available through normal insurance channels, such as liability for death or injury, claims from crews or passengers, damage to docks and quays, risks associated with smuggling and other extraneous hazards. As they were mutual organizations, each member was, as it were, both insurer and insured. With the passage of time, these mutual associations were transformed into Protection and Indemnity Clubs.

What Bowring's did was to create a small market composed of a few insurance companies and an underwriting syndicate at Lloyd's, in order to make available to the American Pacific Coast shipowners insurance cover for their members similar to that provided by the Mutual Protection and Indemnity Clubs. For a while this business flourished – but difficulties arose. There were problems associated, for instance, with the need to find someone on the spot who could investigate controversial claims, some of which involved malingering, and, furthermore, there were lawyers around of doubtful repute, who were not beyond inventing false claims; and, it seems, marine underwriters had difficulties in implementing awards in American courts, especially where weekly payments to dependants were required. So, while this venture was comparatively short-lived, another opportunity arose which would prove to be more successful and of much longer duration.

To replace these unsatisfactory arrangements, a closer relationship was developed with the more enterprising British Shipowners' Mutual Protection and Indemnity Clubs, some of which were prepared to insure American vessels, albeit on somewhat different terms from those applying to their own. Bowring's built up a close relationship with the West of England Club, which had been created by the Holman family at Topsham in Devon in the 1850s and of which Sir John Wimble became a director. As in the case of the original 18th-century Mutuals, these Clubs were non-profit making and were made up of shipowners for their own mutual protection. Each contributed according to his tonnage and was covered against a wide range of risks not insured under normal hull policies. As well as being of immense value to British shipowners, these P&I clubs have attracted and now include a considerable proportion of foreign tonnage. It is not surprising to find that the West of England Club is now located in Luxembourg – a far cry from the origins of its distant forebear at Topsham.

Another small but important addition to the developments, which would help to keep the company's head above water during the prolonged and deepening depression, was attributable to Commander Hawkridge of the Hull Steam Trawler Mutual Insurance Association. He accepted the company's suggestion that his Association's reinsurance protection should be rearranged on an Excess of Aggregate Losses basis, a principle soon to be adopted by other mutual associations.

But the most significant contribution to the company's progress during the twenties and thirties was in the expansion of their reinsurance business with the United States and Japan. American companies seem to have been well satisfied with the attention they received from the executives with whom they dealt and with the enthusiasm of the younger members of the company. This business, which, it will be recalled, saw its origins in the closing years of the 19th century, steadily increased until, at the outbreak of the Second World War, the company's brokers had secured most of the major American marine reinsurances. They also continued to insure direct an increasing number of hulls as they had been doing for many years.

The growing business with Japan had later origins than the American operation, starting during the early years of the 20th century. A major contribution to the association with Japanese companies was the friendship of Sir Thomas Bowring with Mr N. M. Townsend of the Hong Kong and Shanghai Banking Corporation's London Office. Sir Thomas took Townsend's son, Sidney, into his own office, where he showed considerable talent. In 1906 it was decided that he should be sent to visit the Kobe Insurance Company with a view to establishing how best their reinsurance business might be arranged in London.

Townsend, who was the company's first representative to Japan, was to make a second visit in 1908. These were long and tedious journeys including weeks by train through eastern Europe, Russia and Mongolia, and finally by sea from Vladivostock to the port of Kobe and the city of Osaka. After his second visit, his perseverance was rewarded by the Kobe Insurance Company's wish to place all their considerable hull and cargo reinsurance treaties in the London market. This success was followed by a further valuable and long-lasting relationship with another highly regarded organization, the Nippon Fire and Marine Insurance Company. These well-established connections were maintained throughout the twenties. Townsend, sadly, was killed in France during the First World War, but the tireless Edward Stevinson visited Japan and further strengthened these valuable connections, as a result of which the Kobe Insurance Company invited Bowring's to place their fire reinsurance treaties for them in London. But these successes of the 1920s were not to be repeated during the next decade. The activities of Japanese troops in China and growing resistance by the Japanese Government to meet payments in foreign currencies created a decline in dealings with Britain and by the outbreak of the Second World War Bowring's business with Japan had reached its lowest ebb.

Notwithstanding various setbacks during the years between the two Great Wars, caused principally by the worldwide economic depression, Bowring's marine insurance and reinsurance activities developed. During the same period and, again, in spite of adverse trading conditions much of the time, the company and its non-marine syndicate at Lloyd's had prospered since its creation in 1921, although the early years were not easy. However, in 1923 the arrival on the scene of a new resourceful leading underwriter, Mr (later to be Sir) Matthew Drysdale brought new life to the syndicate. A man of rare distinction, Matthew Drysdale was eventually to become six times Chairman of Lloyd's and to be awarded the Lloyd's Gold Medal. Some years later he and I were to be elected, on the same day, with Tom Bowring of whom there will be more to be said later, to the board of the parent company, C. T. Bowring & Co. Ltd. He took great interest in the wider range of the group's activities. We sat side-by-side at board meetings and from time to time he would, in a loud whisper, ask me to explain some trading activity by which he was confused. On one such occasion, prodding a list before him of the transactions of the Fertilizer and Foodstuffs Department, he was heard to enquire, much to the amusement of the other board members: 'What on earth is "batters crap"?' What, in fact, had attracted his attention was a typing error for 'batter scrap', a popular ingredient in animal feed.

At Lloyd's Sir Matthew was universally popular and enjoyed a high reputation with brokers as observed by a member of his non-marine underwriting box:

> He always tried to be constructive with regard to risks. Instead of trying to find reasons for turning them down, he would try to find a reason for writing the business. So when he started off in 1923 in the old Room at Lloyd's in the Royal Exchange it was quite an event. I can remember clearly the queues of brokers that surrounded our box, all wanting to see Drysdale and get a risk placed with him.

Since the inclusion of Crawley, Dixon and Bowring Ltd within Bowring's, the non-marine broking business was developing apace, both at home and overseas, in spite of the vicissitudes of the inter-war years. The variety of risks being put before underwriters was reaching bewildering proportions, some of them quite eccentric.

Shortly after the appointment of Matthew Drysdale and in the run-up to the election of Calvin Coolidge as President of the United States, rumours were being spread around that Henry Ford might be nominated for the presidency. No matter how unlikely this may have seemed, an enquiry was received from someone extremely disturbed by the possibility of his being elected and anxious to take out insurance cover against it to the tune of $30,000. A young broker, who had spent some time in the United States, was dispatched to Lloyd's with the slip, which he placed before an underwriter whom he knew as 'a great character and a very able man'. On returning from Lloyd's he reported:

> I put the slip down and he passed it back as an indication of refusal. I then said, as I had said to Mr Stevinson, 'I think this is one of the best risks you will see in the next few years, because it's really quite clear that Henry Ford hasn't got any more hope of being elected President than you or I have.' He looked a little surprised at this – after all Henry Ford was a great figure in the United States – and then asked me a number of questions very much to the point. Finally he wrote down 6 per cent as the rate and $10,000. So I was home, with only $20,000 left to do.

One of the more memorable stories of unusual risks brought before Bowring's brokers concerns two giraffes, which had been acquired by the Chicago Zoo. Their long journey from the plains of Africa to the concrete canyons of their proposed new home in America was to be riddled with hazards, and the whole exercise was seen by all concerned as likely to present a series of awkward and unforeseeable predicaments. Underwriters were understandably distrustful and, in fact, not one would entertain the risks involved. But Harvey Bowring decided to insure them as a private venture and the transaction was entered in a special 'Office Account'. Reports of progress were received with relief by him and his colleagues as the two giraffes, homesick no doubt for their thorn trees and faced with unfamiliar diet and possibly even *mal de mer*, had reached their American port of entry undamaged and apparently in good shape. But as David Keir relates in *The Bowring Story*:

> . . . though it seemed as if the major hazards had been overcome, and that yet another unusual insurance risk was receding into the company's files as part of the orthodox pattern of satisfied clients, complacent brokers and relieved underwriters, the outcome was very different.

One can only assume that during the completed part of the journey, it had been possible to provide adequate headroom for two of the tallest mammals known to man. From now on the journey from port to zoo would be by rail. Impressively commodious though American freight cars are known to be, headroom enough for giraffes is not one of their strong points, and one can only speculate about the unaccustomed postures that the unfortunate animals were forced to adopt on the last phase of their journey to the care and comfort of their new Chicago home.

Patient and well behaved though the two African ruminants had been throughout their tedious and uncomfortable experience, there came a time when, as in our case we might have wished to stretch our legs, they felt the need to stretch their necks – well at least one of them did. It was unfortunate to say the least that it chose the moment when the train was entering a tunnel to seek relief from weeks of discomfort by sticking its head out of a window. A tall story you may say, but it does have the merit of truth.

The year 1928 and 1929 were years of notable progress, especially in the development of business with the United States. Some of this was due to the arrival at Bowring's of three prominent members of a rival broker who had decided to leave their company over a matter of principle and who brought with them the reinsurance business of several American clients with whom they had become closely acquainted and who wished them to continue handling their business. Another, but very different, area of significant growth resulted from the formation in 1928 of the Eclipse motor syndicate, which was attached to the company's non-marine syndicate at Lloyd's. In step with the ever widening ownership of the motor car, the Eclipse syndicate has grown continuously over nearly 80 years to be one of the largest of its kind.

Stories abound of the exceptional circumstances in which some important business deals were completed in these days of rapid development of the company's insurance activities. One in particular involves a race against time with much at stake. For many years now no Lloyd's business has been conducted on a Saturday; but even up until the late 1940s it was not unusual for Lloyd's, and many other businesses, to be operating, albeit with a reduced staff, typically about one-third, for half of the day. Except for the most senior directors, brokers and other staff members might expect to have to turn up one Saturday in three, and it was entirely possible that quite important business would be conducted on such occasions.

On one Saturday morning in May 1929, a broker on duty turned up in the office at 52 Leadenhall Street to find a cable from one of the company's most valued marine clients in New York seeking to place business of very great importance, which required decisions at the highest level. The Chairman Sir Walter Hargreaves was away in Scotland salmon fishing on the River Naver, and the lodge at Bettyhill, in the most northerly part of Scotland, at which he was staying, had no telephone. We take up the broker's story:

> Having realized the cable's importance I immediately telephoned its contents to Mr Stevinson and he in turn was insistent that Hargreaves' views on the cable should be obtained at the earliest possible moment so that the office might be able to send a cabled reply to New York on Monday morning. The discussion on this point did not take long because Mr Stevinson almost immediately said that the only thing for it was for me to motor up to Sir Walter's fishing lodge. He also said it would be comparatively easy for me to start early on Sunday morning to get to Sir Walter's house if not the same night certainly very early on Monday morning. As Bettyhill was some 620 miles away this seemed to me to be a fairly formidable task, but Mr Stevinson rarely looked at difficulties. He added that he felt sure his son Jim would be quite happy to accompany me and share the driving. This agreed, we set out at 6 a.m. on the Sunday morning in a new Daimler coupe which belonged to my mother. It was

of course obvious that we would have to drive as much as possible with our foot on the floorboards and we started out, as indeed we finished, in this manner. Our first stop – for a hasty breakfast – was at Stamford on the Great North Road, and we then drove without stopping and at a really high average speed to Newcastle where we had an equally quick lunch. If memory serves me right we passed through Edinburgh at what should have been teatime but decided to skip that meal and go straight to Inverness, which we reached as the clocks were striking eleven.

By this time we were both tiring although we had shared the driving. But we went on through Inverness, still maintaining a high average speed, until we came to Dingwall, where after a near accident we felt it was high time we stopped for a few hours rest in a local hotel.

Next morning we were up very early and after a good but long drive reached Sir Walter's lodge about 11 o'clock, only to be told that he was out fishing. However we found him on the river bank, and there and then discussed the problem. Having got his answer, we returned to the car and started our trip home. From the first town with a telephone I gave Mr Stevinson Sir Walter's views with which, as I remember it, he was in complete accord. A cable was therefore sent to our friends in New York, the whole matter was satisfactorily resolved, and still more business flowed in our direction as a result.

At the same time as the American contacts were being regularly added to with profitable results, the insurance directors decided, in 1929, to start a new company, the purpose of which was to create a vehicle for underwriting marine and non-marine business other than through Lloyd's. The company was named the English and American Insurance Company to perpetuate the name of Bowring's shipping company of the same designation, which experienced such serious casualties during the 1914-1918 War. Initially this was not found to be such a good idea; it caused confusion among potential clients who wanted to know what proportion of the capital was American, how many of the directors were American citizens and how much influence they exercised in forming the company's policy. The shareholders were in fact the parent company, C. T. Bowring & Co. Ltd, its main subsidiary C. T. Bowring & Co. (Insurance) Ltd and some directors, senior members of the staff of whom at the start there were very few, and one or two retired executives of the group at large. This new company was soon spreading its wings into the fast growing non-marine field and became well-established in the American market. Whilst in its early years the E&A – as it was generally referred to within the group – dealt only with Bowring brokers, it eventually opened its doors to all Lloyd's brokers, once it had begun writing fire, accident and burglary business.

In spite of the fact that the parent company's head office was still in Liverpool, it wasn't until the early thirties that the insurance needs of the cotton importers, warehousemen and manufacturers were recognized as potential insurance clients. Liverpool and Manchester had for many years been pre-eminent in this industry and it seems that the parent company directors were somewhat delinquent in not paying adequate attention to this fact. They were probably more concerned at the time with the development of a variety of trading and manufacturing activities at home and overseas – of which there will be more to follow – and with the management of the company's ships. Apart from the small internal marine underwriting function, they seem to have considered that new insurance ventures were the domain of the London office. It was, indeed, the directors in the London office who persuaded their colleagues in Liverpool to approach the cotton barons, who traditionally placed their business with the tariff companies, and to try to encourage them to spread their insurances and make savings in premiums by placing part of their fire risks through Lloyd's at non-tariff rates. But unfortunately this was short-lived following the closure of the Liverpool Cotton Exchange. Nevertheless, the Liverpool office was fired with enthusiasm and increased its non-marine business by providing private motor and householders' comprehensive insurance, which it placed through the London office.

In step with the developments taking place during the years between the two World Wars, Bowring's insurance activities moved into two of the most favourable growth areas, aviation and films, both of which opened up promising prospects for the future.

Just as they had been quick to recognize the possibilities arising from the drilling of the first oil well some seventy years earlier, so the company recognized the potential rewards to be gained from the insurance of aircraft and the risks related to their operation. Much development of aircraft took place during the First World War and this was recognized by a number of entrepreneurs who were keen to establish civil air services to the Continent. As in so many new industries, where enthusiasm has outweighed financial wisdom, several of the smaller competing companies, which were established in 1919, were running into difficulties only two years later. However, two of the more substantial pioneering companies weathered the storm and can be seen as the true founders of one of the world's most rapidly developing and technologically advanced industries. The earliest of these, which started the first daily passenger air service in the world, was Aircraft Transport and Travel Limited, offering flights between Hounslow and Le Bourget, whilst Handley Page Transport Limited ran the first service between London and Brussels. Other companies and different routes followed but, in some cases, serious financial problems arose, grave enough to threaten the future of travel by air. Recognizing the possible dangers that lay ahead, the then Secretary of State for Air, Mr Winston Churchill, formed a small group in 1921, known as the Cross Channel Committee, to examine the financial difficulties. The outcome of this committee's deliberations was to give a Government subsidy to Handley Page, Daimler Hire and Instone & Company, which enabled them to open a service between London and Paris. Although the civil aviation industry made progress during the next few years, this assistance proved to be of only fleeting value, and the Government persuaded the various companies involved, with one or two of the other more reliable beginners in the industry, to join in the formation, on 31 March 1924, of Imperial Airways Limited.

Pioneering in this exciting new method of travel, which, in time, would effectively reduce the size of our planet and, for good or ill, bring the peoples of the earth closer together, was riddled with hazards – and with hazard comes insurance. The single-engine aircraft of the early operators commanded weighty insurance premiums. Heavy claims experience meant that insurance costs accounted for as much as thirty-three per cent of overall airline operating costs. But by 1924 the situation had changed. As small individual companies these fledgling airlines had employed a number of different insurance brokers. Now that they had merged it became necessary to obtain professional advice, and the services of Bowring's were sought. It was as a result of discussions between Harvey Bowring and the Imperial Airways Board that the first fleet insurance policy was drawn up. The business was underwritten mainly by two insurance companies of the time, the Union of Canton and the White Cross. A few bold underwriters at Lloyd's also took on some of the business.

In these formative years the Imperial Airways fleet consisted of converted Service aircraft, which had been adapted for civilian use. They had a total value of less than £55,000. The highest valued aircraft, the

Handley Page W9, was valued at £13,550, which makes interesting comparison with today's cost of a Boeing 747 at over £100,000,000. With at least one broker in Bowring's who had flying experience during the First World War with The Royal Flying Corps and, later, the Royal Air Force as it became known in 1918, there was considerable enthusiasm in the company for the energetic pursuit of this promising new field of endeavour, and soon aircraft manufacturers were to be included among those whose business was sought. Among the more prestigious of these clients was William Beardmore and Company, a large Clydeside engineering firm, which had built many of the aircraft used during the war and, subsequently, the airships R100 and R34.

It was not long before the aircraft used by the growing number of airlines became faster, safer and more reliable, and this resulted in smaller but much more valuable fleets. Instead of the earlier method of cover devised by Bowring's, whereby claims were paid on an aggregate loss basis, it became necessary to adopt a more direct form of insurance with premiums being calculated on insured values. In the next few years there were to be many changes in the conduct of aviation insurance. The Union of Canton and the White Cross joined forces to create the British Aviation Insurance Group and in 1928, the United States Aviation Insurance Group was established in New York. Bowring's were soon building up a clientele of airlines both overseas and at home. The names of many have subsequently disappeared, frequently as a result of mergers, but they included the Dutch airline KLM, Misr Airwork, (later to become United Arab Airlines) and Indian National Airways. At home names included Northern Airlines, which ran a service between Liverpool and Belfast, Highland Airways and Scottish Airways, which were linked with Jersey Air Services, Hillman Airways, which brought a number of the others together to form a successful group known as British Airways, and a number of flying clubs and private owners at home and abroad.

During these early formative years of the rapidly growing airline industry, most of the business done by Bowring's was placed with the British Aviation Insurance Group. However, in 1935 there was a feeling that the industry would be better served if there was a more competitive market, and the firm was instrumental in bringing together several of the leading insurance companies to form the Aviation and General Insurance Company, which started life with several of Bowring's accounts on its books. A hopeful view of the future in early promotional literature read:

'Aviation insurance is available today to anyone having an Aircraft to insure, and the money with which to pay the premium, provided the Owner is a satisfactory risk from the point of view of moral hazard'.

In the late twenties and the thirties significant progress was made as the rapidly growing international network of air travel possibilities took shape. In 1926 Imperial Airways began a regular service to India. Between 1931 and 1933 services to Cape Town and Singapore were developed, and, in conjunction with Qantas Empire Airways, to Australia. In 1936 Hong Kong was added to the list, and the following year the recently developed Empire flying boats were chosen to operate the Egyptian, Indian and Australian services; and during the year preceding the outbreak of the Second World War, Imperial Airways joined forces with the recently formed Tasman Empire Airways Limited to run a regular service to New Zealand. Thus it can be seen that the origins of a global network, such as we know today, was rapidly taking shape during the brief twenty-one years between the wars.

This was an exciting and profitable time for Bowring's, no less than for Imperial Airways, and the prospects seemed boundless, which as David Keir sums up in *The Bowring Story*: 'They had certainly taken on a rosy tinge in 1937, a year made memorable when the Imperial Airways flying boat *Caledonia*, making an experimental westward flight across the North Atlantic at the same time as the Boeing *Clipper* flew eastward, threw new, significant writing across the world skies.'

Among the other industries that blossomed in the years between the wars and which provided ample opportunity for the insurer was that of entertainment in general and, in particular, of film-making. The speed of progression from the earliest days of inexpensive silent movies to the multimillion-pound technicolour blockbusters that would follow during the next twenty years bears comparison with the development of aircraft from the W9 to the Boeing 747. As in so many promising areas of endeavour, the ideas of many of the early companies to make memorable films were sadly not matched by the amount of available financial backing. And the ever increasing costs involved could only be defrayed by success at the box-office. The banks were prepared to advance the funds required, but only against the provision of unquestionable security. And this is where the ingenuity of Bowring's brokers came into play.

A scheme was devised by the company, the purpose of which was to enable a bank to provide funding to a film producer only after Bowring's had authorized it. According to a company record, Bowring's, by way of security, were to issue a policy of insurance to the Bank underwritten by various insurers guaranteeing return of the loans with interest at the due dates unconditionally. The due dates were either a stated period from the general release of the film or a fixed date allowing for the film to be produced and distributed. One of the usual conditions was that the producer had to give written authority to the distributor to pay all monies received from the film's distribution direct into a blocked account at the Bank concerned.

The first advance to be made under these arrangements, according to the company record, was made by Lloyds Bank, Lombard Street, to the famous film producer, Alexander Korda's company, London Film Productions Ltd. (Among his many well-remembered films were *The Ghost goes West, Sanders of the River, Knight without Armour* and *The Private Life of Henry VIII*.) The news of this new method of helping the film companies to meet their financial burdens soon got around and other producers, many of them not quite up to the standard of Korda, were soon seeking similar accommodation with the result that the rules agreed between Bowring's and the banks had to be drawn up in sterner terms. Under revised conditions it became necessary for an accountant's certificate to be issued, to the effect that previous advances had been properly spent and that further sums were needed to meet prospective expenditure. However, these new arrangements were not entirely successful and, following a period of losses, they gradually came to an end.

But insurance cover for many of the diverse and frequently eccentric features of the world of entertainment is unlikely to come to an end, whether gradually or otherwise. It is well known that stars of stage, screen and the concert hall have for a long time taken out insurance cover against damage to those of their physical attributes upon which their livelihood depends – pianists' hands and singers' voices, for instance, and at the more eye-catching end of the spectrum, models' busts and dancers' legs come to mind. But moustaches are not commonly to be found on the broker's slip as he presents his case to an underwriter at Lloyd's. The upper lip of the celebrated comedian James Keith O'Neill Edwards, DFC, LLD, MA, otherwise well remembered as 'Professor' Jimmy Edwards, was adorned with a remarkable hirsute growth measuring no less than some 26 centimetres from tip to tip when measured horizontally. A persuasive broker and sympathetic underwriter arranged cover of £5,000 for 50 per cent loss at any point along its length and half that sum for any loss between 20 per cent and 49 per cent. But the policy stated that the luxuriant adornment, whilst it was covered against all risks of accidental damage, would not be considered for compensation for wear and tear nor, indeed, attack by moth or vermin.

Before moving on to the widening range of commercial activities in which the company was becoming involved, there is one further insurance connection worthy of mention. Whereas most of Bowring's growth overseas was in the United States, there was also a foray in the early thirties into Europe. In Antwerp there was a steamship agency called Kennedy Hunter whose principal, John Hunter (not to be confused with John Hunter of Swan Hunter, the Tyneside shipbuilder) was anxious to establish relations with a leading London company in order to develop a substantial insurance business. There was a time before the First World War when Antwerp enjoyed a high reputation as a centre for insurance, but although there was something of a revival after the war this was not entirely successful since much of the old business found its way to London. But Bowring brokers, with their forward thinking and adventurous approach to the creation of new operations, were sympathetic towards John Hunter's ideas. Be that as it may, the initial outcome of the joint efforts of Bowring's and Kennedy Hunter were not blessed with early hoped for success. In the first place it proved difficult to persuade London companies to give the 'partnership' their under-writing agencies. But eventually some six agreed to grant their agencies to the two companies jointly. Thus, in 1934, a new firm, Hunter Bowring, was formed to act as their underwriting managing agents. But still there was no joy. At considerable expense of shoe-leather and with growing frustration, countless visits to potential clients proved fruitless. So attention was diverted to Antwerp brokers; but this was also very disappointing, since the entire Antwerp insurance market adopted a hostile attitude to the newly created partnership. It seems they felt that a long established company with worldwide experience might put them out of business. However, in the fullness of time, recognition of the fact that Hunter Bowring had the experience and confidence to underwrite sizeable business meant that a number of major contracts remained in Antwerp, which after all, was what John Hunter sought to achieve.

Notwithstanding the fact that after the First World War the insurance business showed clear signs of rapid expansion, tradition dictated that the varied trading and shipping activities developed by preceding generations of the Bowring family over the past century would continue to expand and, it was to be hoped, flourish for some years to come, in spite of the fact that the shipping interests had been severely crippled by enemy action.

Chapter 11

IT IS UNLIKELY THAT old Benjamin and his sons could have foreseen in what directions their trading activities might lead; that the products of the Newfoundland fishery would take the company into vitamins and fine chemicals for example, or that a wider range of financial services, spawned by the burgeoning insurance business, would bring with it a Caterpillar earth-moving equipment dealership and a merchant bank; that cod liver oil, rosin and turpentine, teak, rubber, coffee and fertilizers, to name some of the commodities in which the company and its subsidiaries would in due course be dealing, would contribute to a kaleidoscope of trading activities.

Familiarity with the handling of cod and seal oils since the earliest days of Bowring Brothers in Newfoundland led directly to the manufacture of fish oil products and the fishmeal industry at home. Fishmeal had been well known both as an effective animal feed and as a fertilizer since the beginning of the 19th century and in 1917, in order to start production, the company acquired the factory of C. W. Kendall & Company at Pyewipe near Grimsby. Such was the initial success of this venture that, during the following year, the adjoining premises of William Bennett were purchased. The manufacture of fishmeal is ancillary to the production of fish oil and is the substance remaining after the oil has been extracted from the fish under pressure. In 1923 a department was opened in Liverpool specifically for the handling and distribution of fish oils, not only Bowring Brother's oil of Newfoundland origin, which had hitherto been handled by brokers, but also of British oil, including that of the Grimsby plant, and of oils from other producing countries. But at this early stage there was little by way of a coherent link between the two operations, the Grimsby plant being under the control of Clive Bowring in the London office. The Liverpool department was in the capable hands of R. M. ('Robbie') Johnston. Though virtually in the same business, they were run as two quite separate functions. Notwithstanding the lack of logic in this arrangement it was to continue for some years before a more rational operating procedure was adopted.

Apart, possibly, from having been persuaded of the virtues of a regular dose of cod liver oil to keep a variety of ills at bay, there are probably few who have ever given a moment's thought to the existence, let alone the usefulness, of other fish oils. In addition to the well-known pharmaceutical uses of cod liver oil both for human and veterinary purposes, other fish oils have been filtered, blended, purified and treated in a number of different ways for use in the tanning, paint, lubricating oil and other industries. In 1925 it became necessary for the Liverpool department to find premises in which oils could be handled physically rather than just being traded and a suitable building was found in Addison Street. But such was the progress made in the next few years that two further moves were required, the first to Oriel Street and eventually, in 1933, a building at 16 Blackstock Street was purchased, and pumps, tanks and filter presses were installed. Hitherto the blending of oils was achieved by hand-pumping from one drum to another, originally in railway vaults at Seaforth, but this last move, providing a range of new machinery, significantly widened the scope of the business, which soon became the largest of its kind in Europe.

However, these early successes were to be dampened by the outcome of a conference at Ottawa which is best explained by David Keir in *The Bowring Story*:

> Though the progress they had made was heartening, it had become as clear as a good catch of cod that the continuance of the Liverpool department and the Grimsby factory as separate units was a weakness in itself, which the Ottawa Agreements and a spectacular change in the policy of British trawler interests had dramatically exposed.
>
> 'In 1932, at Ottawa, an Imperial Economic Conference, composed of leading Ministers and their advisers from all the British Dominions including Newfoundland, discussed proposals to increase their mutual trade. In many ways this conference could hardly be called a model of brotherly love, for only too quickly it became engulfed in rather inelegant tariff huckstering, which again is understandable since national interests had to be balanced against each other in a traditional oversea setting. On the one hand the Dominions strove to safeguard both their basic agricultural and their new manufacturing industries. On the other the United Kingdom wished to protect her own farmers, as sensitive to Dominion as to foreign competition, and at the same time sell an increasing amount of her own manufactures not only in the Dominions but in the rest of the world, though this last aim depended partly on British

purchases of meat, butter and other products of the land from many foreign countries as well as the Dominions. The results of all this bargaining and the consequent adjustments in Empire tariffs, preferences and quotas need not be recounted here in detail. But one had a strange ending. In accordance with Article 2 of the United Kingdom-Newfoundland Agreement, Westminster imposed an import duty of 1s 4d a gallon on foreign cod-liver oil. Ostensibly this measure was intended to assist the Newfoundland fish oil interests to combat foreign competition. But in the outcome it had precisely the opposite effect. British trawler owners, encouraged by the high protection so suddenly given them, copied their German rivals and quickly produced a high-grade crude cod-liver oil at sea instead of bringing back 'rotting' livers from which only technical grade cod-oil could be produced. As this came to Grimsby in increasing quantities, new plant to deal with it had to be installed in the Grimsby works which not only became a 'cod-liver oil' rather than a 'cod-oil' factory but supplanted a leading German firm which the Liverpool Fish Oil department had helped to finance, one or two concerns in other countries, and above all the luckless Newfoundland which had once been the main source of Liverpool's cod-liver oil supply.

As a result of these rapid changes of fortune the United Kingdom became a net exporter of cod-liver oil, indeed producing more than the rest of the world combined, in contrast to its recent reliance on imported oil.

The fact that the volume of Liverpool's trading and Grimsby's manufacturing activities had increased so rapidly, and that their functions were so closely related, determined beyond doubt that the two enterprises should be operated as a single entity. A new company, C. T. Bowring & Co. (Fish Oils) Ltd, was incorporated at Liverpool on 1 July 1934. The directors were Sir Edgar Bowring as Chairman and Clive Bowring, Frederick Clive Bowring (my father) and 'Robbie' Johnston. At the beginning of the following year responsibility for the oil interests of the Grimsby factory was transferred from the London office to the new Liverpool company.

Experience in the processing of fish, seal and various other products of an organic nature led to the development of an interest in animal protein feedingstuffs and fertilizers and in 1925 a department was opened in London to trade in these commodities. It was the accepted dictum in the early days of this business that the products traded in by Bowring's Fertilizer and Foodstuffs Department would be only of organic origin.

The main source was the *frigorificos*, the massive South American slaughter-houses, where animal waste, after cooking, drying and crushing was exported as a fertilizer to many parts of the world. Eventually the processes involved were improved and modernized to such an extent that the end product was suitable to be incorporated in compound animal feedingstuffs. This meant that in due course practically none of the products of animal waste were used as fertilizer, virtually all of them finding their way into animal feed. And the same can be said for fish meal. What was a crude, stinking product suitable only as a fertilizer became, with similar advances in manufacturing methods, a widely used feedingstuff for many domestic animals including, particularly, pigs and poultry.

Developments in the manufacture and distribution of organic animal feed encouraged Bowring's in 1927 to start a small company in Hamburg. After an inauspicious start under the name of Franz Hollander the company was reorganized eighteen months later as Fischmehl Einfuhr, and it prospered for several years, marketing fish and meat meal. There was trouble, however, when in 1935 the successful and dedicated managing director, Gunther Gienow, was arrested on a charge of contravening one of the many irritating regulations issued by the Nazi Government. He was tried, after spending 18 months in gaol, and was sentenced to six years imprisonment. Bowring's engaged the services of a courageous and capable Hamburg lawyer on Gienow's behalf, but he was forced to give up the case. Although the company were not specifically mentioned in the indictment they were faced with a fine of over one million marks; but no effort was made to extract payment. It became clear that the trial was brought, as were so many others at the time, solely for propaganda and political reasons.

There was no doubt that trading in fishmeal was now an expanding business and Bowring's, spurred on by their success, decided to purchase three small factories in Iceland – at Reykjavic and Isafjord, and, on the north coast, at Siglufjord. Whilst the latter never got into production the other two operated effectively under the name of Fiskimjol Ltd. Their method of production was somewhat unorthodox. The meal was made from the heads and backbones of the catch. In Iceland, except for those fish sold for human consumption, the rest were split lengthwise and placed on rocks to dry. This, in much the same manner as the dried salt cod shipped to Portugal by Bowring Brothers, was sold in various Mediterranean countries where it was made into 'baccalao'. The heads

Clink Wharf

Sir Frederick Charles Bowring, DL, JP, 1857–1936, Chairman 1916–36

Sir Matthew Drysdale

Sir Edgar Rennie Bowring, KCMG, 1858–1943

Eric Aubrey Bowring, CBE, 1884–1959

Sir Edgar Bowring with the Duke of Connaught at the opening of Bowring Park, St John's, Newfoundland in 1914

5 May 1969. Centenary of appointment of Bowring Brothers Ltd as Lloyd's Agent in St John's, Newfoundland. Left to right: A.C. Sturge, Deputy Chairman of Lloyd's; Lambert Sharpe and Edgar Bowring, Directors of C. T. Bowring & Co. Ltd, H.S. Mance, Chairman of Lloyd's, who presented a silver plaque to mark the occasion, Derrick Bowring, Chairman of Bowring Brothers Ltd, Peter Bowring and Peter Stoddart, Directors of C. T. Bowring & Co. Ltd

Frederick Clive Bowring, 1897–1965, Chairman of C.T. Bowring & Co. Ltd from 1957 until his death in 1965

Edgar Bowring and Fred Bowring

Left to right: *Harvey Bowring, Edward Stevinson and W.G. Pedley*

Left to right: *Mrs Milling, Geoffrey Milling, Chairman of The Bowring Steamship Company, and Fred Bowring, at the launching of MS* Orlando, *August 1960*

Fred Bowring presenting the Master and Officers of MS Regent Springbok to Her Royal Highness The Princess Royal, when she travelled on this Bowring ship to Trinidad in January 1953

and backbones, meanwhile, were processed in the two factories and pounded into meal. Apparently the end product strongly resembled shredded white string, but was found to be useful when mixed with barley meal as a 'balancer' to prevent clogging, and was favoured in Germany for pig feeding.

This promising new endeavour was, regrettably, to be dogged by misfortune. In the early thirties the young Icelander who ran the business so well met an untimely and tragic end. From time to time wild goose shooting parties were arranged with officers of the British fishery patrol when they were visiting. Apparently, on one of these occasions, a gun he was holding by its muzzle went off accidentally wounding him so badly that he died from loss of blood before it was possible to obtain medical assistance. Distressing though this appalling accident was in its effect on the future management of the company, hopes for future success were further dashed when competition from Icelandic fish merchants, who were developing state-of-the-art manufacturing methods, manifested itself. This would soon face Fiskimjol with serious difficulties, of which we shall learn more.

There was a third venture into the animal feed business during the years between the wars, this time in Holland. The Dutch company Vischmeel N.V. was established at Rotterdam in 1933 and in its earliest days it was managed by a young man from Fischmehl Einfuhr, Mr K. Lifschitz, who had escaped from Russia with his mother in 1917 at the time of the Revolution. Although Mr Lifschitz was brought up as a German citizen, he was summoned to the Russian Consulate at Hamburg during the twenties and was required to register for service in the Soviet Union. However, he ignored the invitation and, in due course devoted his time and energy to launching and developing the fishmeal business at Rotterdam. He was assisted by Mr Piet Rottinghuis, who was eventually to become the company's Managing Director.

Although there is little doubt that the older members of the family in Liverpool were suitably impressed by the successes being achieved in the insurance business in London, they still pursued their diversification into more trading activities and remained devoutly involved in shipping, in spite of the fact that they must have been fully aware of the greater certainty of the profits to be derived from insurance broking and underwriting than from a variety of commodities traded in or manufactured, or in shipping, where these markets were likely to be more fickle.

It would be many years, however, before those members of the company involved in trading or shipping, at whatever level, would consider C. T. Bowring & Co. (Insurance) Ltd to be anything other than 'the insurance 'branch' or 'department'.

In 1922, probably reflecting the historical and continuing maritime interests, the company moved into the importation and distribution of Naval Stores. To the uninitiated such a description might well evoke visions of anything from 18-inch shells to ship's biscuits. In fact Naval Stores are, broadly speaking, the products of pine trees and the name derives from the use of tar and pitch made from the gum exuded by these trees, used to caulk wooden decks. Since they are, in fact, a residue after the production of other materials, the whole group became known as Naval Stores. Other derivatives include rosin, turpentine, pine oil and, more recently, a host of more sophisticated related derivatives and chemicals used by a wide range of industries.

To carry on this new variation in Bowring's merchandizing activities a new company, Bowring, Jones and Tidy Limited (BJT), was formed. This new addition to the 'group' was created as the result of Mr A. (Archie) Probart-Jones, the manager, and his assistant, Mr W. E. Tidy of a company representing American naval stores interests, which had gone out of business, joining Bowring's, bringing their valuable contacts and expertise with them. Unfortunately, Mr Tidy's early death soon after the formation of BJT, robbed the company of a most able and knowledge-able executive. But in Archie Jones the parent company had acquired a businessman of rare astuteness who proved himself well able to run the business single-handed and, in due course, as the scope of its activities widened, to locate and employ a number of equally capable managers. He was also something of a Lothario and was just as successful in choosing attractive female company as he was in selecting competent business associates, though the former rather more frequently.

Although trading in Naval Stores would always be the main activity of BJT, other commodities were added from time to time, some of them used by the same customers. But it is the products of the pine tree that we shall look at first. The earliest certain knowledge of the start of the Naval Stores industry in North America (the United States were always the dominant producing country) dates back to some fifteen years before the arrival of the Pilgrim Fathers when there was a small production in New England. But there have been many other countries involved in the Naval Stores industry during the past 300 years including France,

Portugal, Greece, Russia, China, India and indeed, notwithstanding their colder climate, Sweden and Finland – and there have been others from time to time, albeit on a smaller scale.

The original method of manufacture was to extract the gum from various species of pine tree (in America chiefly the Long-Leaf Yellow Pine and the Slash Pine) and, by distilling it, produce a residue, rosin, and the condensed vapour, turpentine. These were known collectively as Gum Naval Stores. The collection of gum from the pine trees was extremely labour-intensive work, which would in due course, especially in the more developed producing countries, render this procedure too costly. But new manufacturing methods came along. The first of these was to extract the rosin and its associated products from the stumps of pine trees which had been felled for timber, by using mineral solvents after the stumps had been pounded into very small chips. The rosin and terpene oils, including turpentine, were then separated by distillation and were known as Wood Naval Stores.

The most recent method, which has significantly reduced the importance of the other two, is the extraction of rosin and various associated chemicals from tall oil, a by-product of paper-pulp manufacture. (However the rosin coming from this source had not become popular with customers when Bowring, Jones and Tidy ceased to operate in the 1970s.)

To most readers it is unlikely that the mention of rosin will mean anything more (if indeed anything at all) than an amber coloured substance used in its solid condition by violinists and other string players to apply to their bows and, in powdered form, by boxers and ballet dancers to put on their shoes. In fact the quantity used by all the musicians, pugilists and dancers in one year would not, in all probability, keep a small production plant busy for more than an hour or two. Rosin has been used in a wide range of industries including the manufacture of soap, paint, paper, linoleum, plastics, medical plasters, adhesives, permanent road markings and many articles of everyday use. Whether it is used so extensively today is doubtful. Turpentine, however, has been well known as a paint thinner, and its associated products, derived from the manufacture of Wood Naval Stores, are used extensively in chemical and industrial preparations, including embrocations, disinfectants, solvents and wetting agents. Turpentine, in the twenties and thirties, was usually shipped in wooden barrels of about 45 gallons capacity, which were prone to seepage and consequent waste. In order to avoid this costly loss Bowring, Jones and

Tidy, as an experiment, decided to charter the tanker *Camillo* from the parent company to load a cargo of turpentine from Jacksonville. But, of course, it would be necessary, on arrival of the cargo, for the turpentine to be off-loaded into barrels. Speculation arose as to how BJT would find enough barrels to accommodate a tanker-load and their competitors in London set about 'cornering' all the available barrels they could lay their hands on. However, the ever-resourceful Archie Jones, having foreseen this possible complication, arranged for the purchase in the USA of a sufficient quantity of heads and staves to be shipped ahead of *Camillo* and to have the barrels assembled before the ship's arrival. In due course the accepted container for turpentine and allied products was to become the metal drum, but shipment of turpentine in bulk, especially from Continental producers, continued for many years, sometimes in deep-tanks on ordinary cargo vessels and also in small chartered tankers.

It would not be long before Archie Jones' 'nose' for favourable business opportunities led to the importation and distribution of various commodities and raw materials used by many of those customers who were buying Naval Stores, particularly the paint manufacturers. These products, the handling of which was in the capable hands of my cousin, Robert Bowring, a son of Clive Bowring, included linseed oil and tung oil, otherwise known as China Wood Oil, which is produced from the nut of the tung tree (*Aleurites Fordii*), and a variety of oilseeds and pulses, some of which were sought by the animal feed industry and were marketed in conjunction with the Fertilizer and Foodstuffs Department of the parent company. Most of the linseed oil and oilseeds were imported from India through the Bombay firm of Kilachand Devchand. Tung oil came mainly from China where an association with a well-known Shanghai concern, Arnhold and Company, who were operating in a similar field, was formed and with whom a joint enterprise, Arnhold Trading Company Ltd was entered into following the acquisition of a block of their shares by BJT. The prevailing enthusiasm for tung oil also led to a substantial investment by BJT in a tung oil plantation at Bogalusa in Louisiana.

There is no doubt that an element of professional jealousy existed between the managers of the earlier created Fertilizer and Foodstuffs Department, 'Jock' Smith and Bernard Weil, and the board of Bowring, Jones and Tidy. Smith and Weil were jealous of their status as a department of the parent company to whose board they reported directly, and were strongly opposed to any suggestion that they might become a department of a subsidiary company, an arrangement that would have made good commercial sense.

The energetic pursuit of diversification in trading continued throughout the period between the wars, sometimes in unexpected directions, usually – but not always – connected in some way or other with an existing interest. For example, notwithstanding the failure of a tung oil plantation in Burma, in which it seems Bowring's were involved together with a paint manufacturer (who had established the plantation in order to secure supplies of the oil), a commercial interest in Burma developed. It could not be seen at the time, however, that the conditions for the successful conduct of commercial activity in Burma were to become complex and, indeed, hazardous.

In the early years following the First World War, Bowring's wanted to test the commercial climate in India and opened a small pilot trading company in partnership with the Manchester firm of Ledward and Taylor. With them they jointly acquired, in 1921, Fleming, Shaw and Company, a firm with offices in Bombay and Karachi, mostly involved in the textile business. This led to an association with two experienced businessmen, Alexander (Sandy) Fairweather and W. J. C. (Bill) Richards, both of whom were well acquainted with Burma, and with whom it was decided to open a business in Rangoon, the initial capital of £21,500 being subscribed equally by Fairweather and Richards as individuals and, corporately, by Ledward and Taylor and by Bowring's.

The early years of this new company were modestly successful based mainly on the export of rice and on a varied range of imported products. In order to provide the British market with the better quality of rice it demanded, Bowring's purchased a rice mill, the production of which they marketed. However, the combination of the world depression of the late twenties and early thirties, and fierce competition from European owned rice-milling companies with London based offices, robbed these efforts of any lasting hope of success. In fact, Fairweather's losses were so severe that it became necessary to reconstruct the joint enterprise with Bowring's as the main shareholder.

Probably the most successful of the early enterprises in which Fairweather, Richards – as the newly created company was named – became interested was the management of a number of rubber estates, all registered in London. These included Mergui Crown Estates, King Island Estates Ltd, Moulmein Rubber Plantations, local agencies of Sittang Valley, Tenassserim Plantations and Burma Estates. Eventually the company were controlling the affairs of half of the total area of rubber plantations in Burma, which accounted for some two-thirds of the country's production. A further extension of their expertise in plantation management led to their sponsoring of a tung tree estate in the Southern Shan States. Thus the thread, sometimes slender, of a continuing affinity with existing operations was maintained.

To add variety to an already colourful range of activities, Fairweather, Richards became involved in exporting teak, for which Burma has traditionally been one of the world's major exporters. The history of the use of teak in large quantities goes back to colonial days when, because of its strength and durability, it was employed in the building of wooden ships. Such was the nature and location of the teak forests in Burma that transportation was always a problem. Machinery was never as satisfactory as elephants for moving the timber out of the forests. After the first stage of its journey, on its way to reach the world's markets, the timber would be arranged into rafts, and floated down river to the loading ports. When Fairweather, Richards started in the teak business, there were no political hazards to contend with. Today, however, many countries shun its use because it is produced under slave-labour conditions. Nevertheless, Burma is still the producer of some 70 per cent of the world's supplies.

The company also operated as an active import agent, mainly of manufactured products and building materials, but its operations in this field were confined to those organizations prepared to offer them an exclusive agency. Burma is one of the few countries from which Bowring's were forced to withdraw in later years for political reasons.

While Fairweather, Richards were enjoying a period of successful and profitable business, they maintained a close relationship with the parent company in London, who had acquired warehousing facilities for the rice they were marketing for them. This service was provided for them by the recently created but comparatively short-lived Produce Department, which eventually became part of Bowring, Jones and Tidy. The storage facility was at the historic Clink Wharf in Southwark. The warehouse, on the site of the old Clink Prison – the debtors' gaol, which gives its name to the time honoured phrase 'in the clink' – was purchased in 1936 together with the neighbouring premises, Soho Works. At Clink Wharf the rice was cleaned and re-bagged. Some was sold to food retailers in cartons under the brand name 'KAPPA'. But this was not to be a successful or long-lasting venture, brought to an end by the outbreak of war as much as for any other reason. Soho Works, paradoxically, consisted mainly of space for storage and distribution, though it did possess equipment for cleaning and blending various commodities. A variety of products were handled including coffee and tea. As a result, the parent company became involved in the importation and distribution of coffee and a separate department was created. This was to be followed some years later by a much more significant stake in the coffee business.

Finally, among the variety of trading ventures in which Bowring's indulged between the wars, most, though by no means all of which bore some relationship with activities previously pursued, they took their involvement in their historic handling of sealskins in Newfoundland a stage further by the acquisition in 1936 of the firm of W. Duckworth and Sons Ltd, an old-established tannery in Bermondsey blessed with a small highly skilled workforce, where full chrome seal leather in its natural grain was produced for the English shoe trade. At the same time, seal furs shipped by Bowring Brothers from St John's were treated and marketed by an expert fur dresser.

As we have seen earlier, by the end of the First World War Bowring's were, to all intents and purposes, out of the mineral oil business. In 1912 the Anglo-Mexican Petroleum Products Company Ltd (created to develop exports of the Mexican Eagle output) had acquired a small majority shareholding in the Bowring Petroleum Company. By 1920 Anglo-Mexican were marketing the Bowring products, over which they now had control, in their own name. Bowring's had agreed with Anglo-Mexican not to compete with them before February 1923, and so, after being pioneers in the very earliest days of what was to become the largest business in the world, they found themselves for a number of years without any position at all in the petroleum business. We shall never know what might have been the position had George Bowring, that tireless enthusiast for deeper involvement in oil, not died so young, at a time when his enthusiasm was at its peak and the prospects seemed endless.

However, by 1924, taking advantage of experience of the industry gained in previous years, the company established a department to handle imports and the distribution of petroleum products. The Petroleum Department was operated from offices at 52 Leadenhall Street and managed depots at Croydon, Datchet, High Wycombe, Limehouse in London's East End and at Birmingham. The product first handled by the department was paraffin imported from Romania, usually landed at

Thames Haven and stored in rented tanks before being distributed by road and rail-tank wagons throughout the London area.

In the early 1930s the business was extended to include the distribution of motor spirit, but only for the commercial user rather than becoming involved in the private motorists' filling-station market.

Chapter 12

URING THE TWENTY-ONE YEARS between the First and Second World
Wars, Benjamin's earlier courage and determination, and indeed
that of his successors during the first half of the 19th century, had paved
the way, though I doubt whether the idea would have ever occurred to
any of them, for the development, both by evolution and acquisition, of
what today might well be described as a conglomerate. What successful
company of fish oil processors or of teak importers would have expected
to find themselves rubbing shoulders with a flourishing and aspiring
world-class firm of insurance brokers. While these largely successful
activities were developing during the period between the two wars on
the European shores of the Atlantic, the story from North America was
often rather less than heartening.

Although they were experiencing significant development in some of
their activities between the wars, it was generally for Bowring's a period of
mixed good and not-so-good results. In 1920, for instance, the parent
company showed a loss in the vicinity of £500,000. This was attributable
not only to difficult marketing conditions affecting the commodities
handled by the various trading branches, but has also been ascribed to the
directors' decision to make a generous donation of £250,000 to the
Government's Victory Loan. Unfortunately, both Bowring Brothers at St
John's and, at New York, Bowring and Company suffered significant losses
during the years 1920 and 1921. David Keir compared the ups and downs
of the fortunes of the North American companies' maritime and mercantile
activities in the early post-war years to 'the rise and fall of a big Atlantic
swell'. While Bowring Brothers continued to pursue their traditional
business with varying degrees of success, Bowring and Company had
become engaged in the sale of ores and metals from Europe and sealskins
and cod oil from Newfoundland. They also managed the affairs of the Red
Cross Line before it was sold, and were involved in shipbroking and agency
work for various shipowners, a bewildering variety of activities which, at
times, seemed to be somewhat overwhelming for a small office, and which,
many years later, would lead to its demise through lack of sufficient
management skill and attention to detail.

The Red Cross Line's *Florizel* and *Stephano*, both lost during the war, had to be replaced if the company was to maintain its good reputation with American cruise addicts. In order to make good these losses, C. T. Bowring & Co. bought two vessels, the 2,390-ton *Lady Gwendoline* and the 3,589-ton *Orel*, both built before the war. Their names were promptly changed to *Rosalind* and *Sylvia* respectively, so perpetuating the time-honoured choice of Shakespearean characters. These ships were so successful that, in 1925, the company decided to give the line a new ship, *Nerissa*, built by Hamilton and Company on the Clyde in the remarkable short time of seven months, notwithstanding the intervention of a ten-day General Strike. *Nerissa*, a vessel of almost 6,000 ton gross, was designed to carry both cargo and 200 passengers. In view of the success of the Red Cross Line it is surprising that the three ships were sold in 1929 to Furness, Withy and Company, much to the chagrin of their managers, Bowring and Company at New York, who nevertheless remained busy importing ores for Naylor, Benzon, for whom they acted as sales and distribution agents. They continued to sell Newfoundland cod oil and sealskins and to operate their ship-chartering department.

Mention has already been made of the heroism shown during the war by Newfoundland sailors and by the soldiers of the Royal Newfoundland Regiment at Beaumont-Hamel. In spite of appalling losses, there were many ex-servicemen returning to the colony in search of employment. Fortunately, there was a period immediately following the end of hostilities of exceptional prosperity brought about by the recovery from wartime shortages. The demand for fish rose sensationally, as did the prices. There was promise of jobs aplenty.

In November 1918 Sir Edgar Bowring was appointed Newfoundland's first High Commissioner to the United Kingdom and on his arrival in London he expressed the view that the island's fishery could expect a prosperous future. In March the following year he reinforced his view by stating that the industry was likely to become more reliable and that men were returning to it. In *The Bowring Story*, David Keir enlarges upon Sir Edgar's outlook:

The Newfoundland government's policy was therefore to get people back to the sea rather than back to the land, because an immense quantity of fish was there for the taking. The island also offered great prospects for the pulp and paper industry, and afforestation was a matter of vital importance. Sir Edgar saw, too, a significant place for the island in the future of transatlantic aviation, but struck a cautionary note by making it clear that Newfoundland was unwilling to encourage immigrants from the old country until the problems of settling returning ex-servicemen had been resolved.

But his optimism was soon to be shaken. An impending economic slump manifested itself in 1920 when sales of cod fell dramatically and prices sagged. The situation deteriorated to such an extent that fish was left to putrefy in ships' holds, eventually to be dumped. The government took over the railway and the coastal service (although Bowring Brothers were willing to carry on with the latter), unemployment figures rocketed, and the generous credit facilities, freely available a few years earlier, were slashed. The possibility loomed that the island was about to face economic collapse.

The government of the day, though remembered for its instability, endeavoured to rectify the situation by seeking measures to help the unemployed. Among the proposals to alleviate rising poverty and to provide relief work were plans to build a dry dock at St John's, the construction of new highways and improvements to a railway system of questionable value. In spite of these efforts, life on the dole became the lot of thousands, many being reduced to a meagre subsistence level, a far cry from the comfort and prosperity that many had enjoyed following the war. Ministers, showing every sign of being incapable of providing a basis for rebuilding the colony's economy, resorted to reckless borrowing.

It is surprising, perhaps, that on his return to Newfoundland in 1923, Sir Edgar Bowring should maintain his optimism. It was his staunchly held view that the island was capable of significant development, that wealth was attainable, and that its people could lead happy lives. He asserted, furthermore, that there were mineral resources to be exploited, and even went to the extent of suggesting that, were these hopes to be realized, Newfoundland could become one of the richest countries in the world. In the meantime, however, he pronounced the more modest view that, within a few years, prosperity would surely return. But it would be rather more than just a few years before his aspirations would be fulfilled. There was worse, much worse, to come.

In his delightfully absorbing book, *Theatre of Fish*, (Hutchinson, London, 2005) John Gimlette captures the despair of the 1920s:

> ... Newfoundland was in a state of terminal paralysis. It was wandering into the Depression with its debt doubled, and one in four on the dole.

Outporters were surviving on a third of the income now needed to ward off starvation. The government kept them busy with relief roads, and they fed themselves on seabirds. Relief was paid at a withering 6c a day.

'The country is nearing the breakers,' said the Speaker of the Assembly. 'If it has to be revolution, let it be revolution.'

But political life too had simply seized. There'd been five changes of command since 1923, and soon there'd be only one person left on the wreckage. It was Squires. He was prime minister again, looting the stores whilst Newfoundland went down.

Sir Richard Squires deserves a mention, if only to record his combined incompetence as prime minister and his propensity to flout the law. He was accused of using bribes to win the 1923 election and the Attorney General issued a warrant for his arrest from which he was released on bond; he resigned as prime minister. However, he pegged away at being returned to power and in 1928 was re-elected as Liberal leader, at the expense of the Conservatives. The years that followed, as already mentioned, were little short of disastrous for the colony, and once again there were allegations of corruption levelled at him and his administration. There was widespread political instability and public discontent. In 1932, Squires was accused by his finance minister, Peter Cashin, of having falsified council minutes in order to suppress the fact that he had been secretly receiving payments out of the national pocket. This further aroused public anger, already inflamed by the prevailing desperate economic situation. Organized by the opposition, a crowd of 10,000 protesting citizens of St John's descended on the Colonial Building, then the home of the House of Assembly. Matters quickly got out of hand when no one came out to address them, and a number of the angry demonstrators managed to enter the building. For Squires and several members of his government there was nothing for it but to try and escape from the back of the building. He only avoided surrendering to the crowd's fury as he was trying to enter a taxi by running through someone's house.

These dire conditions, aggravated by the Newfoundland government's improvident borrowing and by the depressed economic situation throughout the world, caused the British government, in 1933, to appoint a Royal Commission to undertake a thorough examination of the island's affairs. It came as no great surprise that the findings of this body pinpointed reckless waste and extravagance, and a political system that lacked constructive and efficient administration and which, for a generation, had encouraged exploitation for personal and party gain. As a result of these findings, self-government in Newfoundland was suspended, and early in 1934, government by commission was introduced. This form of administration was to last for the next fifteen years, in fact until confederation with Canada.

Notwithstanding this new method of conducting the island's affairs, gloom and despair persisted with almost a third of the effective population drawing relief during the winter. But there were glimmers of hope during the next ten years as the paper and iron ore industries were developed and plans were drawn up for the construction of Gander airport (as envisaged by Sir Edgar Bowring). For Bowring Brothers, the future was not entirely doom-laden; indeed they managed to expand their business in a number of ways. The seal fishery, for example, was quite successful during the 1930s, and retailing and insurance were both prospering. It will be recalled that the last two were among Benjamin Bowing's earliest activities, and it was encouraging to see them performing reasonably well in the now enlarged Water Street premises, in spite of the generally depressing economic climate. Whilst they were no longer directly associated with the cod fishery, they nevertheless maintained their support for the industry. This took the form of an alliance with other St John's trading houses through the formation of the Hawes Group, which was created to stabilise the marketing overseas of Newfoundland cod. George Hawes was well acquainted with European trading conditions and was able to give help and advice on establishing a sounder basis for operating in the various European markets. But Bowring's, who in fact had derived very little profit from the cod fishery for more than fifty years, still found it to be unrewarding, and withdrew altogether. They continued, however, to import salt and other products needed by the fishing fleets.

In the early twenties there was an attempt to capitalize on the experience gained in France during the war from the use of spotting-aircraft, by sending scouting planes to seek out patches of seals on the ice. The first trials were unsatisfactory because of the failure of the aircraft engines due to icing. The later introduction of the small Avro aircraft, capable of taking-off from the ice and previously used by Shackleton on board *Quest*, was marginally more successful, and on occasions was carried on the deck of Bowring's *Eagle*. However, aerial spotting never quite fulfilled the hopes expected of it; often, while assisting the captains in pointing out collections of seals, they would be located in ice so thick that the ships were unable to reach them.

The high prices achieved for seals during the war had tumbled by 1921, and sending large numbers of vessels to the ice front each year with large crews became a risky proposition. However, during the next few years, Bowring Brothers nearly always managed to send five steamers and in 1927, the 1,000 ton *Nascopie* was added to the fleet with the Avro on board.

Mixed though the fortunes of sealing had always been, Bowring's felt sufficiently confident in 1929 to introduce to their fleet a new steam ship, *Imogene* (IV), 1,638 tons gross. Built by Smith's Dock Co. Ltd at South-Bank-on-Tees, she was designed specifically for the seal hunt with a crew of 250, and in 1933 she brought back to St John's a record 55,636 pelts. (She ran aground in 1940 off Canso, Nova Scotia, when carrying a cargo of salt from Turks Island to Gaspe, after directional buoys had shifted in a gale The captain and crew of 27 were all saved, but she broke up in later gales before she could be salvaged). A few of the motorized schooners still visited the ice each year and in 1930 they accounted for 22,592 of the total of 241,256 pelts brought back.

Early in 1931, the people of Newfoundland and far beyond were to be devastated by news of a tragic accident at the ice-front. On Sunday 15 March, as some of the residents of Horse Island were walking back home from their evening church service, enjoying a change in the weather from the gales and blizzards of the previous week, they became suddenly aware of the trembling of the earth under their feet followed by the distant sound of a massive explosion. To their horror they could see, some miles out on the ice, the outline of a blazing ship. That night would prove to be one of horror and deep distress.

When the sealing fleet sailed from St John's the previous week for the start of the season, the last ship to leave was Bowring's well-known small wooden coal-fired sealer, *Viking*. She was delayed because, in addition to her usual complement, an American film crew, led by Varick Frissell, a New York film-maker who wanted to obtain shots of colonies of seals and of storm conditions, joined the ship. Frissell had already completed the major part of a film, which was to be called *Northern Knight* (later to be changed to *White Thunder*). *Viking* was under the command of old Captain Kean's son, Abram Kean Jnr.

According to various early reports received in St John's on 16 March, *Viking's* magazine at the ship's stern had exploded the previous evening when she was some eight miles off Horse Island, setting fire to the whole ship. Further messages stated that it was impossible to obtain accurate particulars since those who had been able to escape to the island across heaving broken ice, were so exhausted that they were unable to give a coherent description of what actually happened. Later it was learned that possibly up to twenty had lost their lives. As soon as these reports were received the Newfoundland Department of Marine and Fisheries arranged for the ocean-going tug, *Foundation Franklin*, to leave immediately for the scene of the tragedy with doctors, nurses and medical and surgical supplies. Later that day *Sagona*, a specially equipped rescue ship under the command of Captain Jacob Kean, left St John's with a further three doctors and two more nurses. It was quite clear that many were injured and that it had been necessary for them to be carried, in the face of great danger, across the ice by the other survivors.

In the *Book of Newfoundland* (J. R. Smallwood, Newfoundland Book Publishers Ltd, St John's 1937) there is an eye-witness account, by *Viking*'s wireless operator, Clayton King, which gives a graphic description of an ordeal of unimaginable horror. He had been attending to some news and weather reports that had been coming in, and then went aft to the saloon to join other members of the crew and the film unit all of whom were thinking of turning in for the night. There were substantial stocks of explosives on board and he remembered that he had heard that certain safety precautions were needed, in view of the fact that there were some old, damaged flares, which should be disposed of over the side. King's account continues:

> Carter [*the bos'n*] picked up the flares and left the saloon for his room which was on the after-starboard side of the saloon. The magazine and the toilet were located in a small corridor directly opposite Carter's room. Dynamite and powder were stored in both these places.
>
> A few seconds after Carter's departure the ship gave a terrific lurch and listed to an angle of forty degrees. In an instant all was chaos. All hands were thrown clear of the mess table. The stove capsized.
>
> The ship righted herself immediately. Captain Kean came running out of his state room and headed for the deck to determine the cause of the racket. Getting to our feet we started to clean up the saloon. Almost immediately there followed a terrific blast from the after end of the saloon. For me there followed oblivion.

Fire swept the whole length of *Viking* following a second explosion, which destroyed the crew's quarters in the fore part of the ship. The main deck collapsed trapping the men below and rescuers, because of the fire, which now extended from stem to stern, were prevented from reaching them. King found himself, when he regained consciousness, trapped under fallen timbers with his clothes and hair on fire and unable to move because his legs were badly crushed. He eventually managed to free himself, but the damage to his legs was so severe that he could not possibly stand. Somehow he managed to drag himself away from the inferno of the blazing saloon. His account continues:

> Get clear I must. I either fell or threw myself clear – I do not remember which – and landed in the water. I could not get a grip on the ice-pans. Slippery and hard as steel they afforded nothing to hold to. Sargent [*from the film unit*] who must have been near, came to my rescue and pulled me out on an ice-pan.

Those of the ship's dories that were not too badly damaged were used to convey the injured by the exhausting process of pushing them across the ice to the island. It was in this way that Captain Kean, who had been found on an ice-pan, conscious but badly hurt, was, with the rest of the injured, brought ashore. But for some of the survivors there was a worse situation developing. King and Kennedy, the ship's navigator, and a few others adrift on a very small ice-pan only a few feet square, were being taken away from Horse Island by wind and tide. By using bits of wood from the wreck they were able to build some rudimentary protection from the biting wind, but they were without food, water or adequate clothing and were to suffer these dreadful conditions for the next two days. King, grievously stricken by his shattered legs and a head wound, was unconscious most of the time, and Kennedy was suffering from pneumonia. One of the other members of this small, severely threatened, group managed to rouse King from his near-lifeless condition and was able to make him understand that he thought he could see smoke from a steamer in the distance. He was right. What they saw was the specially equipped rescue vessel *Sagona*.

Unfortunately, Kennedy died from pneumonia before *Sagona* could reach St John's, but King miraculously survived, though he had to suffer amputation of both legs, and Sargent, of the film crew, was able to walk ashore. The sinking of *Viking*, the first Bowring sealing vessel to be lost in over fifty years, claimed, in all, the lives of 30 men including the leader of the film group, twenty-eight-year-old Varick Frissell. Captain Kean made a full recovery and was at sea again the following year. Of those who died in the immediate vicinity of the explosion no trace was ever found.

The fortunes of the seal fishery continued to be variable through the thirties, and the loss of *Viking* left Bowring's in 1932 with a main working fleet of only three vessels, *Imogene, Terra Nova* and *Eagle*. They would be joined in due course by *Beothic*, which they purchased from their friendly competitors, Job Brothers. In spite of the use of larger, better equipped ships, the catches during the thirties could not compare with those of the early years of the century. However, there was no diminution in the export of Newfoundland sealskins, seal oil, codfish and cod oil, nor of the reciprocal shipments of the growing requirements of the St John's Water Street store.

Chapter 13

WE HAVE ALREADY seen how, between the wars, new areas of trading were developed, and involvement in insurance broking and underwriting was expanding rapidly. But Bowring's position in the world of shipping had been substantially reduced, as a result of the war. If the company was to regain its former prominence as shipowners and operators, a monumental task lay ahead. Bowring's losses amounted to some 60 per cent of the tonnage owned and operated by them at the outbreak of hostilities and any hope of rapid recovery was severely hampered in 1919 by widespread industrial action in the shipyards, railways and coalmines. Whereas it proved possible to replace the losses of the Red Cross Line reasonably quickly, those suffered by the English and American Shipping Company were beyond any hope of restoration and reductions in the tanker fleets of the Bearcreek Oil and Shipping Company and the Oil Tank Steamship Company meant that sight of the company's flag on the high seas had become a rare occurrence.

The parent company, in view of the seriously weakened state of the English and American Shipping Company, decided that it should be placed in voluntary liquidation and that its assets and surviving vessels should be transferred to a new company to be called The Bowring Steamship Company, which was incorporated on 5 April 1919 with a capital of £1,000,000. The new company began its long and largely successful career with the ships *Tafna* (II) and *Adra* (II). Of these two *Tafna*, 4,512 tons gross and launched in 1911 by Wm Doxford & Sons Ltd at Sunderland, was the only ship of the English and American Shipping Company to survive the entire war. *Adra*, 4,860 tons gross was launched during the war, in 1917, also at Sunderland by Short Bros Ltd. It was during this year that Bowring's placed an order for a further vessel, *Ronda*, 4,943 tons gross. Built at South Shields by John Redhead & Sons Ltd for the English and American Shipping Company, she should have been delivered two years later but, because of the industrial unrest that followed the immediate post-war boom, she didn't come into service until 1920. That the country should have enjoyed a brief period of commercial and industrial renaissance in 1919 was perhaps understandable following the privations and controls of war, but it didn't last long and probably owed its origins more to a surge of euphoria than to down-to-earth planning and common sense. In fact, as early as January 1919, when the rest of the country was basking in the warm glow of peace, the shipyards and engineering shops of Clydeside were at a standstill following strike action for a 40-hour week. The shipbuilders suffered not only from the problems in their own industry, which spread to London, Newcastle and Belfast, but also from the knock-on effects of other disputes. Railwaymen, workers on the London underground, and even the police were withdrawing their labour in order to draw attention to their working conditions. Many of the new companies connected with shipbuilding, which were started during the war, failed and share values and dividends in the industry hit new lows; to make matters worse, there was withdrawal of labour in a number of related trades, all of which contributed to a couple of years of depressed conditions.

A serious and lasting side effect of this labour unrest in Britain was to deflect many of the orders for the vast amount of new tonnage required to replace wartime losses to foreign yards, particularly in America and Japan. It was not long before the competition thus created led to a noticeable and unwelcome reduction in the United Kingdom's erstwhile leadership in the world of shipping and shipbuilding. But not all of the industry was in the doldrums. There was a growing demand for tankers.

The global appetite for oil, the increasing use of which had been boosted by the war, gave rise to an intensive search for supplies, and new oilfields were springing up in many parts of the world. As a result new tanker operating companies were being created to meet the transport requirements of burgeoning output. At this stage in the development of Bowring's involvement with tankers they were, for the time being, more engaged in ship-management than in ownership. It was as managers that they had developed strong relations with the Admiralty both before and during the war. This association was further enhanced when the company took over the management of five 'War' class tankers for the Admiralty, an arrangement that lasted until 1937 and included, at various times, the vessels *War Diwan, War Alfridi, War Brahmin, War Pindari* and *War Bahadar*. These ships, known as 'Z' type steam tankers, although built at different yards, were of virtually identical specification, and some of them were still in service well into the late 1950s, though, at that stage in their lives they were no longer managed by Bowring's.

Although the relationship with the Admiralty was generally perfectly benign, it could not be said that this was always the case. The principal, quite understandably looking for ways to impose economies, informed Bowring's that they considered the management fee of £2,083-6s-8d was too steep, and asked if they would 'agree to a reduction and if so, to what extent'. Regrettably, there is no trace of any detailed response, but some indication of what it might have been can be derived from a fragment that read: '. . . Firm willing to consider any definite proposal made by the Admiralty.' That the relationship was, by and large, a satisfactory one is evident from the willingness of the company to provide technical advice on matters such as the improvement of safety measures on tankers by providing the necessary expertise.

The steady growth of the oil industry understandably encouraged the building of tankers and by 1923 the world's oil tanker fleet had increased to such an extent that many of them were being laid-up on delivery, in spite of the continuing discovery and development of new oilfields. This erratic performance of an evolving industry gave rise to fluctuations in oil prices and freight rates, but such was the speed with which the production of oil increased, laid-up tonnage was soon back in business and, indeed, for a time there were even signs of a tanker shortage.

When, in the late twenties, the demand for tankers returned, Bowring's rose to the occasion by placing an order with William Hamilton and Company at Port Glasgow for *Cymbeline*, a 9,450 ton tanker, which was launched in 1927 and went into service with the Oil Tank Steamship Company Ltd. She was followed by a diesel driven ship, *Benedick*, 10,300 tons, which was completed at Scotstoun by Blythswood Shipbuilding Company for the Bearcreek Oil and Shipping Company and was launched by my mother, Agnes Walker Bowring, in 1928. In addition, a number of contracts were entered into, the first of which was arranged by the parent company with Lobitos Oilfields Limited for whom they acted as fleet managers. Under the contract an order was placed with the Blythswood Shipbuilding Company for a tanker, *El Mirlo*, which was delivered in September 1930. As an example of the currently mercurial nature of the industry, she was promptly time-chartered to The Anglo-Saxon Petroleum Company Ltd, who, having approved the ship at her acceptance trials, then decided that she should be laid-up in the Gareloch. Meanwhile, Bowring's negotiated on behalf of their own two companies – The Oil Tank Steamship Company and the Bearcreek Oil and Shipping Company – with Swan, Hunter and

Wigham Richardson for the construction at their Wallsend yard of two tankers, *Cordelia* and *Capulet*. At the time of ordering these ships the tanker market looked promising, but by the time they were launched the prospects had become unfavourable, and both ships suffered the same fate as *El Mirlo* and followed her into lay-up berths. There was, apparently, an opportunity in London to obtain charters for these two ships on favourable terms if, in 'shipowner-speak', they could be 'fixed' promptly. This implied the broker acting on behalf of the owners being able to close business quickly on the Baltic Exchange with the potential charterer. However, at the company's head office in Liverpool the Chairman, Sir Frederick Bowring (he had received his knighthood in 1928 following his second year as Lord Mayor of Liverpool), pronounced from on high that if business were to be done it should be at a rate higher than that ruling in the market at the time. So the opportunity was lost and the two ships continued to languish in their lay-up berths for a further 18 months. Sir Frederick, my great-uncle, was, as they say, 'his own man' and his utterances were frequently unconventional if not downright eccentric, a characteristic of which there will be more to be said in due course.

In 1927 the company suffered yet another loss of one of its most able directors when, at the height of his ability and influence, Sir John Bowring Wimble died at the age of only fifty-nine when he was Chairman of C. T. Bowring & Co. (Insurance) Ltd. He held many directorships and performed a number of public duties as befitted his energy and amiable disposition. He was the son of the John Wimble who, it will be recalled, married Charles Tricks Bowring's daughter Harriet Jane. His appointment to the Boards of other companies included Lobitos Oilfields, The Bowring Steamship Company, the Metropolitan Life Assurance Society and the World Auxiliary Insurance Corporation. Among his numerous public appointments were Deputy Chairman of the Port of London Authority, Chairman during the War of the Shipowners and Transport Workers Military Service Tribunal, Honorary Treasurer of the King George V Fund for Sailors and Chairman of the Metropolitan Library.

Although Bowring's shipping interests following the First World War were mainly concerned with tankers, cargo carriers had not been ignored and two, *Urla* and *Anthea* were built at Ardrossan in 1925 to the order of The Bowring Steamship Company. Of 5,197 and 5,186 tons gross respectively, they were the last two freighters to be built for a Bowring company for some years to come because of the worldwide depression that followed the 1929 economic crash and the serious long-term effect it had on the shipping industry generally. Depressed freight rates on the one hand and the unrestrained output of the shipyards in the past on the other, led to severe recession throughout the industry. This gloomy situation prompted Sir Edgar Bowring to proclaim: 'There is a big depression in the shipbuilding industry, owing to the inactivity of the freight markets of the world, and I do not see how it will be able to show any lasting improvement so long as there is such an excess of surplus tonnage.' At the same time as he made these observations, the press reported that 416 ships totalling 892,000 tons net were laid up in the British Isles.

This was a bad time in the company's shipping life and, in his position as Chairman, Sir Frederick (he had succeeded his cousin, Sir William following his death in 1916), who remained at Liverpool for personal preference and because of his many public duties in the city, was shouldering a heavy burden. He had come a long way since those early days in New York when, as a raw recruit to the world of shipping, he will be remembered for his supervision of the loading aboard *Juliet* of a cargo of molasses in leaking barrels over a large consignment of bacon, and for which he incurred the extreme displeasure of his uncle, Charles Tricks.

I must have been seven or eight years old when I first encountered my eldest great uncle, when he would have been about seventy-five. The two things that I remember most clearly about him when he visited us at our home, Trepassey in Heswall, on the Wirral, were his very watery eyes and his generosity – he gave each of us, my younger brother, two sisters and me, half-a-crown. It seemed to us to mean that he was probably very rich, which of course he was. He noticed that we were all blue with cold, with dripping noses and, in my case a fine crop of chilblains to accompany one of my frequent attacks of asthma. He forthwith instructed my father to have central heating installed at his expense. To do things by halves was not in his nature. Fortunately there was a cellar with enough space to house the plant, which included a boiler of such gargantuan proportions that it could probably have produced enough steam to propel a small ship. In preparation for winter, great quantities of coal would arrive, and the sacks were emptied down a chute into the cellar where there would otherwise have been plenty of room for wine racks; but in those days, it seems, the preference at

Trepassey was for gin, and the beckoning call of the church bells on a Sunday morning was drowned by the rattle of ice in the cocktail shaker; the Dry Martini had arrived. 'Billy the Bart', one time President of the United Kingdom Temperance Alliance, would not have approved, although, as a staunch Unitarian, he might have been awarded a few brownie points for avoiding Anglican matins.

It wasn't until 1935 that there were signs of an improvement in the fortunes of the shipping industry and of a revival in world trade generally. A return to long awaited optimism gave rise to the decision to increase the size of the tanker fleet and Bowring's were soon to place orders with Swan, Hunter and Wigham Richardson for three ships, *Regent Lion* launched in December 1936, *Regent Panther* in February 1937, each of 14,540 tons deadweight, and, in 1938, *Regent Tiger*, 14,259 tons deadweight. With Sir Frederick at the helm the company had weathered the vicissitudes of the twenties and thirties and there is no doubt that his prudence and commercial wisdom had much to do with its emergence unscathed from the bad years. But, sadly he was not see the new ships at sea. He died after a few years of indifferent health on 24 March 1936 when nearly eighty.

Although there has been a tendency within the family — and possibly outside it — to characterize 'Uncle Fred', as something of an oddball, he was without doubt an extremely able and highly respected citizen of Liverpool, and his benevolence was legendary. Born at St John's in 1857, he was the eldest son of Benjamin's youngest son, John. At the tender age of twelve he was sent to England to be educated at Liverpool and Scarborough. Thereafter, in 1874, he joined the Liverpool office as an apprentice and worked under his father for a princely £10 a year. This rose to an annual salary of £100 after four years, no doubt awarded in recognition of his potential ability and probably seen in those days as a meteoric rise. In accordance with accepted family custom he was dispatched to Newfoundland in 1878, and thence after a few years, to New York where he joined his cousin Thomas in the management of Bowring and Archibald. He returned to Liverpool in 1888, where for the next forty-eight years he led a distinguished life both as the leader of a growing family business and in the public domain.

As an enthusiastic Liberal, he was elected a member of the Liverpool City Council in 1909 representing the Exchange Ward, and he continued in this capacity for the next eleven years; thereafter he represented the Granby Ward until 1934. On two occasions he stood, albeit without success, as a Liberal candidate for parliament, on the first occasion for the Abercromby division and later for East Toxteth. In 1925 he was elected Lord Mayor of Liverpool and was so popular that he was elected for a second successive term, a unique instance in the city's history at that time. His generosity is well illustrated by his support for the Walker Art Gallery. When, shortly after he assumed his mayoral duties, the gallery mounted an appeal to raise funds for an extension, he promised to match the contribution of any other donor. A certain Mr George Audley of Southport promptly donated £10,000, whereupon Sir Frederick gave a similar amount, in recognition of which the Bowring Gallery at William Brown Street was named after him.

His unquestionable love of the Arts took a rather whimsical turn when, on the occasion of the launch of the tanker *Benedick* at Glasgow he thoughtfully offered to take my mother, who was to name the ship later in the day, on a tour of the city. When they had seen all that he thought she ought to see and since they had some time left, he decided that it would be to her advantage if she were to meet one or two of his old business cronies. On entering a particularly drab office building, the Chairman of Bowring's and erstwhile Lord Mayor of Liverpool, addressed the elderly commissionaire with the request that he would like to see his old friend Sir John Cargill. 'Oh,' said the somewhat perplexed functionary, with due respect and solemnity, 'that will be difficult for, d'ye see, sir, Sir John died some three years back.'

'In that case, Agnes,' said the ever unruffled Sir Frederick, 'we shall go to the Art Gallery.'

During his two years as Lord Mayor he became well known for the splendour of the official dinners he gave, especially on the occasion of the visit of King George V and Queen Mary for the opening of the Gladstone Dock. He was no less renowned for the lavish dinners he hosted at his home, Terra Nova, though his generosity and other virtues were sometimes tempered by stubborn determination not to be found wrong. As he was unmarried, his sister, Charlotte Hope, performed the duties of lady mayoress. At one of his famous dinners his distinguished guests were standing around restlessly waiting for him to appear. He was often, quite probably on purpose, a few minutes late. When eventually he did appear and everyone was ushered hurriedly into the dining room, Charlotte noticed that his white bow tie was missing. A bright shining brass collar-stud, visible to all, was the cause of much whispered comment.

'Frederick,' Charlotte said for all to hear. 'You have forgotten to put on your tie.'

'Nonsense,' he is said to have replied, sitting down and unfolding his napkin. 'I never had any intention of putting it on.'

And there was the occasion when he was catching a train from Liverpool's Lime Street Station to London. As he walked down the platform, splendid in silk hat and spats, he was greeted by the stationmaster who, properly bedecked with much gold braid as was his custom when meeting distinguished travellers, said that he was very sorry that Sir Frederick had missed the 11.30, the tail of which could be seen disappearing out of the station and on which he had intended to travel. 'I do not happen to be late for the 11.30,' said he who never wished to be found to have erred, 'I simply happen to be a little early for the 12.15.'

He had appointed as his personal assistant his nephew J. E. B. (Jack) Hope, Charlotte's son. From time to time, usually at the end of the week, he would summon Jack to clear up a few outstanding matters and to empty his briefcase. One Friday afternoon, following a lengthy lunch at his club, the ritual was being customarily pursued at Sir Frederick's desk, the briefcase open in front of him and Jack sitting on his right. The contents, which consisted mostly of business papers and old letters, were passed hurriedly one by one to Jack, accompanied, more often than not, by the command 'File that away, Jack, file that away,' and so on. Suddenly, as related by Jack something very hard and rough hit him across the bridge of his nose removing a sizeable slice of skin, accompanied by the words, 'File that away.' The missile proved to be an ancient railway sandwich which had been lurking at the bottom of the brief case quite clearly for several weeks, such was the rasp-like condition of the crust.

Sir Frederick Bowring was especially generous to his relations and having no children would often give expensive presents. Many nephews and nieces and other relatives would assemble at Terra Nova to celebrate Christmas. Each year he would call the family together on Christmas Day around the billiard table, on which were laid a great variety of beautifully wrapped gifts. When all were present, standing expectantly around the table, he would position himself at one end and, with a billiard cue, propel each gift across the table to the excited beneficiaries, who, of course, had no idea what they were about to receive. 'This is for you, Betty,' or 'that is for you, Tom,' he would pronounce in majestic tones. Since he could not necessarily recognize from the shape of the parcels what they contained, it was almost certain, for example, that Betty would find herself clasping a gold-plated razor while Tom would be not a little surprised to receive a diamond ring. Heated discussions would follow to decide who should claim what, during which the seasonal spirit of peace and goodwill was at some risk.

But it was not only as a public-spirited, extremely competent businessman, that Sir Frederick Bowring would be remembered, but also for his philanthropy. He made countless gifts to charitable organizations and gave valuable time serving on the museums', art galleries' and public libraries' committees. He would have found himself moving at some speed between the boardrooms of well-known Liverpool companies, spirited hither and thither in his immaculate dark red Sunbeam coupe with his faithful, reliable and patient chauffeur, Mr Craig at the wheel. As well as his chairmanship of C. T. Bowring & Co. Ltd and its growing number of associated companies, he was a director of Barclays Bank, the Liverpool & London & Globe Insurance Company and the Liverpool Overhead Railway Company; he was president of the Shipbrokers' Benevolent Society, the Liverpool Domestic Mission Society, The Adult Deaf and Dumb Society, the Florence Institute for Boys, the Liverpool branch of the Royal Society for Prevention of Cruelty to Children and of the Reform Club. His other interests, which were many, included committee membership of Lloyd's Register, the Gordon Smith Institute for Seamen, the Liverpool Merchants' Guild, the Hospital for Diseases of the Heart, the Liverpool School of Tropical Medicine and he was a member of the University Council.

Of Uncle Fred, the Bishop of Liverpool, Dr David, said: 'He was a man of very attractive simplicity with which was combined a native shrewdness that sought no concealment, and never worked in hidden ways. He was transparently honest, and his plain common sense was a surer guide to success than brilliance often is in other men. He was eminent among those who have made Liverpool great in commerce and have faithfully served her.' Under his leadership Bowring's made great strides on all sides; he would be a hard act to follow. But, in the safe and competent hands of his younger brother, Sir Edgar Bowring, who succeeded him in London as Chairman, the company pressed on in good shape to face the difficult years that lay ahead.

I am indebted to David Keir for one final anecdote, quoted in *The Bowring Story*, which throws an amusing light on Sir Frederick's simplicity of approach: 'He was travelling in Italy in the twenties with a

civic delegation which was duly presented to Il Duce at an early stage of
the Fascist dictator's career. Portentously the Duce gave them the Fascist
salute. There was then a pause which ended suitably when the Liberal
Sir Frederick, after digesting all the rodomontade, calmly held out his
hand and said: 'How do you do, Mr Mussolini?"

Chapter 14

A T THE ONSET OF the Second World War there was much apprehension among those in Bowring's who remembered the previous war, especially those who were specifically involved with shipping and insurance, that there would be a repetition of the devastating losses suffered between 1914 and 1918. And their concern was not misplaced. During the first six months of hostilities more than five per cent or over 150,000 tons of the British tanker fleet had been sunk – and the first to go was Bowring's *Regent Tiger*, when she was on passage from Trinidad to Avonmouth with a cargo of motor spirit and diesel oil. She was already at sea when war was declared and on 8 September, at 10.20 a.m., when less than 250 miles from home, she was ordered to heave to by a U-Boat which, having ordered the crew to abandon ship, set her ablaze with one well-aimed torpedo. The U-Boat then submerged, leaving Captain Roberts and his crew of 43 men to the elements. Fortunately they were soon sighted by a Belgian ship, which picked them up and put them ashore three days later at Ramsgate.

A year later, on 15 September 1940, *Regent Lion*, also on a voyage from Trinidad with a similar cargo, was extensively damaged by bombs and gunfire from enemy aircraft when off Mull of Kintyre with the loss of two men killed and one wounded. For his part in this action Captain Jury was appointed an OBE. This was but the first of *Regent Lion's* wartime misfortunes.

On 16 December 1942, as part of an Atlantic convoy, she was torpedoed by a U-Boat (U–610) in rough weather. When the crew were ordered to abandon ship one of the lifeboats sank, and two men were crushed to death when an escorting destroyer came alongside in an attempt to pick up survivors. But *Regent Lion* was not to be defeated; she refused to sink and was towed back home to be repaired. However, having performed sterling service for nearly the whole war, she met her end on 17 February 1945 seven miles south of Cape Trafalgar, when on passage from New York to Bizerta with 12,440 tons of gasoline. Three men were killed following a direct hit on the engine-room by a torpedo from a U-Boat (U–300), but most of the crew, under the command of

Captain Colin Pitt OBE, were taken off by an America destroyer. A salvage party attempted for six hours to lighten her by discharging some of her cargo of high-octane fuel. At some considerable risk, HM Trawler *Arctic Ranger* came alongside and, with the help of a tug, tried to make for the shore. However, the weather deteriorated and with the damage now becoming terminal, *Regent Lion* ran aground on La Perla Rocks one mile south of Carnero Point just twelve hours after being torpedoed. For several weeks further salvage work was attempted, but to no avail. She was finally towed into Tangiers where she was declared a total loss. After surviving two U-Boat attacks, *Regent Lion* finally succumbed.

Other ships owned or managed by Bowring's, like the two already mentioned, were to meet their end as a result of enemy action during the earliest weeks and months of the war. On 11 January 1940 *El Oso*, a Lobitos Oilfields tanker under the company's management, struck a magnetic mine and sank six miles west of the Bar lightship at the entrance to the Mersey when bringing a cargo of crude oil from Peru to Stanlow on the Manchester Ship Canal. The next victim on 19 September 1940, this time sunk by a German surface raider, was the steam tanker *Cymbeline*. She was under Admiralty requisition and on passage from Gibraltar to Trinidad in ballast. Her master, Captain Chadwick, suspected from daybreak that he was being shadowed, but it wasn't until 8.30 in the evening that the enemy vessel, *Narvik*, struck, killing seven of the crew of 35, the rest being taken prisoner. The Master however, with his Chief Officer and the Third Engineer, managed to escape capture by seizing one of the ship's lifeboats in which they were adrift for two weeks before being picked up by the tanker *Yolanda* and landed at Covenas in Venezuela.

And so the gloomy news of losses continued to reach the company's London offices at 52 Leadenhall Street. Towards the end of the year yet another of the company's cargo vessels, *Anthea*, was sunk in the Atlantic in unusual circumstances. Under the command of Captain Watts she had joined an Atlantic convoy after loading a cargo of timber from Newfoundland. At 3.00 a.m. on the morning of 8 December, a Dutch ship, sailing independently in the same area, cut across the convoy and collided with *Anthea* with such force that she sank very soon afterwards. The next Bowring ship to be lost was, coincidentally, *Anthea's* sister ship, *Urla*, torpedoed and sunk on 28 January 1941. She was carrying a cargo of steel and timber from Boston and Halifax to Manchester and had left the convoy because her speed had dropped owing to inferior coal. It was some days before the office received any news beyond the fact that a British warship had rescued a number of survivors. Information followed, however, that the Chief Officer and 13 members of the crew were landed at Londonderry after being two days adrift, and on 3 February the office heard that Captain Marsden and a further 27 members of his crew, after almost a week in a stormy Atlantic, had been landed at Oban. *Anthea* and *Urla* were named after two of the daughters of Edward Hugh Bowring Skimming, the son of Dr Skimming who was married to the eldest daughter of Edward Bowring, Fanny Charlotte.

Marie Maersk, the next to be lost was, in fact, a Danish ship, which had been seized at Gibraltar as a Prize of War and handed over by the Government to Bowring's for operational purposes. On 22 March 1941 she sustained serious damage in an air attack off Crete and was again bombed on 12 April at Salamis Bay after which she was escorted by the Royal Navy into the harbour at Piraeus. Here she was captured with her crew of 37 when Germans occupied the port on 27 April.

The Lobitos tanker, *El Mirlo*, under Captain Pedersen, suffered bomb damage, both in March and November 1941, in raids on Liverpool and the Manchester Ship Canal, but survived the rest of the war. Captain Richardson's *Capulet*, however, was not so fortunate, and was torpedoed in the Atlantic on 28 April 1941 on passage from Curaçao to Scapa Flow with a cargo of fuel oil while under Admiralty requisition. Her back was broken and she was eventually sunk by gunfire. Of her complement of 39 crew, two gunners and three passengers, eight crew and one passenger were lost. In 1942 two ships managed by Bowring's for the Government became casualties. In September *Empire Oil* was torpedoed and sunk off St John's and in December, a Belgian tanker, *President Francqui*, which had been placed under Bowring management when Belgium was invaded by the Germans, was sunk by a U-Boat.

There were to be two more casualties before the loss of *Regent Lion* in 1945. On 3 February 1943 *Cordelia*, on a voyage from Curaçao and New York to the Clyde with 12,000 tons of Admiralty fuel oil, was torpedoed and sunk whilst under Admiralty charter. All her crew of 39 and eight gunners were lost with the exception of one engineer who was captured. This was a particularly disturbing loss for the company since it was the first time that virtually an entire ship's complement had died without there being any radio warning. *Cordelia* had left her convoy to carry out repairs and, in a severe Atlantic storm, was struck by two torpedoes from a U-Boat, which in spite of the appalling conditions, surfaced. With the aid of its searchlight it apparently picked up a life-raft on which a number of the crew were drifting. When the Captain of the U-Boat found out that one of them was an engineer he took him prisoner and left the rest to the mercy of the storm. They were never heard of again. Some months later a card arrived at the Leadenhall Street office from the Chief Engineer, Mr Bingham, reporting that he was a prisoner of war in Germany and it wasn't until he was repatriated at the end of the war that he was able to give an account of the tragic end of *Cordelia* and her crew.

The last recorded wartime loss of a Bowring owned or managed ship (apart from *Regent Lion* reported earlier) was due to air attack. The Lobitos tanker *El Grillo*, while under Admiralty requisition and carrying a cargo of 8,500 tons of fuel oil and 285 tons of diesel oil, was sunk by bombs from German aircraft at Seidisfjord, Iceland on 10 February 1944. Her guns did their best to ward off the raiders, but it was not possible to save the ship and she sank very quickly, but without any serious injuries to the crew of 40 and nine gunners, all of whom were saved.

That commercial endeavour should become hedged about with controls and restrictions of one kind or another soon after the outbreak of war came as no surprise to anyone, and it was natural in order to ensure the safe and fair distribution of commodities and essential goods, and to conserve foreign currency, that the Government should introduce import licensing for a wide range of products. For Bowring, Jones and Tidy the privations caused by government intervention came in August 1941. Until then the importation and distribution of Naval Stores, chiefly from the United States because other sources were cut off, had continued, subject to Import Licences, through normal trade channels. But a ship, the *Bradglen*, carrying what turned out to be the last privately imported cargo of rosin and turpentine for the duration of the war, was sunk by enemy action in the Thames estuary. BJT, who had worked at all times in close touch with the Government in order to ensure that those customers in urgent need would receive their supplies, had frequently borrowed from a customer with ample stocks to supply another in a less fortunate position. With the sinking of the *Bradglen*, the company found it was unable to 'pay back' the supplies it had borrowed, which were dependent upon the vessel's safe arrival.

This situation gave rise to the formation of the United Kingdom Naval Stores Association Ltd, and involved the seconding of a senior member of the Bowring Jones and Tidy staff to the Ministry of Supply.

The Association remained in existence until the abolition of controls in 1949, and was responsible during that time for holding and distributing, as agents of the Government, every ton of Naval Stores imported. There was a constant reminder for several years after the misfortune that befell *Bradglen* of the need for the Association; drums of turpentine were frequently washed up on the south and east coasts of England during stormy winter weather.

A somewhat similar arrangement was made for the distribution of oils and oilseeds, in this case the organization acting as agents for the Ministry of Food and enjoying the rather inflated designation of the United Kingdom Oil and Oilseed Brokers Association Ltd. Although the manager of BJT'S Oils and Oilseeds department played a leading part in this Association, ultimate control was in the hands of the Ministry of Food.

During the mid 30s BJT had entered the coffee business, probably as a result of this commodity being stored at Soho Works. (There would eventually, however, be a much larger involvement in this trade.) The normal activity of this small, seemingly unrelated department was to purchase coffee from shippers overseas, acting as their European representatives, and to sell it on to buyers in the UK and across the Channel. But the business was totally frustrated by the German occupation of the importing countries, and it wasn't until many years after the war that it was partially resumed.

Fish oils and fishmeal both came under Government control to some extent. The fishmeal factory at Grimsby was earmarked as being of national importance from the beginning of hostilities because of its contribution to animal feed production. For this reason most of its staff were exempted from military service, though it is likely that in their spare time they would be serving in the Home Guard, Civil Defence or one or other of the numerous voluntary services such as Air Raid Precautions (ARP), nursing or fire-watching.

The activities of C. T. Bowring & Co. (Fish Oils) Ltd also came under the partial control of the Ministry of Food. Feeling very uneasy about the low stocks in the country of cod liver oil and of its apparent wastage, the company put forward a plan, which was readily accepted by the Ministry. The suggestion was that the Ministry should not be thinking of cod liver oil in isolation, but of the nation's nutritional requirements in terms of vitamin oils in general. Other plentifully available oils such as whale oil and seal oil could be used as carriers for natural and synthetic vitamins or blended with cod liver oil. It was also thought that, as a consequence of this concept, vitamin oils should be assessed not in terms of quantity but of their potency or vitamin content. Robbie Johnston, the managing director of the Fish Oils Company, was one of the Government's marine oil advisers, and the company was given the special duty of buying any marine oils which were specially needed. The company also bought large quantities of fish liver oils for the Ministry from South America. The premises at Oriel Street, where fish oils were stored, were completely destroyed by enemy bombing in May 1941, and the refinery at Blackstock Street suffered severe damage.

With war raging over the Continent it was unlikely that the news emanating from Bowring's fishmeal companies in Germany and Holland could be anything but depressing. The Nazi Government blocked all the funds of Fischmehl Einfuhr in Hamburg and Gunther Gienow, the managing director, was drafted into a labour battalion in 1941 following his earlier arrest. After the war, when it became possible to re-establish contact, management was restored and the company was revived under Gunther Gienow who, though his health had suffered during the war years, continued successfully to run the business until his retirement in 1964.

Vischmeel NV in Rotterdam, on the other hand, continued to operate throughout the war despite the destruction of its office in the bombing of the city in 1940 and, as we shall see, considerable variations in the character of its trading. The company's auditor had kept duplicate records, thus enabling the business to continue after the bombing under the direction of Piet Rottinghuis, though he was faced with mounting difficulties following the German occupation. The Nazis, in an exchange of prisoners, had arrested his predecessor, the Russian immigrant Mr K. Lifschitz, and sent him back to the Soviet Union. The authorities had appointed an official trustee whose sole interest, it appears, was to turn up once a month to collect the salary that the company was required to pay him. Since all animal foodstuffs were eventually placed under total Government control the company sought alternative business opportunities and became engaged in trading such unlikely items as toothbrushes, wooden brooches carved by members of the Dutch resistance movement and, perhaps oddest of all, talcum powder.

There was one more short-lived business which was started during the war and survived for a short while thereafter. This was a company called Underwater Welders & Repairers Ltd, which Bowring's had acquired just after the war started and which owned the patent rights to an invention which ought to have been a greater success than it turned out to be. As its name implies the process, which was invented by a Frenchman domiciled in Egypt, allowed welding to take place under water, which made it possible to salvage wartime wrecks. This could have been of particular value in the removal of vessels that had been sunk in the entrances to harbours. But its application was limited, even in wartime, and it ceased to be of further interest to Bowring's shortly after the end of hostilities.

While the trading companies were doing their best to prosecute their businesses successfully under difficult conditions, Bowring's main offices didn't escape the attention of the *Luftwaffe*. The port of Liverpool suffered grievous damage from German bombing during 1940, and in mid-March 1941, two successive nights of blitz set much of the docks and the city ablaze. There were further raids in May and Bowring's along with many other companies were seriously hit. The offices in India Buildings, Water Street were set on fire with disastrous results. All but a few scorched remnants of the company's records were destroyed and in the three days it took to recover what remained, it was found, when the safes were opened, that the money in the cash boxes had been melted and fused by the heat. Because of the helpfulness of the Liverpool business community, office space, albeit spread about the city, was soon found. Account books were acquired and new company records were opened. However, it was not until 1943 that all departments in Liverpool were reunited in offices at Tower Building, Water Street.

In London, frequent air raids brought business to a halt. It had been one of the duties of the shipping department in London to pay out allotments to seamen's wives and families. The need for prompt payment to the beneficiaries was seriously threatened by these raids on London and the responsibility had been transferred to Liverpool. Fortunately, before this became necessary, the London office had made duplicates of the relevant records and, during the disruption in Liverpool, saw to it that the expected allotments were paid on time. In due course it was possible to return this duty back to the Liverpool office.

As with most offices in the City arrangements were made among those members of the staff for whom it would not be too inconvenient and who were also willing, to volunteer for night-time fire-watching at the office. This generally boring but not infrequently frightening chore on the roof of the Leadenhall Street office, armed with rudimentary fire-fighting equipment in expectation of the arrival of incendiary bombs, seemed to attract a number of senior directors and managers, perhaps because they were more likely to have houses or flats in London and were not faced with too much travelling. But it seems more likely that, when not actually on duty they could walk across the street to a subterranean club of which they had all become members, where there was a snooker table and adequate and varied supplies of morale raising beverages. In a number of cases it was perfectly clear that what was claimed after a night on duty to be post fire-watching fatigue was quite simply a thumping hangover.

Although spared the perils of bombing raids and the ever-present threat of invasion – at least, during the early part of the war – Bowring's subsidiary companies on the other side of the Atlantic played a significant part in the struggle against the Axis powers.

From their office at 17 Battery Place, New York, overlooking the entrance to the Bay and the Statue of Liberty, it was for Bowring and Company very much a case of 'business as usual' though with rather more responsibility, in as much as the company's ships' agency department was involved in handling tankers and ammunition carriers as well as pursuing the firm's other business of importing metals and ores from those sources not made inaccessible by hostilities.

In Newfoundland the impact of the war was inevitably more immediately felt. The island had no direct defences of any kind, no arms and no training equipment. But it became obvious in the spring of 1940 following the military collapse in Europe that, from a North American perspective, an undefended Newfoundland posed a serious hazard. Soon the Governments of the United Kingdom and Newfoundland established a naval base at St John's on behalf of the Admiralty, to be managed by the Canadian Navy. And, in September 1940, the British Government sanctioned the construction of United States bases in Newfoundland. A civilian airport already existed at Gander and this was quickly modified for military purposes. Henceforth, the island was to play an increasingly important part in the Battle of the Atlantic, and St John's harbour soon became strategically significant. Among the many contributions that it would make throughout the war, the harbour became a safe haven for the convoy escort vessels which protected the merchant ships carrying the much-needed food and equipment upon which the Allies in Europe would depend in the years ahead.

In May 1940 Eric Bowring, who was Chairman of Bowring Brothers, received a cable from the Ministry of Shipping in London, which read:

> I shall be glad to know by telegram whether you are willing to accept appointment as Ministry of Shipping representative in Newfoundland. It is expected that a large number of ships will be sent to load each month under Ministry of Shipping instructions to lift timber, pit props, pulpwood, wood pulp, iron ore and zinc concentrates. Duties of Minister's representative would be to supervise such shipping whilst in Newfoundland and assist as far as possible in ensuring ships are properly handled with a view to quickest despatch and are dealt with in accordance with the Ministry's instructions.

The comparatively straightforward instructions in the cable belied the complicated and time-consuming nature of the task with which Eric was faced. He had barely cabled his acceptance of the appointment when the first vessel requiring his undivided attention arrived to load a cargo of iron ore and pit props. He always made sure that such ships carried a fair quantity of codfish, cod liver oil and pickled herring, to accompany their industrial cargoes.

However, it is unlikely that Eric could have had the remotest idea of just how complicated the problems with which he was to be confronted would become. Berths had to be found for unexpected arrivals together with facilities for loading and discharging cargoes; fuelling and repairs needed to be dealt with; consideration had to be given to ways of accommodating survivors from torpedoed vessels and crews awaiting the completion of repairs to their ships. While he had these personal responsibilities to deal with, the office of Bowring Brothers, over whose functions he presided in addition to their normal trading activities, were required, in their capacity as ships agents and as agent at St John's for Lloyd's and the Salvage Association, to deal with an endless stream of shipping casualties. A director of the company wrote later of these diverse duties:

> We were complementary to him (Eric). We supervised damage repairs, paid the bills and reported to owners by code through the naval authorities. Although the Representative was looked to for the care of survivors brought into St John's it was the company which had to clothe, feed and house them and arrange their repatriation. Certificates of seaworthiness had to be arranged through Bowring Brothers as Lloyd's Agents. And at one very critical period when there was a grave shortage

of ships' lifeboats we even set up a factory which built many hundreds of lifeboats and so fulfilled a pressing national requirement.

So busy did St John's harbour become that there were times when it was possible to cross from one side to the other by stepping from ship to ship. In fact when *Gloucester City* arrived in November 1940 with survivors from torpedoed vessels, to be followed by more ships crowding in, it became necessary to redirect them to the nearby harbour at Bay Bulls. Congestion soon became critical. Halifax, Nova Scotia and St John, New Brunswick, were soon suffering the same problem and there was no clear answer other than to improve and extend the harbour, for which Eric Bowring made an urgent appeal to the Newfoundland Government. He also asked the repair yards to attend first to ships that were not too severely damaged so as to get them away as quickly as possible in order to reduce the acute overcrowding. So successful were these measures that, within six months the dockyards were looking for more work.

This greatly improved state of affairs was not, however, to be long lasting. The Admiralty decided that St John's was needed as a more permanent home for the escort destroyers and that the harbour should continue to be designated a naval base. This inevitably brought back overcrowding and Eric Bowring's suggestion, supported by the Ministry of Shipping, that some other Newfoundland harbour, such as Heart's Content for example, should be used was dismissed by the Admiralty who insisted that it should be St John's.

Although there remained a demand for seal oil during the war, the number of ships at the ice in 1941 was, as mentioned earlier, reduced to four, three of them belonging to Bowring Brothers, *Terra Nova, Eagle* and *Ranger*. But in 1942, for the first time in over a century, there were no Bowring ships at the ice front. While the company's vessels occasionally sailed from St John's for the ice in future years, the days of the seal hunt as it had been during Bowring's developing years in Newfoundland had virtually come to an end.

Chapter 15

THE FACT THAT London was a prime target for the Luftwaffe, and that the majority of Bowring's staff worked there for C. T. Bowring & Co. (Insurance) Ltd had exercised the minds of the directors ever since the possibility of war had become apparent. It was clear that the company would have to bear the brunt of the inevitable, routine-destroying changes that wartime conditions would bring. During the early part of the two years or more before America joined the Allies there was much concern as to whether or not American companies would be willing to continue using the London market, having regard to the many complications that would surely arise. What would be the position, for example, if communications were to break down – or how would it be possible to conduct marine insurance business under the shroud of secrecy demanded by wartime conditions? To some extent these anxieties had already been foreseen by Lloyd's who, with commendable vision shortly before the outbreak of war, had created the Lloyd's American Trust, a fund the size of which was believed to be sufficient to meet the needs of underwriters.

The American market, too, took precautionary measures by the introduction of the American Cargo War Risks Reinsurance Exchange. This was virtually a pool into which American insurance companies placed their cargo war risks insurance. The reinsurance of the pool was then placed in the London market. In order to expedite the implementation of this procedure, the companies were asked to suggest a London broker to act as their sole representative there, and they chose Bowring's.

But this was not the only occasion on which preferential consideration was given to the company by the American market, further enhancing the already well-established mutual confidence and trust that had been building up over the years. When the United States joined the Allies in December 1941 the US Government's Maritime Commission took on the marine insurance for American merchant vessels. This business was duly handed to a group of domestic insurers, known as the American Marine Insurance Syndicate, who, on the basis of a complex agreement, serviced it for the Government. This arrangement required the appointment of a single American broker to handle the technicalities of the scheme agreed between the Commission and the Syndicate – and it was Marsh & McLennan who were selected. Since the Syndicate had decided to forgo a share of the business to the London market by way of reinsurance, it was resolved that a single broker should be involved – and Bowring's, once again, were chosen.

Whilst Lloyd's, in spite of inevitable wartime doubts and misgivings, continued to enjoy the confidence of the market generally, there were one or two overseas companies whose nervousness became apparent during those dark, uncertain early days of the war, and who withdrew their business from the London market. One such company in the United States, which had for many years placed its reinsurances with Bowring's, decided early in the war, to take its business elsewhere. As it happened, Bowring's were able to retain half of the business; but the other half went to the American market. By an ironic twist, the American insurer decided to reinsure at Lloyd's – and nominated Bowring's as the broker.

Office work in wartime London presented far reaching administrative and organizational problems. By no means least among them was the evacuation from the City of large numbers of staff. In an article for the *Bowring Magazine*, which was revived in 1952 after a short pre-war existence, Harry Chapman, a well-remembered and long-serving member of C. T. Bowring & Co. (Insurance) Ltd, wrote in an article entitled *The Great Exodus*:

On Monday (4 September 1939; war was declared the previous day) the staff assembled at 52 Leadenhall Street as usual, quite ignorant of impending events. At a hurriedly-called meeting of all departmental managers and seniors, it was announced to their astonishment that the bulk of employees, numbering between 450 and 500, complete with records, typewriters and equipment would forthwith move to Boreham Wood (*now known as Borehamwood*). Lorries had been engaged beforehand and were in attendance under the control of a senior who assumed in masterly manner the orderly dispatch of each vehicle as it was loaded.

It was a case of all hands to the pumps. All members of the staff took a hand excitedly parcelling and labelling, and, department by department, the office was gradually stripped. The staircases were thronged with an endless chain of laden personnel conveying parcels from the office to waiting lorries. As they were filled, so they were dispatched with male

guards perched precariously on top complete with bowler – or trilby –
hat, striped trousers and umbrella. Fortunately, the weather was perfect.

Only the broking staff, underwriting accounts personnel and a few others,
whose presence in London was essential, remained at the Leadenhall
Street office. The 'evacuees' had to be provided with office accommodation, housing, restaurant facilities and some opportunity for recreation.
Harry Chapman continues:

> This was no two – or three-day picnic – it was for the duration so far as
> one could see and nobody could foretell the duration of the war. In the
> event, the staff was evacuated for nearly six years.

Nobody, it seems, knew much about Boreham Wood or, indeed,
where it was. At that time it was a small village, some fourteen miles
outside London, near Elstree, with whose film industry it was associated.
'It is interesting to note', the narrative continues:

> that the discovery of Boreham Wood for the firm's purpose was largely a
> matter of luck plus a certain amount of foresight, and was the outcome of
> a chance telephone conversation following much fruitless searching by
> those who had been given the formidable task of finding suitable office
> accommodation and housing in competition with many other business
> houses engaged upon similar problems.
>   A film studio, which at that time was not operating, had been taken over by
> the Ministry of Food. Following negotiations, the firm were given permission
> to use such portions of the studio as were not required by the Ministry.

Communication with the London office was a serious problem; there
was only one telephone line. This problem was overcome to some extent
by the engagement of a single telephone operator assisted by an army of
runners. This somewhat tenuous arrangement was supplemented by the
acquisition of a car and chauffeur to maintain daily physical contact with
the City by carrying records and personnel.

The greater problems, however, were those of housing and feeding.
For the majority of members of the staff to have to travel from their
homes would have taken up so much time as to absorb most of the
working day. So acceptable sleeping accommodation had to be found.
Once again, Boreham Wood was able, fortuitously, to provide the
answer. Recently built blocks of flats were found to be unoccupied and
were secured, against the likely possibility of being taken over by the
Army, by the simple exercise of squatters' rights. A gallant group of male
volunteers took them over and secured them until they had been made

suitable for occupation by the female members of the staff. This involved the purchase of great quantities of beds and bedding, carpeting, kitchen equipment, furniture of various kinds, and other items appropriate to a reasonably civilized existence.

While some of the girls decided to make their own arrangements and to do their own housekeeping, for which they were given a billeting allowance, the majority decided to move into the flats. For many of them this would be their first time away from home, but the strange new lifestyle was accepted joyfully in a spirit of adventure, any inconvenience suffered being seen as their contribution to the war effort.

The men, however, sought their accommodation separately, some of them establishing their quarters in the star's dressing rooms of the studio and others being given lodging in a house nearby, which had been made available by one of the company's directors. For the convenience of all, the working week was condensed into five days so that everyone had the opportunity of spending a full weekend at home.

Without doubt the most challenging aspect of the move, was the problem of feeding nearly 500 members of the staff at midday, Monday to Friday. Restaurant facilities in Boreham Wood village were virtually non-existent. So Bowring's were faced with their first venture into catering. Harry Chapman takes up the story:

> A tiny restaurant of sorts was being operated within the studio for the benefit of the maintenance staff, and the proprietor and his wife were co-opted. A large, somewhat dirty shed, formerly the plasterers' shop, was reconditioned, furnished with up-to-date kitchen equipment, as well as tables and chairs, and under the initial supervision and guidance of an expert loaned by the A.B.C. (a then well-known nation-wide catering company) an efficient cafeteria was installed capable of seating some 100 odd at a sitting. Prices subsidized by the firm were moderate and the food offered was varied and adequate, especially in the early days before the impact of rationing began to be felt. The canteen, as it became known, was a veritable godsend, as it not only catered primarily for the needs of the staff, but later, when the studio began to operate, it supplied the wants of the hordes of 'extras' who, without warning suddenly descended upon Boreham Wood ... The manager's foresight in buying before rationing became acute was perhaps not always fully appreciated, but the least of his admirers must admit that he fulfilled a difficult task under most adverse conditions and meals were provided during the whole of the war.

★   ★   ★

It would, I think, be fair to say that up until the outbreak of the Second World War Bowring's were still probably as well known as shipowners and traders as they were in insurance. But the loss of ships in both wars and the curtailment of trading opportunities had seriously reduced the significance of these two areas of endeavour, while insurance continued to prosper, albeit somewhat hamstrung by regulations and reduced scope of activity. Nevertheless, the company continued to build new ships and to carry on developing its varied trading activities; but as expected, it was the insurance business that would grow most rapidly in the years ahead. As the company embarks upon the next thirty-five years of general expansion, though not, it must be said, in all areas, it might be worthwhile to catch a glimpse of the major players.

At the outbreak of war Sir Edgar Bowring was Chairman of C. T. Bowring & Co. Ltd having succeeded his older brother, Sir Frederick, on his death in 1936. 'Uncle Sir Edgar', as we called him, was a quiet, unassuming man of considerable charm, who had spent many years in Newfoundland where his devotion to the island manifested itself in countless acts of outstanding generosity. His eventual departure from his birthplace was prompted to some extent by medical advice; it was thought that he should seek a less rigorous climate. But, notwithstanding unidentified health problems, his taking up residence in England can be attributed, as much as anything else, to his being appointed from 1918 to 1922, Newfoundland's High Commissioner in London, and again from 1933 to 1934. In both cases he gave his services gratuitously, as he also did from 1912 to 1914 when serving on the Dominions Royal Commission, which was set up to foster closer links between the Commonwealth countries and involved visits to Australia, New Zealand, South Africa and Canada. Following his second appointment as High Commissioner he was created a Knight Commander of the Order of St Michael and St George.

In addition to his being responsible for the gift of Bowring Park, for the benefit and enjoyment of the citizens of St John's, he commissioned for the park a sculpture by Sir George Frampton of Peter Pan, identical to the one in Hyde Park, London, in memory of his goddaughter Betty Munn who, it will be recalled, was drowned with her father when the steamship *Florizel* sank off Cappahayden on 24 February 1918. Further-more, as a tribute to and in undying memory of the Royal Newfound-land Regiment, of which he was a loyal and generous friend, he gave a memorial statue, The Fighting Newfoundlander, which also stands in Bowring Park.

His domestic arrangements seemed to us when young to be rather mysterious, perhaps because we were thought not to be old enough to understand the circumstances. He lived for many years after leaving Newfoundland in a luxurious apartment which he shared with a handsome, statuesque lady whom we knew as 'Cousin May', on the top floor of what was then the Hyde Park Hotel. What we didn't know was that on 11 January 1888 he had married at St John's a widow, Flora LeMessurier Munn. It was her son, John Shannon Munn, who with his small daughter, Betty lost their lives in the *Florizel* disaster. They were on their way to New York to be with his wife who was in hospital undergoing treatment. John Munn had married Alice May McCowen in January 1908 in the Anglican Cathedral at St John's, an occasion described by the local press at the time as one of the city's more memorable social events. Edgar's wife, Flora, had died in 1898. He took compassion on his deceased wife's widowed daughter-in-law, Alice ('Cousin May') and she became his constant companion and remained with him for the rest of his life. Their partnership was shared, in some degree, with May's personal maid, the rather emaciated and lugubrious but devout Roman catholic Alice Kerridge, who followed her everywhere at a discreet distance casting covetous eyes on her mink coats, of which there were more than one and which, in the fullness of time and to her undisguised delight, she inherited. They were, however, at least six inches too long and for the next few years played their part in sweeping clean the pavements of Hove whither Cousin May had gravitated following Sir Edgar's death on 23 June 1943.

My few recollections of 'Uncle Sir Edgar' are, nevertheless, very clear. In the thirties, around Christmas time my brother, two sisters and I would enjoy an excursion to London with the specific object of being treated by him to a visit to the pantomime. My inordinate and growing passion for the motor car was, on our way to the theatre, well satisfied by being allowed to sit in the front of his huge black Phantom II Rolls Royce with my brother Henry and the faithful chauffer, Mr Whitall – plenty of room for all three. Memories of such occasions, as we weaved our majestic way through the London traffic, are far more vivid than any recollection of the actual pantomimes. But even memories of these occasions fade into insignificance when I recall the morning of my seventeenth birthday. 'Uncle Sir Edgar' had obviously noticed my interest in cars and rang up to ask me what car I would like to have as a birthday present. So generous was he that had I said I would like to have his Rolls Royce, I believe he would have given it to me. But rare and, in the circumstances, inexplicable modesty prevailed and I asked for and was given a small Standard 8 which cost him £128 delivered with a full tank of petrol, which during strict wartime rationing was probably worth almost as much as the car.

But my last and clearest memory of him is of a visit I made to the Hyde Park Hotel a few days before embarking for service overseas early in 1943. He had apparently told my father that he would like to see me before my departure. However, when I reached his bedside – he was now in his eighty-fifth year, very frail and mentally confused – he thought I *was* my father, although I was in uniform. I found that conversation with him was very difficult, being uncertain as to whether I should go along with his delusion or try and explain who I was. It eventually transpired that he thought I was on my way to Newfoundland and he implored me to be absolutely certain to visit Quidi Vidi Lake, at St John's, and make sure that his skiff was being properly looked after. It is unlikely that he would have seen the boat for many years, even if it still existed. My first letter from home when I arrived in Egypt brought the sad news that he had died a couple of months after my visit. He was a good if not outstanding chairman, some of his time being devoted to voluntary extramural activities, among which was his close association with the War Graves Commission. Outstanding among his many virtues were his thoughtfulness for others and his exceptional generosity.

The next chairman of C. T. Bowring & Co. Ltd was Edward Hugh Bowring Skimming (son of Charlotte, Edward Bowring's daughter). He was the first chairman of the company not to bear the Bowring name. Soon after joining, 'Ted' Skimming had been sent in 1903 to San Francisco to the West Coast branch of Bowring & Company. His main interest throughout his long business career was in shipping, a subject of which there were few more gifted specialists. He was made a Chevalier of the Legion d'Honneur for his services during the First World War on the Inter-Allied Chartering Executive and represented the London General Shipowners' Society on the General Committee of Lloyd's Register from 1934 to 1946. Although Bowring's would continue to operate a small but significant fleet of modern ships for many years, he was the last of the firm's representatives to uphold the international reputation earned by his forebears during the past 100 years of being among the world's major shipowners.

'Ted' Skimming, though aged sixty-eight when he became chairman, and no longer as energetic or of pioneering outlook as he had been as a younger man, was nevertheless thoroughly supportive of those ambitious members of his board of directors who, during his thirteen years in the chair, were responsible for creating an unprecedented period of expansion. The most active and apparently inexhaustible of these was undoubtedly my father, Frederick Clive Bowring, who had joined the company at Liverpool in 1920 at the age of twenty-three following four years with the army in France. His father, who was Henry Alfred, the youngest son of John and a grandson of the founder, left Newfoundland before the First World War. He died of pneumonia in 1919 aged sixty-three when he was managing the affairs of the Liverpool office. He was well known for his rather boisterous nature and, when returning home to the family residence in Sefton Park, more often than not in a somewhat inebriated state after an hour or two at his club, was known to take pity on the driver of the horse-drawn cab, whose seat was outside and exposed to the elements, and to give him his overcoat. Among those present at his well-attended funeral were, apparently, a large number of cab drivers elegantly and warmly clad in my grandfather's cast-offs.

When 'Ted' Skimming retired as chairman in 1956 it was my father who succeeded him. Frequently referred to as 'Young Fred' or simply 'FCB' by his colleagues, and as Mr Fred by the staff, he would confess never to have achieved even the most modest academic success, claiming that during his four years at Shrewsbury School he remained in the bottom form; and his awareness of most of what was happening in the world was derived solely from the business pages of the *Daily Express*. He nevertheless possessed a unique instinct for recognizing propitious business opportunities, which he would pursue relentlessly until they were brought to fruition or, as was rarely the case, reluctantly but sensibly laid aside. To the extent that restraint might, from time to time, seem appropriate, this was provided by his younger brother, Edgar, known as 'Egg', Uncle Egg, ERB or Mr Edgar, who was cautious to a fault. Never was there a more recognizable manifestation of the descriptions proactive and reactive. But they respected each other's points of view and seldom came to blows. I recall an occasion when I was privy to an eloquent example of their different personalities. They were leaving the office together for a business appointment and were standing waiting for the exasperatingly slow lift. After a few moments FCB took off down the stairs, two at a time, bowler hat at a jaunty angle saying 'Come on, Edgar, we're going to be late', to which his brother replied as he carefully pulled on his gloves, 'Slow down Frederick, gentlemen never hurry' – and continued to wait for the lift.

In fact Edgar was only pulling on one glove. His right hand was severely damaged by shellfire in France at the end of the First World War and he always wore a knitted woollen mitten to cover the scars. Of these mittens he had a great variety to suit any occasion and whatever clothes he happened to be wearing, and they were made of the best and most luxurious soft wools available. The story is told of a rare occasion when the two brothers found themselves in a well-known London nightclub after attending an official dinner where, no doubt, they would have acquired sufficient Dutch courage for one of them, probably my father, to suggest such a diversion. Of the hostesses available for their enjoyment that night only one was not already engaged and she sat between them in a shadowy corner of the club from which to watch the cabaret. It was not unknown for my father, on such occasions, to indulge in a little under-skirt exploration and, indeed, after a short time he was thus occupied. There came a moment when he thought that he had, as it were, struck home only to find that he was holding hands with his brother.

Neither of them would claim the insurance business as their chief interest although ERB was a director of a number of insurance companies including the Royal, the Liverpool & London & Globe, and the London and Lancs. He was also a director of the Cunard Steamship Company and of Martins Bank. FCB went from Liverpool to the London office in 1938, when the headquarters of the parent company was moved and ERB, who had started his career with Bowring Brothers in St John's shortly after the First World War, returned to England in the mid thirties to take charge of the Liverpool office. He didn't move to London until the mid fifties, which no doubt accounted for the fact that he had become a director of a number of Liverpool based companies, but in virtually every case, in a non-executive capacity. He was also appointed High Sheriff of Cheshire for the year 1948–49. FCB's 'outside' directorships, whilst probably not so prestigious, were almost certainly more numerous. Both were steeped in the traditional trading and shipping philosophy of previous generations, but they were nevertheless unstinting in their support of those responsible for the rapid progress and geographical spread of the insurance broking and underwriting activities and of the proliferation of subsidiary companies spawned by these developments.

The fortunes of C. T. Bowring & Co. (Insurance) Ltd were presided over by its chairman, Harvey Bowring. He had joined the company in 1904 shortly after its incorporation as a separate company and became a director in 1913. He was appointed to the board of the parent company in 1922. He was assisted by an extraordinarily able team of directors and brokers headed by Sidney Buckenham and including such well-experienced colleagues as Fred Bromley, James Steel, Laurence B. Stoddart, and Leslie Wimble, all of them in their own particular spheres of expertise worthy successors to those great pioneers Walter Hargreaves and Edward Stevinson. They would be followed in due course by a group of younger brokers, including Ian Skimming, Ivor Binney, Bruce Jenkinson, Ronnie Cottle, Simon Tonge, Richard Webster, Tom Bowring, Edgar Bowring and others whose names are likely to be mentioned again, and all of whom made significant contributions to the company's development.

Harvey Bowring was a big man by any standards and of a rubicund countenance which gave him a slightly pastoral benignity. He was, indeed, well liked by all with whom he came in contact, whether socially or in the course of business, and this may well account for his success, with his colleagues, in building up Bowring's growing reputation in the insurance world. The combination of his kindly demeanour and his highly developed knowledge of the business undoubtedly led to many years of the company's close relations with a number of the most important insurance organizations in the United States and, no doubt, his familiarity with baseball in general and with the World Series in particular would have contributed to the many lasting friendships that he made during his countless visits to America. He travelled extensively to all parts of the world for the company and enjoyed a facility for combining holidays, frequently accompanied by one or more of his grandchildren, with his business trips.

Both his sons, Peter Raphe and Ben joined the company after the war, the former becoming a well-respected and extremely able Lloyd's underwriter and Ben, an affable but somewhat unreliable marine broker, who transferred his unquestionable skill as a wartime fighter pilot to the almost equally lethal handling of a series of very fast cars. He possessed a well-developed talent for entertaining American business visitors who would often stay overnight at his home in Woking and suffer the drive into London the following morning, frequently after a hectic frolic the previous evening. There was an oft-repeated anecdote which claimed that, as the massive and indecently rapid supercharged 4½ litre Bentley wove its growling way through the suburbs, one of his terrified American guests said: 'I guess we must be getting pretty close to London.' – 'Of course we are' said Ben 'Why do you say that?' – 'It's just that we seem to be knocking more people down,' replied his panic-stricken guest. It was, in fact, a motoring offence that ended Ben's career with the company and he moved to another Lloyd's broker prepared to accept his somewhat cavalier attitude to life in general and his business responsibilities in particular. But for all his carelessness he was popular, loyal and generous friend. He was massively built and a comfort to sit next to on the train from Woking to the City on cold winter mornings; but to be avoided at all costs in summer.

Ben was yet another member of the family to escape narrowly from the hungry waves. He was flying with a group of motoring enthusiasts to Le Mans for the 24-hour car race. For reasons unknown their aircraft came down in the Channel. All but two of the passengers and the pilot lost their lives, but Ben, being well upholstered, was able to withstand the cold and supported a fellow enthusiast for several hours until they were miraculously picked up by a passing cargo vessel. The following day, still shivering like a jelly but wanting to do something to rid his mind of a frightening experience, he invited three of us to accompany him on a day's outing in the fearsome Bentley. If the terrors of the previous day could have been extinguished for him by instilling them into his passengers his day was a resounding success. It seemed that for three hours the wheels never touched the ground. We returned to our homes quivering wrecks while our intrepid driver was understood to have enjoyed a peaceful night's sleep.

During and after the Second World War a few non-executive directors joined the parent company board from outside. The first was Arthur Bowring Leather who was the son of Charles Tricks' youngest daughter, Edith Bowring who had married William Fishwick Leather. Popularly known as 'Tosh', Arthur Leather was a most valuable member of the board in his capacity as a distinguished solicitor and was the senior partner of the Liverpool firm of Alsop Stevens and Co. His son, another Arthur, was also with the company and was much involved in setting up Bowring's insurance activities in Australia. Geoffrey Milling, who had been a director of Bowring Brothers at St John's for many years, returned to England soon after the war to become the company's first non-family director and was soon appointed Chairman of The Bowring Steamship Company. Another post-war non-executive director to join the company was Philip Shelbourne, a director of N. M. Rothschild & Son and a barrister specializing in tax matters. During the middle sixties it was decided that the company should engage the services of a top ranking finance director, and in February 1965 Lambert Sharp, a highly experienced accountant, joined the board.

With the conduct of the company still under the direction of a mainly 'traditional' board there remained a strong desire to stay in shipping; but there was a growing tendency for those members whose main interest was beginning to veer towards insurance to question whether it was wise to spend a large part of profits, more and more of which were being derived from insurance, on ships whose return on the capital invested was far less certain. But Bowring's was still a private, family-owned company and the majority of the directors of the parent company were members of the family. They believed, and with some justification, that the prestige derived from a long history of successful shipping and trading could only be of advantage to the further development of the insurance interests.

In 1945, very soon after the end of the war, an order was placed on behalf of The Bowring Steamship Company Ltd with Swan Hunter & Wigham Richardson Ltd for a successor to *Regent Tiger*, the tanker sunk in September 1939. She was delivered the following year but was renamed *Capulet* in 1954, the third Bowring ship to be so called, thus returning once again to the traditional use of Shakespearian names.

During the next few years a number of tankers were built, both for direct ownership and for other owners, but under Bowring management as in the case of *Regent Hawk* built in 1945, also by Swan Hunter, for Trinidad Leaseholds Ltd. In 1946 Bearcreek Oil and Shipping Company purchased *Empire Trinidad* from the Ministry of War Transport. She was built by Blythswood Shipbuilding Company Ltd and renamed firstly *Regent Lion* and later *Camillo* in 1955. *Regent Leopard* was built in 1949 by Blythswood and later named *Prospero*; they also built *Regent Caribou* and *Regent Springbok* which were launched for The Bowring Steamship Company in 1951. All these ships traded under long-term time charters either with Trinidad Leaseholds or Lobitos Oilfields. It was generally reckoned that, all being well under these terms, a ship would lose money in its first three years of operation, break even during the second period and be profitable from then on.

In *The Bowring Story* David Keir records an exceptional and rather bizarre incident in the working life of *Regent Lion* before her name was changed to *Camillo*:

Soon after the end of the war this ship was caught up in one of the finer flights of bureaucratic mystification. There was at the time a shortage of edible fats in Britain. Imports had been cut during the war, and one of the important sources of supply had dried up altogether when whaling was suspended. With the end of hostilities, however, there came a determined move to make amends for the lean years. But though whaling was started as soon as possible the industry was seriously handicapped by the shortage of suitable tonnage.

In 1946 a certain South African company was having particular difficulty in operating its factory ship *Empire Victory* – a wartime prize from the Germans which had been known as *Unitas II*. She had set off on an Antarctic expedition without her owners being able to charter a tanker to service her with fuel oil and bring back as much as possible of the badly needed whale oil. At this point the Ministry of Food, with its eye on margarine as a vital foodstuff, stepped in with a request that the Ministry of War Transport should provide the tanker required. The Ministry of War Transport in turn discovered that Bowring's *Regent Lion* was the nearest vessel available. She was therefore diverted to the Antarctic, despite urgent petrol-carrying commitments.

When her sailing orders arrived *Regent Lion* was discharging oil at Rotterdam. She then went to Southampton and three days before Christmas duly sailed for the Canary Islands to load fuel oil for *Empire Victory*. En route her crew worked night and day throughout Christmas week, cleaning and treating the tanks in preparation for the expected cargo of whale oil; and at Santa Cruz 10,000 tons of fuel were loaded in less than twelve hours. As she headed south the crew continued to clean the tanks till New Year's morning when an unofficial and unexpected relief squad was found in the picturesque shape of twelve Spanish stowaways, who emerged from the lifeboats with the firm impression that they were on their way to the United States. Instead they were immediately put to work in return for bed, board and a cigarette ration. But at least they got a glimpse of sunny Cape Town on 15 January when *Regent Lion* topped up her own fuel supply, took on mail and supplies for the whalers and then set out for her Antarctic rendezvous with *Empire Victory*.

The last leg of the trip ran through the bad weather zone of he southern ocean, where gale force winds normally blow three days out of four, and without any land to break the wind a massive ocean swell builds up. To make matters worse, southern icebergs, especially in the dark hours, are more of a menace than their northern fellows, since they are larger when they break away and have no mellow Gulf Stream to shorten their lives. *Regent Lion's* passage was made all the more hazardous by having to steam as near full speed as possible to keep her rendezvous; and to heighten the tension, *Empire Victory* had radioed that her fuel would be dangerously low by the appointed date, the 1st of February. On 31 January anxiety in the tanker heightened again when she ran into heavy pack-ice, but after a difficult night of nudging through the pack, the rendezvous was accomplished in time.

Using sperm whales as fenders the two ships were manoeuvred alongside each other and immediately started exchanging whale oil for fuel. The weather, which had been relatively moderate, was degenerating and the whaler captains were anxious to get some fuel before it broke altogether, since it began to look as if they might be called on to ride out the storm. Their fears were justified. By noon the following day a driving blizzard engulfed the two ships, and they had to part company to seek shelter of a kind in the pack. Thus it was that for two nerve-racking days *Regent Lion* courted the lee of an iceberg before she was able to rejoin *Empire Victory* to complete the transfer of the oil.

The other misadventures of the trip need not be detailed here. But it should be put on record that it took *Regent Lion* two whole weeks to tow a crippled whale-catcher back to Cape Town where she could be dry-docked. From Cape Town *Regent Lion* was then ordered up the coast to Durban. And there, after more than two months' hard labour in some of the roughest ocean weather in the world, having survived encounters with icebergs, breathed in assorted odours of a whaling factory, and even put up with stowaways, the crew of *Regent Lion* dutifully discharged the precious edible oil – into the vats of a soap factory!

A more benign engagement awaited *Regent Springbok* when, in 1953, she was chosen to take HRH The Princess Royal in her capacity as Commander-in-Chief of the British Red Cross Society to Trinidad where she was to present new colours to the Red Cross Society of Trinidad and Tobago. Her Royal Highness was borne across the Atlantic described on the ships articles as a supernumerary, but was sometimes referred to later, in terms even less complimentary, as the company's most distinguished 'pier-head jump'. There was some suggestion that she might well herself have coined the nickname.

Princess Mary joined *Regent Springbok* at Wallsend on 24 January 1953 and in so doing became the first member of the Royal Family to travel aboard a Merchant Navy tanker. Throughout the voyage, during which the ship was at times subjected to heavy weather, Her Royal Highness took a keen interest in the work on board and in the routine ship's activities. She was, in fact, the guest of Trinidad Leaseholds Ltd to whose subsidiary company, the Regent Petroleum Tankship Company, the ship was chartered. In his capacity as a director of Trinidad Leaseholds and Chairman of The Bowring Steamship Company Ltd, Fred Bowring was at Wallsend to wish Her Royal Highness bon voyage. When she disembarked at Port of Spain she gave the Master, Captain V. A. R. Jury, OBE, her personal standard, which had flown from the mainmast throughout the journey, with the request that it should remain with the ship as a souvenir of her voyage.

While tankers can be seen to have been playing a major role in the company's maritime activities during the post-war years, The Bowring Steamship Company's *Cape Breton*, a 9,280 deadweight ton freight carrier completed by W Gray & Co. Ltd of West Hartlepool in July 1940, was regularly employed carrying coal on the St Lawrence for the Dominion Steel and Coal Corporation. Successful results in this trade persuaded the directors to place an order with Swan, Hunter for a bulk carrier, *Trinculo*, for delivery in 1957. Of 15,297 tons deadweight she was the third Bowring vessel thus named, the first, a 310-ton iron barque built in 1858 and the second, a 5,200-ton tanker, commissioned in 1908. In her day the new *Trinculo* was a truly modern ship, incorporating many up-to-date features such as automatic ventilation and air-conditioning throughout the crew's quarters, power-operated folding hatch covers and a 'listometer' to show the attitude of the vessel during loading and discharging. Her virtues were soon apparent and she was in more or less continuous employment covering over a quarter of a million miles and carrying over 700,000 tons of cargo during her first four years.

The next ship to join the Bowring fleet was *Orlando*, 14,154 tons gross, a motor tanker with three 'firsts' to her credit. She was, in 1960, the largest vessel to have been built at Lithgow's yard, she was propelled by the most powerful diesel engine yet designed and built by John G. Kincaid and Company Limited, and was the largest ship to be commissioned by The Bowring Steamship Company. Once again special attention was given to the crew's quarters and, another 'first', she boasted a swimming pool on her after deck. As might be expected of British shipbuilders, striving to maintain their worldwide supremacy as it then was, Lithgow's ensured that *Orlando* was technically 'state of the art', and she was provided with the very latest in navigational and communications equipment.

Bowring's long history of shipowning at the end of 1961 was still very much alive and well, albeit on a smaller scale in terms of the number of ships being operated, though in size they exceeded anything Benjamin could, in his wildest dreams, have imagined. Although, at the end of that year, the future of international shipping was anything but promising, all the company's ships were employed. At about Christmas time the fleet was positioned as follows; *Orlando*, with a cargo of crude oil was on passage from the Gulf to Portland, Maine, *Trinculo* was carrying ore from Algeria to Middlesbrough, *Regent Caribou* and *Regent Springbok* with fuel oil from Trinidad were headed, respectively, for the Thames and Avonmouth, *Capulet* was en route to London from Puerto Miranda in the Gulf of Maracaibo with a cargo of crude oil and *Cape Breton*, loaded with wheat from Quebec, was on her way to Hull and Leith. Meanwhile, Bowring Brothers' sealer *Algerine* was involved in survey work when not at the ice front.

While the company's ships were, for the time being at least, enjoying full employment, many of the varied trading activities were still hindered by restrictions which had been imposed during the war, and it was not until 1951, for example, that the distribution of petroleum products was released from the wartime pooling system.

This business was still handled by a department of the parent company, C. T. Bowring & Co. Ltd. The Petroleum Department was never in fact accorded corporate status. When the wartime pooling arrangement came to an end and branded products returned to the market, the department was once again restricted to the commercial user and gave up its connections with the motor spirit side of the business. Such reduced distribution services as were retained were with haulage contractors, farmers and various organizations running their own fleets of vehicles. The pattern of the department's modus operandi was substantially changed as far as sales of paraffin were concerned and this brought about a relationship with the Esso Petroleum Company. Henceforth, in order to satisfy a public demand for branded products, Bowring's became distributors of 'Esso Blue'. Existing arrangements to import refined petroleum spirit were dropped and in their place negotiations took place to import crude oil direct into the Esso refinery and to collect requirements from Esso installations when needed. The company gave up its rented storage space at Thames Haven and built a new facility at West Ham.

At Liverpool C. T. Bowring & Co. (Fish Oils) Ltd had survived serious war damage to its office and factory premises and was operating successfully from Tower Building in Water Street and in reconstructed works with a capacity of 4,000 tons of oil at Blackstock Street.

My first experience of the business world, reluctantly entered into in February 1947 after abandoning with much regret a regular commission in the army, was with the Fish Oils company as a clerk in their Liverpool office. The art of writing out invoices or delivery orders was lost on me, and after one morning at it I was only too glad to accept an invitation to lunch with one of the more senior members of the Liverpool team, a marine underwriter called Ben Squirrell, whose clear purpose was to give me an appropriate baptism. Ben, who had lost both his legs at Gallipoli in the First World War and was universally loved and respected, underwrote, as a one-man operation, marine insurance for the account of C. T. Bowring & Co. Ltd. He had been given this job in the early 1920s by my father and Edgar who had befriended him. He had earned a reputation for being an exceptionally generous host. The consequences of his kindness need not be retold here in all their painful detail, but when I returned to the office in a semi-anaesthetized state, with half a bottle of vintage port under my belt, it was made clear to me by my employers, one of whom was a strictly teetotal member of the Plymouth Brethren, that in future there was to be a much more rigid observance of regular office hours, which ran from 9.00 a.m. to 5.00 p.m. with an hour for lunch, and I settled down to a routine which at first seemed dreary and stultifying. Fortunately the spirit of rebellion wore off as the work became more interesting.

Ben Squirrel, who lived to be over eighty, managed to do so with exceptional courage on his two artificial legs, about which he never complained in spite of the fact that he occasionally suffered great pain. Nevertheless, he was renowned for his considerable success with the ladies. In this pursuit and for other joys of life he and my father shared some enthusiasm and, from time to time, would repair to the South of France for a few days of pleasure and respite. But success did not always come Ben's way. A lady with whom he was keeping company on one such excursion, for some undisclosed reason, displeased him and he refused to pay her what she claimed she was justly due. By way of expressing *her* displeasure at his stinginess she placed his artificial legs on top of a wardrobe where he could not possibly reach them, and he remained immobilized until he was able to rouse his fellow philanderer.

The processing and blending of a variety of fish oils from many different sources continued both at Liverpool and Grimsby – where fishmeal was also manufactured – for use in a wide range of industries including paint and lubricant manufacture, and in leather tanning, as well as cod liver oil of pharmaceutical quality for human consumption and, in increasing quantities, for domestic animal and poultry feeding. One of the recognized virtues of cod liver oil, as indeed is the case with other fish oils, is its content of vitamin D, which is an essential ingredient in the development of the bone structure of human beings and of domestic animals. A growing realization among the major animal foodstuff manufacturers of the virtues of the vitamin as an additive to their products created a demand for yet more of it than occurs naturally in fish oil. This gave rise to the development of a synthetic vitamin D, known as D3. Quick to recognize the importance of this discovery, C. T. Bowring & Co. (Fish Oils) Ltd went into partnership with the Premier Yeast Company and Crookes Laboratories with the joint purpose of manufacturing D3, and to this end the firm of Peboc Ltd was launched in 1947, with each partner holding one third of the equity.

The first factory to be operated by Peboc was at Greenford, Middlesex. It was technically an elaborate plant incorporating a number of advanced features made necessary by the fact that hitherto D3 had only been manufactured on a laboratory scale. D3 was produced by the irradiation of cholesterol, which was obtained from the spinal cords of cattle. The very latest equipment was installed to eliminate the ever present fire hazard, including flame-proof electric apparatus, ample ventilation and air-conditioning. It wasn't long before demand exceeded the Greenford plant's capacity and in 1954 plans were drawn up for a new and larger factory to be constructed at Northolt. Once again built-in safety, in view of the inherent risks involved, was given priority and, for example, the irradiation equipment was to be fitted with an alarm system connected to automatic fire extinguishing devices, and some of the floors were to be laid at different levels to avoid 'creeping' by heavier-than-air gases.

In 1956 the Fish Oils Company acquired the shareholdings of Premier Yeast and Crookes, and Peboc became, for the time being, a wholly-owned subsidiary company. The new Northolt plant came on stream in 1957 and it soon became clear that Peboc was blessed with a very promising future. Expansion, not only in the production of synthetic vitamin D3 but, possibly, in a wider range of chemical products was foreseen. Soon a new partner was sought in order to maximize this potential and C. T. Bowring & Co (Fish Oils) Ltd became an equal partner with Duphar Ltd, a subsidiary of the highly regarded and world-renowned Dutch company, N.V. Philips Gloeilampenfabrieken of

Eindhoven. Duphar brought particular expertise in the field of irradiation, the basic requirement in the production of D3 and a range of other
chemical products.

Substantial progress was made by Peboc during the next ten years and,
towards the end of the sixties, larger premises were needed once again.
Much of the company's successful progress since it was created some
twenty years earlier can be attributed to the leadership and technical
expertise of Mr Evan Roberts, who was with the company since its
inception. His lifelong association with North Wales was instrumental in
a decision being taken, after a search of possible redevelopment areas in
many parts of the United Kingdom, to move the operation to a site at
Llangefni, on Anglesey. Not only did the chosen location on a new
industrial estate allow for further expansion, there were also clear signs
of co-operation from the local authority and an abundant supply of help
in solving the many problems associated with a move to new premises
and the relocation of staff. The highly sophisticated nature of the plant
soon lent itself to the manufacture, not only of vitamin D3, but to an
ever widening range of specialized fine chemicals to the specific
requirements of individual customers. The factory still remains on the
same site at Llangefni though ownership has passed to Eastman Chemical
Company.

During the fifties and sixties Bowring, Jones and Tidy continued with
their importation and distribution of Naval Stores and various vegetable
oils and oilseeds. In the case of the former the company acted as agent
in the United Kingdom for two producers in America: gum rosin and
turpentine came from Columbia Naval Stores Company in Savannah,
Georgia, and wood rosin, turpentine and their various derivatives were
supplied by Crosby Chemicals whose plants were at Picayune, Mississippi
and De Ridder, Louisiana. I frequently visited both of these companies,
sometimes in the earlier years with Archie Jones. On our first visit
together we were greeted on our arrival at Savannah as we stepped off
the Eastern Seaboard Express by an old friend of Archie's, who liked to
be known as *Colonel* Dan Cushing, though I suspect the title had little if
anything to do with military service. After greeting us warmly the *colonel*
invited me to find a taxi and have the luggage loaded while he and
Archie remained on the platform, deep in conversation. Finding a taxi
and loading the luggage with the help of a cooperative driver was
achieved within minutes and he and I chatted amicably while waiting for
the others. Quite unexpectedly, as Dan and Archie emerged from the

station the hitherto quiet and genial *colonel* bellowed, 'What in hell d'you think you're doin', Peter, fixin' us up with a damn nigra jitney?' Having engaged a taxi with a black driver I had put my foot in it quite spectacularly. Fifty or more years ago in the Deep South, that was totally unacceptable. During the next few weeks I became more aware of the full implications of this unhappy state of affairs.

Neither Columbia Naval Stores nor Crosby Chemicals exists today, their products being more economically manufactured from tall oil, a by-product of the sulphite pulp industry. However Gum Naval Stores continued to be imported from the other sources already mentioned, especially France, Portugal, Spain, Russia, China and Greece, where the costs of the labour intensive production were less onerous.

Bowring, Jones and Tidy continued to deal in their other principal commodities such as vegetable oils, tung oil, and various oilseeds, and their coffee department flourished.

The fortunes in Burma of Fairweather, Richards and Co. Ltd were, however, to be irreparably damaged as a result of the war. Japanese forces had destroyed most of those plantations the products of which they had previously handled. In 1941 their rice mills and go-downs were razed to the ground, and the post-war constitutional changes created a situation in which the continuation of their traditional business became imposs-ible. Nevertheless, under the guidance and determination of their local managing director, Rennie Francis, the business was able to continue for some years, albeit on a much reduced scale, trading with reasonable profits in a diverse range of goods which included tinned milk, baby food and bicycles. This, among other effects of the reduction of Bowring's trading activities, resulted in Clink Wharf losing the storage of Burmese imports and its business reverted to general warehousing which it continued to carry out until the premises were eventually sold and converted into luxury apartments. Much of the past success of Fair-weather, Richards can be attributed to the energy and the wide negotiating and business skills of the company's chairman and managing director, Bill Richards who, during the years when it became clear that the business in Burma could no longer survive in its original form, turned his eyes towards Africa, where he could see promising trading possibilities in some of the developing countries.

In 1955 Bowring's had established an insurance broking subsidiary, C. T. Bowring & Co. (Nigeria) Ltd, with its headquarters in Lagos. One of this company's first clients was the Cameroons Development

Corporation whose agents in London were Rubber and Mining Agencies Ltd, a Bowring subsidiary with a close relationship to Fairweather, Richards. With these connections, there was a natural inclination to establish a company in Nigeria to operate a business similar to that hitherto carried on by Fairweather, Richards in Burma. The prospects seemed promising in a country where there were considerable natural resources awaiting development and where, provided tribal and religious differences could be contained and regional frictions overcome, a rise in the standard of living and growing general prosperity could be foreseen. During the 1950s private overseas investment in Nigeria steadily increased, indicating growing confidence in the country's political and financial stability.

In October 1958 a company named Rubber and Mining Agencies of Nigeria Limited was incorporated, shortly to be renamed C. T. Bowring Services (Nigeria) Limited, and a somewhat eclectic assortment of agencies for several British and overseas manufacturers was secured. These included Saab cars, Black & Decker power tools, Botved motor boats, Hoffman ball-bearings and West Bend outboard motors, together with other imported products of interest to a developing country with a prosperous future. In London the affairs of this company were managed by my brother, Henry.

About the same time that Bowring's trading activities were established in Nigeria, Bill Richards' growing confidence in the future for trading in Africa led him to the opposite coast, to Kenya. Here he came upon the well-established company, R. S. Campbell and Company (1950) Ltd, whose head office was in Mombasa. Founded in 1918 by Mr R. S. Campbell (known to his many friends simply as 'RS') to import and distribute British textiles, the character of the company eventually changed when it became one of the largest exporters of East African coffee, counting among its customers the largest importers in Britain, Germany, the United States, Australia, South Africa and Egypt. Campbell's bought mainly at auctions which were organized by the marketing authorities in the three established East African coffee growing countries, Kenya, Uganda and Tanzania. Campbell's tasters, or liquorers, knowing the particular types of coffee sought by their customers, would taste countless samples before each auction, a procedure which involved much sipping, slurping and spitting. Bill Talbot, the company's chief taster, was a heavy chain-smoker, a habit which one might have thought would have ruined his ability to exercise his profession efficiently. He found, however, that on the rare occasions that he tried to give up smoking he could no longer distinguish one sample from another.

The textile business, upon which the company was originally founded, continued alongside the importation of building materials and paints, an insurance company agency and a clearing and forwarding department which handled a wide range of commodities and motor vehicles.

RS, whose sale of his company was, perhaps, a hint of his thoughts about retirement, nevertheless stayed on as chairman; he found it difficult to hand over the reins. Although Bowring's had been successful in securing the services as managing director of Harold Fabian, who had gained great experience in the years following the war running an import/export business in Hong Kong, RS found it difficult not to interfere. As often as I could, during my frequent visits to Mombasa, I would persuade him to leave Harold in peace, and to spend several days calling on his many friends and businesses in Nairobi and Kampala, taking in the occasional 'safari' in one of the many game parks en route. RS became a very good friend and, when back in Mombasa, we would frequently spend long evenings with his cronies in one of his clubs, playing atrociously bad snooker. If, on these occasions, as the evening wore on, one were to offer RS a drink, his usual response would be, with enthusiasm, 'Yes please, but it must be *one of the last*'. When in Mombasa I almost invariably stayed at Nyali with RS and his charming wife, Mary. During one of my visits, Mary called me in great distress early one morning, just as I had returned from a swim in the Indian Ocean, because RS was clearly in a very bad way. In fact he had suffered a severe stroke which totally immobilized him. In spite of this he lived for several years, unable to move or speak. His interest in the business he had founded never waned and the frustration he endured as a result of not being able to discuss the company's progress was shared by Harold Fabian and all those of the company's staff who had previously been able to profit from his advice and experience.

While these new ventures were being established in Africa, the possibility of a trading operation in Australia was being considered. An insurance broking subsidiary was already in existence there and one of its local directors, Hector McCowan, who already had considerable trading experience, came up with a convincing case for the creation of a merchandising company. He consequently visited several of the Bowring trading subsidiaries in the United Kingdom and overseas and, as a result in 1961, C. T. Bowring Services (Australasia) Pty. Ltd was registered in Sydney to import and distribute some of the goods and commodities handled by other Bowring subsidiaries and to export Australian products including kangaroo hides, wool, vegetable oils and synthetic fibres.

Kangaroo hides provided an interesting alternative to the sealskins, hitherto the main interest of the Leather and Fur Department which the parent company had created in 1947 to handle sealskins shipped to England by Bowring Brothers in Newfoundland. Since 1936, as mentioned earlier, a close working relationship had developed between Bowring's and W. Duckworth and Sons Ltd whose tannery produced high grade seal leather for the British shoe trade. Duckworth had become a wholly owned subsidiary company in 1952. Further involvement in the leather trade took place when, at the beginning of 1965, Bowring's acquired Southwark Hide & Leather Co. Ltd, a company whose business for over a century had been marketing and factoring the products of some of the largest and best known tanneries both at home and abroad.

The wholly owned subsidiaries, Fischmehl Einfuhr at Hamburg and Vischmeel NV at Rotterdam, both having recovered from the vicissitudes of wartime, continued to operate satisfactorily in close cooperation with the Fertilizer and Foodstuffs Department in London which was incorporated on 1st January 1969 as C. T. Bowring (Fertilizer & Feedingstuffs) Ltd. The Icelandic venture, on the other hand, had to be abandoned after the war. Instead of salting and drying their catches, during which process the heads and tails of the fish were used to manufacture fishmeal, the Icelandic fish merchants were now filleting and freezing the catch and the wet offal left over was unsuitable for processing into fishmeal in the existing plant. The view was taken that the cost of new plant could not be justified and the factory was sold.

An example of how one activity within The Bowring Group of Companies, as it was now generally becoming known, could lead to another which, while seeming to be unrelated, might find itself comfortably at home within the widening scope of 'trading', was the close association with Rhein-Chemie GmbH of Heidelberg in Germany.

In the thirties C. T. Bowring & Co. (Insurance) Ltd had come to an arrangement with a company in Berlin, Krafag GmbH, which financed Berlin taxi-drivers to purchase and run their own cabs. CTB (Insurance) had agreed with the company's founder and owner, Herr Richard Emondts, to put up part of the funding, something over thirty per cent

– the balance continuing to be held by Emondts – in return for being given the placing of the insurance of the drivers and their vehicles in the London market, such cover, no doubt, being a necessary part of the drivers' agreement with Krafag. In view of the wide-ranging devastation of Berlin during the war and, in the absence of any contact with Krafag, it was assumed in London that the company no longer existed.

To the surprise of all, however, there came a message from Heidelberg in the early fifties to the effect that not only did the company still exist, but that it was flourishing, albeit in an entirely different form, and Bowring's were invited to increase their participation to 40 per cent and were offered representation on the Board. During the war Germany had no access to any supplies of natural rubber and relied, to a great extent, on regeneration from old tyres and other sources. Richard Emondts had transferred Krafag's financial strength from taxi-drivers in Berlin (whose survival, it must be assumed, was in doubt) to a plant at Mannheim-Rheinau whose business was rubber regeneration. This led to further industrial involvement, including the manufacture of rubber soles and heels and, surprisingly, pharmaceuticals. Among the highly sophisticated medicinal products manufactured by the latter was a product for the relief of haemorrhoids, the virtues of which were widely advertised on radio to an appropriate jingle, and also a preparation made from the gonads of unborn lambs which was reported to have remarkable rejuvenating effects and was believed to have been administered to such luminaries as Winston Churchill, Konrad Adenauer and even Pope Pius Xll.

Richard Emondts, a man of foresight and wisdom, saw in the seventies that the industries in which Rhein-Chemie was involved had a questionable future and over quite a brief period they were disposed of. Under German tax legislation the proceeds of the sales of capital assets have to reinvested in a limited range of enterprises, including property, if penal taxation is to be avoided. So Rhein-Chemie became an investor in institutional and commercial property and the name was changed to Rhein-Chemie Holding GmbH.

After the war Bowring Brothers in Newfoundland had ceased to participate in the salt cod trade but maintained their interest in the seal fishery. However it had become clear that their future would be in retail trading and to this end the store in St John's on Water Street was modernized and marketing methods were thoroughly overhauled. Under the chairmanship of Eric Bowring, his nephew Derrick Bowring, who was managing director and Fred Ayre, who was in charge of retailing, set about broadening the scope of the company's merchandizing, and in 1955 a small retail branch was opened at Churchill Park, a suburb of St John's. This led eventually to their establishing larger branches at Grand Falls and on Bell Island. Having overcome the hazards of unfamiliar branch management, their teeth were now firmly embedded in the concept of developing smaller retail outlets. Their grasp of modern retailing methods was greatly enhanced by guidance and advice from the long established department store of Owen Owen Ltd of Liverpool, from the Allied Merchandisers of Canada and the National Retail Merchants Association of America. Emboldened by this fund of assistance and by their recently acquired experience of running smaller retail outlets, further development was rapid. There followed the opening of gift-shops at Gander, Halifax and Montreal airports, and the road was clear and the concept well enough established to give consideration to the creation of similar shops well into the Canadian mainland and, indeed, beyond.

While these developments were taking shape two new branches of the Water Street store were opened, in Labrador and in northern Quebec. These two new outlets were following the fortunes of the evolving iron ore industry and were the outcome of connections born in London. Not only was The Bowring Steamship Company agent for the Iron Ore Company of Canada's ships, but Bowring's were members of the development consortium known as BRINCO (The British Newfound-land Corporation Ltd). Both these connections were conducive to closer cooperation on the other side of the Atlantic. By the end of 1960 the Iron Ore Company had invited Bowring Brothers to open stores at Shefferville, at Knob Lake on the Quebec side of the border, and at Carol Lake in Labrador.

It was while these developments were taking place in Newfoundland that Eric Bowring died in 1959 at his home in St John's at the age of seventy-four. There is no doubt that his enthusiasm for Newfoundland, where he had lived and worked for over fifty years and, in particular for the success of Bowring Brothers, inspired his colleagues to press on with the development of the company even if, at times, the auguries may have seemed rather less than favourable. He was noted for his many charitable and philanthropic endeavours and for his valuable contribution to shipping during the war in his capacity as representative in Newfound-land for the Ministry of War Transport, for which he was appointed CBE. It is sad that he was not able to enjoy the 150th anniversary in

1961 of Benjamin's courageous decision to start a business in Newfoundland, for it would surely have pleased him to have been able to read the
message from the Hon. J. R. Smallwood, Premier of Newfoundland,
received by Fred Bowring in London. It read:

> IT IS A GREAT HONOUR FOR ME TO SEND FROM YOUR ST. JOHN'S OFFICE
> CORDIAL GREETINGS AND CONGRATULATIONS ON THIS HISTORIC OCCASION
> STOP IN ALL OUR NEWFOUNDLAND HISTORY THERE HAS NOT BEEN ANOTHER
> FIRM LIKE BOWRINGS STOP LONG MAY YOU CONTINUE IN NEWFOUNDLAND
> STOP PERSONAL REGARDS

It will be recalled that from the very earliest days of Bowring's in
Newfoundland, the business came near to complete ruin as a result of
the devastating fires that swept through St John's. Benjamin's perseverance and that of his successors ensured that the business that he had
founded would survive. But early in 1963, seventy-one years after the
last serious outbreak, there was a fire in the Water Street building, which
was on the same site as the one that had been occupied by the company
during the previous fires and, indeed, since its inception. Fortunately, on
this occasion, the fire was confined to only part of Bowring Brothers'
building and was brought under control after nine hours of strenuous
fire-fighting. After no more than a month it was a case of 'business as
usual'. Nevertheless, after giving the matter full consideration, the
directors felt that the damage was sufficiently extensive to necessitate
tearing down the entire building and erecting a new one. This was
carried out in phases over a period of two years. The new building,
which now housed the department store and the headquarters of the
three main divisions – retailing, insurance and exports – was opened by
the Hon. J. R. Smallwood, on 11 May 1965.

From this fine new and technically up-to-date premises Bowring
Brothers embarked upon a new and exciting period of development that
would take them clear across Canada and into the United States. The
success of the gift shops at Gander, Halifax and Montreal was so
encouraging that Fred Ayre, now managing director under the chairmanship of Derrick Bowring, conceived the idea of establishing
high-class boutiques in regional supermarket developments and urban
shopping malls. These extremely attractive and colourful shops were
designed to display in a warm and elegant atmosphere fashionable home
furnishings and related goods such as chinaware, lighting and a wide
range of household accessories of the highest quality and sophisticated

design. So successful was this venture that over the next few years over 100 such outlets, known as Bowring's 'Little Shops' were opened across Canada and into the United States. This is the only remaining commercial activity to bear the Bowring name, albeit now under different ownership.

The post-war years for Bowring & Company at New York cannot be seen as their most successful and their contribution to group profitability was, to say the least, generally disappointing. The business was in the hands of the rather less than dedicated but charming, generous and hospitable Charles Warren Bowring Jr., generally known as Warren or simply 'Wa'. His father of the same name and a grandson of Charles Tricks was born, it will be recalled, in Newfoundland and was a leading light in Bowring Brothers until he joined the New York office in the 1890s. Warren's mother, a large lady, sometimes impolitely referred to as 'Elephant Amy', dwelt in an over-furnished and gloomy New York apartment in fashionable Manhattan. Her husband had died in 1940. Before my first visit to America I was advised that, when in New York, a visit to cousin Amy was mandatory. Having been greeted with a viciously potent dry-martini when I called I was subjected to a searching inquisition, the purpose of which was to extract from me as much family gossip as I could offer. 'Now let me see,' from the foggy depths of the other end of the room, 'you are Fred's son aren't you; who's he sleeping with these days; and Archie Jones, you never know with him, he has half-a-dozen of them over here?' Her knowledge of the nocturnal habits of us all was thus kept well up-to-date and was sufficient to fill a sizeable anthology of the sexual exploits of as many Bowring executives as managed to survive her lethal martinis.

The chief reason for the mediocre performance of the New York office rested with the management. Warren's workday seldom got underway before 11 o'clock and came to a temporary but lengthy halt at around midday when he would repair to the Whitehall Club at the top of the office building at 17 Battery Place, at which address the company occupied part of a floor. Here he would meet several of his cronies, many of them distinguished members of New York's business society, for the first of several rounds of those vicious martinis. On my first of many visits to the Whitehall Club there was another unforgettable experience when I was invited to join them for lunch. This time it turned out to be a family occasion, including Warren's two brothers, Bonner and Tom (so called though his name was, in fact, Douglas),

MS Capulet, the last ship to be built for The Bowring Steamship Company Ltd

Bowring Brothers', Water Street, St John's, before being destroyed by fire in 1963

Bowring Brothers' premises as rebuilt after the fire in 1963

A typical interior of one of Bowring's Little Shops. The Shops adopted the legendary 'Terra Nova' as their logo

Derrick Bowring, Managing Director of Bowring Brothers Ltd, discusses with Christopher Hope, manager of the Grand Falls retail store, the arrangement of hand tools in the hardware section

Orlando, *motor tanker built in Glasgow, 1960*

MS London Bridge, *bulk carrier, built at Belfast 1967*

Harvey Bowring, 1885–1971

No comment

Gilbert A. Cooke with Peter Bowring

*Ian Edward Skimming 1920–1973, Chairman of C. T. Bowring & Co. Ltd
from 1965 until his death*

Edgar R.H. Bowring, MC, Chairman, 1973–8

*John M. Regan, Chairman of Marsh & McLennan when they acquired
C. T. Bowring & Co. Ltd*

The PLA launch, Royal Nore, brings HRH The Prince of Wales and the triumphant Transglobe Expedition team to their final landing place at Greenwich on Sunday 29 August, 1982

neither of whom were in the Bowring business. On arrival I was asked what I would like to drink. I said I would be happy with whatever they were having. This turned out to be a serious mistake. When my drink arrived it was a fair sized glass of the same colourless liquid as they were drinking accompanied by a small carafe of the same beverage. This, it seemed, was one drink, albeit a double; and, of course, it was the Whitehall Club's particularly potent version of the ubiquitous dry-martini. It soon became clear that I had made a tactical error, if for no other reason, because I was required to visit, for the first time, two important business associates during the afternoon; and, because there were four of us for lunch, there wasn't going to be just one aperitif. Of what we ate I have no recollection. That I had carried out my business obligations during the afternoon there was proof in the two letters I received on my return to London, thanking me for calling in. As to whether the visits served any useful purpose I am extremely doubtful for I remember very little of them. One visit was to someone who, I had been previously advised, had only one working eye, the other being false. In my stupor I had spent most of the time I was with him trying to make out which of the two eyes it was that was fixed on me.

Warren's return to the office after lunch was but for a short session, in order to sign a few letters written for him in his absence. Around 4 o'clock the club life was resumed each day by a visit to the Racquet Club on Park Avenue for a game of squash in the vain hope of working off the midday excesses – and then to the bar for a couple of replacements before taking the subway back to Long Island and his loving and lovable wife, Lorna who, without fail, would have another little dart of evil, as my father used to call a martini (for which he had an equally robust thirst) waiting for him. Were it not for the fact that his kindness and help towards any visitor from the London office to New York could at all times be relied upon, it would probably have been in the company's better interests to have pensioned him off. But Warren's willingness lavishly to entertain his guests from London and to maintain his own expensive life-style were dependent on substantial borrowings from the company for the success of whose performance he was responsible. However, it seems that this was a state of affairs to which the parent company directors were prepared to treat with Nelsonian disregard. He was, after all, one of the chairman's closest friends.

When Warren retired in the sixties nepotism prevailed and, in the uncertain belief that, if the good name of the company was to be maintained, the management and direction of the New York office should remain in the hands of a member of the family, his son Charles Warren Bowring 3rd, otherwise known as Lu, took precarious hold of the reins. His adventurous spirit and lack of sound business principles led him and the company into a number of doubtful ventures, and he would have been better advised to concentrate on the existing areas of endeavour where modest profits were being made, and where sounder leadership and management could have ensured that the business would not have to be brought to a premature close.

During the post-war years Bowring & Company continued to pursue, with varying degrees of success, three main lines of business. These comprised the Ship Brokerage department, the Ore and Metal department and the Trading department. The first of these was involved in arranging dry cargo and tanker business on the one hand and, on the other, the purchase and sale of ships. The department also acted as owners' agents for ships arriving at New York and in this capacity was involved in arranging for tugs, docking facilities, stevedores, bunkers and ships' chandlery. The years immediately after the war were particularly difficult because of the worldwide depression in the charter market, but the company was able to participate in the considerable growth of American exports.

The Ore and Metal department had excellent connections. The oldest and most successful of these was the association with Naylor Benzon and Company which came about in the early years of the 20th century and for whom Bowring & Company acted as American agents. With their worldwide representation from their head office in London of a number of important European mining interests, including the French Compagnie de Mokta, and Comolog, a company in which the United States Steel Corporation had a substantial interest, this was a valuable connection.

The Trading department was started in the mid fifties when Bowring's bought Arnhold and Company, the New York branch of the London and Hong Kong based Arnhold Trading Company in which Bowring, Jones and Tidy were shareholders. Among a wide range of commodities handled by this department were raw materials for the paint and varnish industry, tallow, wattle bark, hardware from Canada, peas and beans for the canning industry, carpet wool and tanning materials.

These three departments, with energetic and diligent management, could have been major contributors to the overall fortunes of The

Bowring Group. Unfortunately, as the business went into steady decline, it was decided in the seventies to wind the company down as painlessly as possible and in these depressing circumstances a major part was played by a brilliant accountant, Don Bernard, who skilfully brought the business to a close with minimal dislocation or hardship.

There were one or two additional excursions into unfamiliar 'trading' territory during the seventies, none of which, though interesting, made much of a contribution to the overall wellbeing of the group. The most significant of these, an electronic device developed in America for detecting shoplifters, was brought to us by my step-brother, Pat Robinson, who was Chairman of Herbert Morris Ltd, a company chiefly involved in the manufacture of cranes but, at the time, interested in diversification. The principle was developed in Florida by a company called Sensormatic. A joint company, Senelco, was set up with Herbert Morris to market and distribute the product, Bowring's share being 49.3 per cent of the equity. Many major department stores were soon persuaded to install the device and today it and many similar products are in retail operations throughout the world.

Chapter 16

M<small>Y FATHER</small>, Fred Bowring, died unexpectedly at the early age of sixty-eight in April 1965 when Chairman of C. T. Bowring & Co. Ltd. Though he was a traditionalist when it came to considering fundamental variations in the group's structure he nevertheless was quick to foresee the inevitable and far-reaching sea change when it became necessary to seek a quotation for the company's shares. An important milestone in the firm's history, the year before he died, was an offer to the public to purchase '1,425,000 "A" Ordinary Shares of 5s each at 19s per share'. In other words, what had been a wholly family-held company for over 150 years could henceforth expect to see the unfamiliar faces of members of the public at its annual general meetings. The reason for creating an 'A' share was to provide a market for the shares held by members of the family, some of whom were now very old and had extremely large holdings. It was felt that on their deaths there would be few, if any, younger members sufficiently wealthy to purchase these shares, which would otherwise have to be sold to the public under duress. The 'A' shares carried one vote each whereas the Ordinary Shares remaining in family hands carried four votes, thus assuring continued control. This was not at all popular with the London Stock Exchange and, when eventually a quotation was sought on various European bourses, steps were taken to equalize the voting rights throughout. There were those family shareholders who gloomily saw this dispersal of the company's capital as the beginning of the ultimate end of their ownership of the company. They would be proved to be right.

Fred Bowring was succeeded by Ian Skimming, son of Ted Skimming, who had been chairman from 1943 to 1957. Whilst the growth of virtually all parts of the group under Fred Bowring's chairmanship had been greater than at any earlier period in the company's history, and much of it the result of his lively and incisive business mind, Ian had broader vision than the previous generation and was bursting with ideas for expansion in directions hitherto barely dreamt of. He also saw ways of reorganizing the group to increase the efficiency of the many and varied operations. He shared and encouraged the view that the success and prestige of The Bowring Group depended on expansion not only in insurance broking but also in the development of financial services generally.

In order to put the development that took place in the ensuing years into perspective it is worth noting that at the end of 1954 the group had consisted of some 20 companies of which 13 were involved in trading or shipping and the remaining eight (including C. T. Bowring & Co. (Insurance) Ltd, their parent company) in insurance. Five years later the number of companies had risen to 27 of which those involved in shipping and trading, or some other non-insurance activity, were still in the majority having risen to 16. The rate of expansion in the years that followed would render this rate of progress to be unremarkable.

Before moving on to the impressive increase in the size of the group during the sixties and seventies it seems appropriate to give some space to the company's most enduring and unbroken involvement in shipping. Ships were still being built during the sixties and seventies and there was a gradual change from tankers to bulk carriers. In 1954 The Bowring Steamship Company owned seven tankers, ranging in size from 8,133 to 12,117 tons gross, all on charter to Trinidad Leaseholds. The first bulk carrier, *Trinculo* (III), 11,206 tons gross, was launched from Swan Hunter's yard in 1947. The last tanker to be owned and operated by the company, *Orlando*, 14,154 tons gross, was purchased in 1960 from A/S Hektor, Tonsberg, whilst still under construction, complete with a five-year time charter to British Petroleum. Thereafter seven ships were built for the company between 1965 and 1978, all bulk carriers varying in size from *Stephano* (II), 16,166 tons gross to *Sydney Bridge*, 35,868 tons gross, the latter being launched from the yard of Harland & Wolff Ltd at Belfast. Two identical bulk carriers, *Forth Bridge* and *London Bridge*, each of 28,467 tons gross, were ordered from Verolme's yard at Rotterdam in 1967. The last two ships to be ordered for The Bowring Steamship Company were *Trinculo* (IV), 17,835 tons gross and *Desdemona* (II), 17,940 tons gross both built by Swan Hunter and launched from their yard in 1977 and 1978 respectively, thus bringing to an end as long and happy a relationship between shipbuilder and owner as could ever have been wished for. Sir John Hunter, Chairman of Swan Hunter, and my father had become close friends and he was a frequent lunch guest at Bowring's office on his visits to London.

In addition to the ships owned by The Bowring Steamship Company they had managed some ten ships for Lobitos Oilfields Ltd and four for

Trinidad Leaseholds, in addition to 12 vessels on behalf of the British Government during the Second World War. Between 1818 and 1983 Bowring's had owned and managed well over 200 vessels from the smallest, Benjamin's little *Charlotte* in 1818 to the largest, the bulk carrier *Sydney Bridge*, 35,868 tons gross, built in 1970.

As already mentioned there were among the rapidly increasing number of insurance executives those who mildly disapproved of the profits derived from insurance broking being used for the purchase of new ships. Happily, however, there were still those members of the Board of C. T. Bowring & Co. Ltd, including the new chairman – although his main interest had, up till now, been in insurance broking – who were prepared to recognize the value of maintaining a well-earned reputation as an internationally recognized shipping and trading organization, notwithstanding its clearly recognizable prominence in the insurance world. Fortunately, overall profits were sufficient to increase the group's share of the 'insurance cake', nationally and internationally, by the purchase of well-established brokers at home and overseas as well as achieving impressive organic growth.

After the war many young men chose to become insurance brokers, and several came to Bowring's to join those older members of the firm who had returned from active service. There is little doubt that they would have been impressed by the ever increasing number of cables and letters that arrived each day from all parts of the globe with requests for insurance cover, with renewal instructions or amendments to existing covers; and in due course, under the guidance of their older, experienced colleagues, they would have hastened on foot to Lloyd's – or possibly to one of the London based insurance companies – with a bundle of 'slips' summarizing the various risks to be placed. As one of the young post-war brokers on his first working visit to the Room at Lloyd's asserted '. . . I naturally watched the company's own brokers circulating among the underwriters, and at first it seemed rather strange that usually they made no approach to underwriters representing Bowring-managed syndicates but got their slips filled in elsewhere.' There was, indeed, no obligation on the part of the Bowring brokers to seek the support of the company's syndicates. Their clear duty was to go to whichever underwriter would give their clients the desired cover at the best rate. The number of Bowring syndicates had increased since last mentioned and three new ones were added following the war, in 1948, 1957 and a third in 1960.

Although Bowring's and other Lloyd's brokers sought wherever possible, to give first consideration to their clients rather than to favour those syndicates whose affairs they managed, there was nevertheless seen to be a potential clash of interest and this, among other shortcomings in the overall operation of Lloyd's, was considered when the Council of Lloyd's, in 1980, commissioned Sir Henry Fisher to produce the basis for a new Lloyd's Act. The outcome of this and successive examinations of the institution's internal imperfections have been well documented and there is no need to recount them here.

In the fifties, sixties and seventies there was a steady increase in all aspects of the group's insurance activities. Business was continuously coming in from all parts of the world. Not only was the geographical spread so impressive, but the variety of risks seemed to be infinite as industrial and commercial developments gathered pace. The ever-widening global presence of Bowring's in the insurance broking world needed the creation of a group-within-a-group. The business would be conducted through a number of subsidiary and associate companies and divisions under the umbrella of C. T. Bowring (Insurance) Holdings Ltd. At the end of 1977 the holding company controlled three major subsidiaries, C. T. Bowring & Co. (Insurance) Ltd, C. T. Bowring (UK) Ltd and C. T. Bowring (Overseas) Ltd, all based in London. Each of these three companies was itself a 'holding' company and had acquired or created a group of subsidiary companies or divisions covering virtually every aspect of insurance and reinsurance. For example, C. T. Bowring & Co. (Insurance) Ltd controlled four divisions, American Non-Marine, International Non-Marine, Marine and Aviation, as well as three subsidiary companies, Undersea Projects Insurance Brokers Ltd, C. T. Bowring Space Projects Ltd and C. T. Bowring Offshore Oil (UK) Ltd.

The UK Company had a controlling interest in 22 companies, either acquired or created, including Bowring Tyson Ltd in Liverpool, R Martin Son & Co. Ltd in Belfast, James M. Macalaster & Alison Ltd at Glasgow, Matthews Mulcahy and Sutherland in Dublin, C. T. Bowring (Midlands) Ltd in Birmingham, and several others in major towns throughout the United Kingdom. In London Muir Beddall & Co. Ltd became part of The Bowring Group in 1964. As an example of the events that were taking place around that time, which were contributing to the steady expansion of the business, the following is not untypical. In October 1964 a report appeared in the National Press: 'Following the recent announcement that talks were taking place between the C. T. Bowring & Co. Ltd Group and the Noble Lowndes Group consequent upon the former's acquisition of Muir Beddall & Co. Ltd, the two groups are now pleased to announce that they have agreed to establish an equal interest in the equity of Lowndes Beddall Ltd, and that as from 1 November, 1964, the name of that company will be changed to Lowndes Bowring Ltd. Talks are continuing with the object of establishing associations between various subsidiaries of both groups in other spheres of their respective activities.'

The Overseas Company had a controlling interest in 25 companies in Australia, New Zealand, Fiji, France, Japan, Malaysia, Nigeria, South Africa, Zimbabwe (then Rhodesia), Singapore, Switzerland and West Germany – and the number was growing.

And Bowring's involvement in underwriting had also been expanding since the incorporation of the previously mentioned English and American Insurance Company Limited in 1929, in addition to the company's long standing relationship with its Lloyd's syndicates.

In 1954, under Harvey Bowring's Chairmanship of C. T. Bowring & Co. (Insurance) Ltd, a 75 per cent interest was acquired in the Crusader Insurance Company. The Crusader, which was founded in Scotland in 1899, started life as the Mutual Property Recovery and Accident Company Limited and, over the years, occupied offices in Manchester and a series of locations in London, as became necessary during its continual growth, until finally, on leaving Whitehall, it came to rest in 1939 in rural surroundings in Surrey at Woodhatch, Reigate. But 'resting' was not a luxury for which the company had much spare time. When Crusader became part of The Bowring Group its main business was in Group Pension, Life, Sickness and Accident insurance, and in its particular areas of expertise it was growing rapidly. The company was developing overseas especially in Africa, and by the late sixties had opened branches in Lagos, Nairobi, Kampala, Johannesburg, Salisbury (now Harare), Kitwe, Accra, Ibadan, Akure, Aba, Enugu, and Onitsha, and in Australia, at Sydney. Much of the inspiration for the development of Crusader can be attributed to Mr Harry D. Day who joined the company in 1920 and succeeded Harvey Bowring as Chairman in 1964.

The third underwriting company, launched as a wholly owned subsidiary of C. T. Bowring & Co. Ltd, the Terra Nova Insurance Company Ltd, was incorporated on 1 October, 1970. In an article written for *The Bowring Magazine* shortly after the company was formed Mr Theodore Landon describes its origins: 'The Terra Nova, which has an authorized capital of £1,000,000, of which £500,000 has been paid up, has been formed to Underwrite in the London Market, through Lloyd's Brokers, a worldwide Account of Non-Marine, Marine and Aviation Reinsurance business, to which will be added in 1972 a portfolio of Direct business in the Marine and Aviation branches. We hope that the company will be able to make some contribution towards reducing the present shortage of capacity . . . The Directors of the Terra Nova believe firmly in the long term future of London as a stable and profitable market for worldwide business . . .'

Two other important aspects of Bowring's involvement in underwriting were C. T. Bowring (Underwriting Agencies) Ltd and C. T. Bowring Underwriting Services Ltd. The function of the former was to manage the affairs of the Bowring syndicates at Lloyd's of which, at the end of 1978, there were over 900 individual members, or 'Names', and, in the case of the Underwriting Services company, to offer underwriting agency and management facilities in London to a number of overseas and UK based insurance groups.

By the early sixties the Head Office at 52, Leadenhall Street had become far too small for such a rapidly expanding group, and with an ever increasing number of insurance related branches in and around London, Ian Skimming was convinced that a move was inevitable in order to bring as many as possible of the outlying offices under one roof. He was at this time Chief Executive Director of C. T. Bowring & Co. (Insurance) Ltd and there were few who doubted his aspirations, eventually, to become Chairman of the Group. Meanwhile he demonstrated by his energy and perception that such hopes were by no means out of place, although it cannot be said that his peers were unanimous in wishing him well in the fulfilment of his ambition. However, few would take issue with him in his belief that more and better designed space was essential if the company was to maintain the steady progress achieved in the past two decades.

Ian had observed a site on Tower Hill, close to the Tower of London, where he could imagine a prestigious new Bowring office building might stand. The area was previously occupied by warehouses which had been totally destroyed by the *Luftwaffe* in the war and for some reason had escaped the developers eye for nearly twenty years. Local authorities, planning departments and other organizations likely to impede the progress of what, in 1962, had become for him a cherished ambition, were anathema to Ian. By a combination of tact, persuasion and, at times, a facility for riding rough-shod over those who spent too much time trying to prevent him from doing what he wanted to do, he eventually overcame all obstacles. However, in general terms, the shape, size, alignment and heights of the development as a whole had to conform to the regulations laid down by the Town Planning Department of the Corporation of the City of London – and there were no less than 23 other authorities that had to be consulted before a start could be made. Ian was not one for doing nothing while these time-consuming deliberations were taking place and was quickly seeking suitable architects, and George Wimpey & Co. Ltd were appointed to clear the site.

Having accepted with some enthusiasm his plans, the Board of C. T. Bowring gave Ian virtually a free hand to proceed, subject to their receiving regular progress reports. The development of the site was to be a joint project by Bowring's and the City of London Real Property Co. Ltd (CLRP). The firm of architects chosen, more because Ian knew one of the partners well than for any other reason, were George, Trew, Dunn, better known for their design of hospitals and university buildings than of offices. However, one of the better known and highly praised examples of their work was the redesigning of the Guards Chapel in Wellington Barracks after it had been severely damaged by wartime bombing. Well aware of their lack of experience in the commercial field they made a close examination of modern office buildings in New York, Dusseldorf, Milan and Caracas before submitting their designs. The building contract was awarded to the well-known civil contractors, Taylor Woodrow.

Because of its close proximity to the Tower of London, the building was constructed, with sympathetic intentions, mainly of the same material – Cornish granite – though in this case not using the natural granite but with slabs reconstituted from the crushed stone, which did little if anything for the claim that it would be self-cleansing. The overall design comprised a four-storey S-shaped block with a fourteen-storey tower at its western end which was shared with CLRP. Though of modular design based on a grid with reference to desk layout, it never fulfilled its promises and there are many who will recall the tiresome hike along a serpentine passageway from one end of the building to the other should it be necessary to visit someone at the farthest point. But, at least for a few years, it sufficed to accommodate most of the London based branches of the group. However, it was not long before the inexorable expansion overtook Ian Skimming's farsighted plans and as CLRP were in fact seeking space elsewhere, Bowring's acquired their 50 per cent of what remained of the 999 year lease. It was now possible to bring into the building various units of the group that had evolved and developed during the intervening years.

Fred Bowring had given Ian full support during the two year's gestation period as, indeed, had the whole Board but, sadly, he didn't live to see it completed. That he would have given the final result his general approval there is no doubt. But there was one aspect of the move from the Leadenhall Street office with which he would have felt anything but comfortable. Throughout the construction period Ian had taken personal responsibility for the decoration and furnishing, of what was now to be known as The Bowring Building, and had approached FCB with temptingly illustrated catalogues of desks, chairs, tables and other items that a modern executive's office should contain, seeking his choice from a comprehensive selection. My father had become 'glued' to the ancient roll-top desk that he had sat behind since he joined the company at 20 Castle Street, Liverpool, some 40 years earlier and, in spite of Ian's powers of persuasion, was not to be separated from it in any circumstances. But Ian, I learnt later, had other ideas. Come the move to the new premises, the ancient bureau would fail to survive an unfortunate accident at the hands of some careless and inept removal men and, in view of its great age, would be wrecked beyond repair. It is a little ironic, perhaps, that the office that would have been my father's and the desk at which he would have found himself sitting, albeit unwillingly, in the new building, would now be the habitat of his successor, Ian Skimming.

Seen from the air, when approaching Heathrow over the City from the East on the frequently used flight-path, The Bowring Building could be easily identified because of its proximity to the Tower of London. There have been many who have interpreted the juxtaposition of the fourteen storey tower, known as Vincula House, and the S-shaped lower block as portraying the letters IS, Ian's initials. Some of them still presume that this was preordained as an icon to associate his name in perpetuity with the building. It is certain beyond doubt that this was not the case; this apparent visual relationship between the two parts of the building was purely coincidental. And, in any case, as far as there might have been any hopes of a lasting memorial, however well it might have been deserved, the building no longer exists.

During Ian's distinguished reign as Chairman of The Bowring Group there were two major developments which confirmed beyond peradventure that Bowring's had become primarily a financial services oriented group. These were the acquisitions of the credit finance company Bowmaker Ltd in 1969 and of the merchant bank, Singer and Friedlander in 1971.

Early in 1969 Bowmaker had come under pressure from a persistent predator whose demanding attention and desire to purchase the company were wholly unwelcome; indeed Bowmaker were in search of a 'white knight'. Founded in Bournemouth in 1927, they had become a leading finance house providing medium-term instalment credit for industry, commerce and agriculture, and also banking and instalment credit facilities for individuals. In fact it seemed that they were the perfect addition to Bowring's fulfilling, at least in part, the prevailing desire to become more involved in financial services – and successful negotiations soon followed. The broad spread of their clientele would also be of considerable interest to Bowring's insurance broking activities.

During the war Bowmaker's energies were diverted mainly to the war effort and much of the company's funds were devoted to the purchase of a large fleet of contractors' plant and earth-moving equipment which was bought by or hired out to companies involved in essential defence work such as airfield construction. This brought about the formation of Bowmaker (Plant) Ltd to operate and maintain the fleet. Much of the equipment used was made by Caterpillar of Peoria, Illinois, and the business reached such proportions that, in 1950, they awarded Bowmaker (Plant) Ltd. the dealership for the Midlands, Wales and South-West England. The company went on to develop an international trade. In 1959 they supplied 80 of the largest Caterpillar bulldozers to Cuba, while two years later they were appointed Caterpillar dealer for the vast Indus Basin project in West Pakistan where the Tarbela Dam was being constructed, at the time one the largest civil engineering contracts ever undertaken. Early in 1965 Bowmaker (Plant) was successful in selling a variety of Caterpillar equipment to a major state-owned civil construction company in Poland. The overseas trade spread further to the Middle East and to Africa.

The plant company's Managing Director, Charles Jackson, and I made a visit to the Tarbela Dam project in February 1972. The somewhat tortuous journey by a very rough, hilly road between the site and the home of the resident Bowmaker (Plant) manager, John Brown, gave rise to a most unusual coincidence which took me back to the early wartime years when my sisters were at school in Shropshire and I had driven my mother to Oswestry to visit them. On the journey home, driving along the A5, the semi-somnolent parent suddenly awoke and advised me that she had noticed that there were elephants in the neighbourhood; she had apparently observed droppings by the roadside of sufficient significance to confirm her belief. I did my best to disabuse her of any such ridiculous notion by explaining that anything resembling an elephant hadn't been seen in Shropshire for many thousands of years. However, a few moments later, much fresher evidence added some credence to her, by now, very strongly held assertion. Well, to come to the point of this story, there, around the next bend, to our utter amazement, swaying majestically down the middle of the road, was a very large jumbo. To return to West Pakistan, on our road to the Tarbela Dam site we came across a pile of practically spherical rocks which had landed neatly in the middle of the road and which reminded me immediately of my experience on the A5 thirty years earlier. So I related the story to Charles and John. No sooner had I finished than Charles, without any sign of surprise, said, 'That was Rosie'. Somewhat taken aback, I asked, '*Who* was Rosie?'

'That elephant,' he said, 'that was Rosie.'

'What on earth do you mean, that elephant was Rosie?' I asked, fearing that perhaps the strength of the Pakistan sun had begun to affect him.

'That elephant' he continued with some emphasis 'was mine and her name was Rosie.'

I could hardly believe what I was hearing. It emerged that during the war Charles was working on a site near the A5 where land was being cleared to make a runway for troop-carrying gliders, and elephants were being used to uproot trees. He was in charge of Rosie and she had escaped on the morning that my mother and I were heading home on the A5, which perhaps Rosie may have thought would lead her back to India.

When Bowmaker became part of The Bowring Group they controlled from their headquarters in Bournemouth some 14 companies in England and in Ireland. Their Chairman was Sir John Cowley GC KBE and the Managing Director Gilbert A Cooke. Sir John retired in 1971 and Ian

Skimming succeeded him as Chairman. There was no doubt that, having achieved his ambition, at least in part, to bring Bowring's into the broader field of financial services, Ian was especially delighted and soon after becoming Chairman of Bowmaker Ltd made a four day helicopter trip to visit their various branches throughout the United Kingdom.

The arrival of Singer & Friedlander Holdings Ltd in The Bowring Group in 1971 completed the sought-after deeper involvement in financial services and, once again, provided fertile ground for coordination and synergy. This highly reputed merchant bank came as a group in itself with no fewer than 17 subsidiary companies. The bank's origins go back to 1907 when Julius Singer founded a stockbroking firm in the City of London. He was joined from South Africa in 1912 by Ernst Friedlander whose family had been bankers in Berlin since 1832. Ernst had become Chairman of the Johannesburg stock exchange, and he founded South Africa's first merchant bank. With the termination of their membership of the London Stock Exchange on the outbreak of the First World War, these two financially experienced businessmen turned their minds to banking and so gave rise to the founding of the influential merchant bank, embracing their two names, which became such a valuable part of The Bowring Group in 1971.

Thus Ian's dreams of a financial services group had become a reality and the time had come to bring all the strands together. Early in 1972 a Group Conference was convened in order, as Ian put it at a dinner on 4 February, to bring together the 277 Executives from the various subsidiary companies in Great Britain and Ireland so that they could get to know each other and learn about the many activities of the Group other than their own. This event did much to harmonize the functions of what to many might have seemed to have become a somewhat disparate group of businesses.

It was also felt that the nature of Bowring's as a fully-fledged financial services group was deserving of a wider audience and later in the same year the leading banks of France, Germany, Italy, Belgium and Holland, at that time the chief members of the Common Market, were each invited to send senior representatives to a conference to be held at The Bowring Building on 8 August. This received a positive response and a large space on the 14th floor of the tower block, normally used for recreational purposes, was converted into something akin to a United Nations debating chamber with simultaneous translation facilities, the interpreters working in all the respective languages except Dutch, on the assumption, presumably, that their representatives would be able to understand English.

This successful conference led to intensive negotiations being under-taken by a team of Bowring and Singer & Friedlander directors and senior executives, which resulted in the Ordinary Shares of C. T. Bowring & Co. Ltd being introduced simultaneously on 5 December 1972 to the bourses of Paris, Frankfurt, Amsterdam and Brussels, and an application for a quotation on the Milan Stock Exchange was made at the same time. The reason for the delay in Italy was that statuary regulations there required any company seeking a stock exchange quotation to advertise the basic statistics of their Balance Sheets in the national press for six weeks before an application would be recognized, and in Bowring's case a quotation when granted would be unique for a foreign company in Italy. So far as the other countries were concerned, it was the first time ever that any company had achieved a simultaneous quotation on five major European Bourses (London included).

As these negotiations were drawing to a close Ian Skimming invited members of the financial press to The Bowring Building to explain to them the reasons for this complicated and noteworthy exercise, which he did as follows:

> . . . Firstly, because we felt that this initiative was consistent with the spirit of the Treaty of Rome, and in accordance with the Universal desire for European economic and monetary union.
>
> Secondly, because we felt that if we wish to become a European Company we should have European Shareholders, both private and institutional.
>
> Thirdly, because we hope to make available to European industry and commerce wishing to enter Great Britain, the financial and allied services which The Bowring Group can offer, and
>
> Fourthly, because as a long term objective we hope to be able to enter into partnership with European financial service organizations operating in the same spheres as The Bowring Group . . .

The Economist, at the time, described the complications of the exercise as 'mind-boggling'. But those physically and practically involved in com-pleting the operation hadn't the time to contemplate such a description. These pioneers were dashing round Europe attending meetings and conferences with bankers and other advisory bodies, breaking new ground and wrestling with a mass of regulations and legal requirements.

When the exercise was completed Ian Skimming and a small team of Bowring and Singer & Friedlander directors and senior executives spent two weeks on an extensive tour of Amsterdam, Frankfurt, Paris, Brussels and Milan. At each city the party addressed groups of market analysts, stock brokers, members of the Press and many others whose interests lay in the day-to-day financial and investment affairs of their respective countries. These occasions attracted much public interest and Bowring's name became well known throughout a large part of Europe – where previously it was scarcely heard of – as a prominent financial services group. It must be said that the presence of Anthony Solomons and his team from Singer & Friedlander at these gatherings, where they were already well known, was an important factor in bringing this about.

The years following Ian's appointment as Chairman saw more successful development than any other period in the company's history and there can be no doubt that that this was due in large measure to his complete dedication to the Group's progress and his exceptional vision and unswerving leadership. With everything going so well it came as a devastating shock to learn late one Saturday morning in February 1973 that Ian had died suddenly and totally unexpectedly at the early age of fifty-three.

At this point in the history of the company it becomes necessary to include two members of the family who deserve special mention, Thomas Arthur Bowring and his younger brother Edgar Rennie Harvey Bowring, whose father Arthur, youngest son of John Bowring, never joined the company, preferring to grow oranges in California. Tom had been with Bowring's virtually all his working life. For much of it he ran the Aviation Insurance Broking Department and eventually, until his retirement, became Chairman of The Bowring Steamship Company. But Edgar didn't join until January 1956 when, at the age of forty-one, he came as Deputy Claims Manager after many years as a solicitor in Tunbridge Wells where he had gained considerable knowledge of the insurance business, his firm having represented various insurance companies. In due course he became Personal Assistant to Sidney Buckenham the Managing Director of C. T. Bowring & Co. (Insurance) Ltd under the Chairmanship of Harvey Bowring. In the years that followed Edgar very quickly developed a broad awareness of all aspects of the business and joined the boards of a number of subsidiary companies including the English and American and Crusader Insurance Companies. He became very enthusiastic about the development and expansion of the broking side and was directly involved in the rapid spread of the Company's business throughout the country and indeed overseas. By late 1965 he had become a Director of C. T. Bowring & Co. Ltd and was joint Chief Executive with Ian Skimming of C. T. Bowring & Co. (Insurance) Ltd. In addition to his increasing responsibilities, he became Group Administration Director and, in this capacity, was directly concerned with the move from 52 Leadenhall Street, and from other offices in London, to the new Bowring Building. During the years of rapid development, Edgar's steadying influence and negotiating ability were of inestimable value. Though he could always be counted upon to support Ian to the full, it could not be said that he was wholly relaxed about Ian's determination to expand in the world of financial services and I suspect he viewed the acquisition of Bowmaker and Singer & Friedlander with some unease.

Chapter 17

ON THE SATURDAY MORNING of Ian's death, Tom Bowring rang me to give me the very distressing and sad news. In our capacity as the two longest serving members of the Board of the Parent Company we both decided that we would do our utmost to persuade our fellow directors to agree to the appointment of Edgar as Group Chairman. They agreed unanimously. As we settled down to maintain the momentum built up in recent years, led by Ian's confident and persuasive nature, we all, I think, felt that it was time for a steady hand at the helm and for the wisdom and cautious nature of a well proven administrator; the time had come, perhaps, to consolidate on past success.

Edgar asked me to be his Deputy Chairman, an appointment I was happy to accept. We got on extremely well. By his own admission he knew little about trading and shipping, but was wholly supportive of these activities for which I had become responsible under Ian Skimming's reorganizing of the Group, as part of which all trading operations were placed within a new company, C. T. Bowring Trading (Holdings) Ltd.

It came as a cruel blow when, less than a year after his becoming not only Group Chairman but also Chairman of Bowmaker, Edgar should be faced in late December 1973 with the secondary banking crisis which hit Bowmaker so seriously that, had it not been for prompt action by the Bank of England, it might well have proved catastrophic for them as for many other banks. The possible effect of this well documented national emergency on Bowmaker was so serious as to cause Bowring's share price to fall from 180 pence to 18 pence. Edgar, while facing this appalling situation with characteristic calmness and courage was, nevertheless, understandably shaken and distressed. Many have wondered how he must have felt after such a short time as Chairman; and he might well, at times, have been haunted by recollections of his reservations concerning the acquisition of Bowmaker in the first place. With something of the order of £150 million at stake, it must have been for him and many others a uniquely unhappy Christmas that year. However, his strength of character and that of Gil Cooke, who as Chief Executive of Bowmaker was equally concerned, prevailed and immediately after the holiday break they, with representatives of other similarly affected organizations visited the Bank of England for discussions. As a result of these talks the Bank launched what became known as the 'Lifeboat', which successfully provided the necessary funding to underpin the worst affected secondary banks while they regained their strength.

On a happier note it was during Edgar's time as Chairman that Bowring's undertook their first major sports sponsorship. Although a lively and well-supported Bowring Sports and Social Club had been in existence for more than 50 years, providing facilities for soccer, cricket, golf, bowls, archery, rifle shooting, dancing and other leisure and sporting activities, rugby football had never been one of them until 1975 when the Bowring Rugby Football Club was formed. By happy coincidence the following year saw Bowring's taking on full and sole sponsorship of the annual 'Varsity Match' fought out at Twickenham each December between Oxford and Cambridge Universities, henceforth for *The Bowring Bowl*. At a press conference in the Summer of 1976 Edgar described the agreement arrived at between Bowring's, the Rugby Football Union, and the two Universities. He explained that C. T. Bowring & Co. Ltd had been approached by the Rugby Football Union earlier in the year to see whether they would be prepared to sponsor the match. He went on to say:

> I am delighted that my Board have accepted this invitation to sponsor the University match each year. The Bowring Group has taken this decision with two objectives; one, to increase the public's knowledge of our company name and, two, to become better known in academic circles not only in the two great Universities, but with the tens of thousands of schoolboys of all ages who follow this great match each year, and thereby hopefully attract recruits and graduates of the highest possible capability to join The Bowring Group.

Reports of some of the many press comments appearing in the Autumn 1976 issue of *The Bowring Magazine*, quoted *Lloyd's List*, as saying:

> For just £10,000 per year the name of Bowring is likely to be put into the minds of thousands and possibly millions of people. This publicity coup will be the direct outcome of one of the shrewdest sponsorship deals ever arranged.

And Terry O'Connor writing in the *Daily Mail* was reported as saying:

This is one of the most fiercely contested matches of the season and for the first time the winners will receive a Trophy – a silver rose bowl. The 'Varsity' game was a big money spinner until five years ago, and helped to finance other Universities sport. Rising costs have made it difficult for the Rugby Clubs to meet expenses. Oxford intend to spend some of the sponsor's money to encourage some of their junior teams, while Cambridge need to improve facilities and ground at Grange Road. Both Universities would like to finance more home matches against teams they are asked to visit overseas.

This sponsorship lasted for 25 years, at the end of which it was one of the longest sporting sponsorships on record and the two Universities were each receiving over £80,000 annually.

During the next four years as Chairman, until his retirement in 1978, Edgar was much involved in a series of discussions between Bowring's and other insurance brokers, significantly Marsh & McLennan, which turned out to be abortive. Whatever the outcome of these discussions might have been, Edgar was determined that The Bowring Group should remain intact. Though no trader or shipping man he was, nevertheless, fiercely protective of the Bowring heritage and would not countenance any deal that would result in the breaking up of the Group. When I succeeded him as Chairman in 1978 I was greatly comforted by the fact that he remained on the Board in a non-executive capacity. His knowledge, experience and, above all, his support were to prove invaluable during the next two years when further discussions took place with Marsh & McLennan.

In the meantime, however, in the limited spare time he could afford, he became deeply involved in the restoration of Bowring Park in Liverpool which, it will be recalled, had been given in trust to the Liverpool City Council in 1906 by Sir William Bowring and was threatened by an obstinate and illegal attempt by the current Council to develop the land. Edgar came to the support of a small group of enthusiasts, energetically organized by Mrs Audrey Wilson MBE, who were determined to preserve the park for the benefit of the inhabitants of Liverpool and its neighbouring boroughs and, by rallying as many members of the family as he could find, he managed to raise sufficient funds to restore the park to an orderly and pristine state.

★   ★   ★

Little, if any, mention has been made hitherto of financial results, but it will have been apparent from the steady growth during the early years of the original Company and ultimately of the rapidly developing Group that the trend, with one or two interruptions, over a period of 165 years has been in financial terms steadily upwards. It is hoped that reference throughout to the steady development of an increasing number of generally related enterprises will suffice to satisfy the reader who may not be particularly interested in the presentation of precise figures. However, if we presume that when Benjamin Bowring arrived at St John's his wealth was not, as a clockmaker and jeweller, all that great, then figures for the organization he founded in three of the last years of its existence as an independent commercial enterprise would surely have astonished him. The consolidated Group profit for 1976 was £25,847,000, as compared with £15,409,000 for the previous year. For the next year the accounts showed a profit of £32,756,000, a figure that must have gladdened Edgar's heart as he was about to step down as Chairman at the Annual General Meeting. Furthermore, in 1977 C. T. Bowring (Insurance) Holdings Ltd won The Queen's Award for Export Achievement in recognition of their contribution to the country's invisible earnings overseas. For 1978 the consolidated profit figure was £37,657,000. In 1979 the going began to get rough. Inflation shot up, interest rates rose several points and trading conditions deteriorated almost everywhere in the world where the Group was operating. And troubled waters lay ahead. It was the last year in which Bowring's were to enjoy their independence.

Happily we were able, in 1978, to celebrate the 200th Anniversary of the birth of the founder. The bicentenary was celebrated in several different ways including a Founder's Holiday for all members of the Staff; pensioners received a Gift Voucher and a Thanksgiving Service was held at All Hallows-by-the-Tower. A splendid dinner was arranged at the Savoy Hotel for 430 guests, of whom no less than 244 were either shareholder descendants of the Founder or related to him by marriage. Lord Orr-Ewing proposed the toast to the Company which was responded to by Edgar, and Warren Bowring from New York, as the senior living descendant of Benjamin Bowring, also spoke, though with a degree of incoherence commensurate with his apparent enjoyment of the occasion. Finally a reception was held at Lloyd's for some 300 friends of the firm. Among them were to be seen an impressive selection of the great and the good, most of whom were valued insurance clients either as senior representatives of a wide and varied range of commercial, industrial and other organizations or as individuals.

Chapter 18

Before recording the events that led to Bowring's loss of independence during the next two years, it seems fitting to give a brief account of the sponsorship of an event strongly reminiscent of a somewhat similar adventure with which the company was associated 68 years earlier, when they provided *Terra Nova* for Captain Scott's ill-fated expedition to the South Pole in 1910.

Early in 1978 I received a letter from Sir Ranulph Fiennes, the greatest explorer of our time, asking if Bowring's would sponsor an expedition which, under his leadership, was proposing to traverse the earth as nearly as possible along the Greenwich Meridian, crossing both poles. It was to be called the Transglobe Expedition. My reply was on the lines that we might be interested when we knew more about it and could be informed as to whether he had been successful in finding any other sponsors. I put his letter in my desk in the personal hope that we might hear more in due course. A week or two after receiving the letter, my son Antony appeared in my office asking me if by any chance I knew or had heard of the peripatetic baronet since he wanted to join his expedition as a deckhand on the support ship. I was able to give him Sir Ranulph's temporary address at Chelsea Barracks and sent him on his way. On presenting himself to the expedition leader he was told that there was as yet no ship, but that if he wanted to join the expedition and could find one, he might be considered for the job of Marine Co-ordinator.

The Board, after giving the matter much thought, indicated that they would be prepared to be one of the major sponsors and would consider purchasing a ship for the expedition if the price was right. Meanwhile Antony, after much travel and many disappointments, found the ice-strengthened *Kista Dan* lying in Halifax, Nova Scotia. She appeared to be suitable and was brought back to the UK to be prepared for the arduous months that lay ahead. But there was a nail-biting delay before acquisition could be confirmed because the asking price was too high. All this was happening while the discussions taking place with Marsh & McLennan over the matter of closer cooperation, were approaching an impasse. Nevertheless I thought it worthwhile to approach Jack Regan,

Chairman of Marsh & McLennan, to find out whether they might be prepared to share the sponsorship. He eventually obtained his Board's agreement on the condition that the vessel bore the names of both companies on either side of her upper deck, which might indicate that a good relationship existed between the two companies, and which we all agreed was desirable. However, the fact that the shorter name of Bowring appearing in much larger letters than Marsh & McLennan was considered at the time to be very much in our favour. The ship was renamed *Benjamin Bowring* and it was agreed that she should sail under the Bowring house flag.

As part of the sponsorship, which included initially some 400 companies, mostly British, rising eventually to 867 companies of many different nationalities, the *Benjy B*, as she became affectionately known, carried a British export trade exhibition which was set up at each port of call and which, over the course of the expedition accounted for sales of British goods and services amounting to over £2 million. These exhibitions were held in London at St Katharine Docks before departure and thereafter at Paris, Abidjan, Cape Town, Auckland, Sydney, Los Angeles and Vancouver. In addition to the ice team when they were not tackling the earth's extremities and, in order to stay as close as possible to the Greenwich Meridian, including the Sahara Desert, the ship also carried a number of scientists, who carried out zoological and oceano-graphic research, and a film crew.

HRH the Prince of Wales agreed to be Patron of the expedition and showed his enthusiastic support throughout its duration. On 2 September 1979 he took the helm of *Benjamin Bowring* as the expedition set off down the River Thames from the Pool of London for the start from Greenwich. He visited the ship when she was berthed at Sydney after the Antarctic crossing and finally brought *Benjy B* up the Thames to Greenwich when the expedition returned to London on 29 August 1982, almost exactly three years after their departure. The team were greeted by a vast crowd of cheering Londoners, which included most of Bowring's staff for whom a small fleet of pleasure boats had been hired.

Much has been written about the Transglobe Expedition and it is admirably described in great detail with many magnificent colour photographs in Sir Ranulph Fiennes' book, *To the Ends of the Earth*, which was published in 1983 by Hodder and Stoughton. Last of a long line of Bowring ships and the one which had the longest single journey of them all, *Benjamin Bowring* was, for most of her time as the expedition's support ship, under the command, for two separate periods, of Captain Les Davis of The Bowring Steamship Company. When waiting for the ice team to complete its crossing of the Antarctic the ship found herself in somewhat alien surroundings, earning her keep by trading, on charter to the New Zealand Government, in the South Pacific. A second charter took *Benjy B* to the Ross Sea with a group of New Zealand scientists, and she was still in New Zealand waters when the intrepid expedition team completed their crossing of the Antarctic some six weeks earlier than expected and she was able to pick them up at McMurdo Sound early in February 1981.

The *Benjy B* then took the team across the Pacific Ocean to Los Angeles and to Vancouver, for the last two of the trade exhibitions. In order to begin the most hazardous parts of the expedition, the approach to and reaching the North Pole, the ship then took the team to the mouth of the Yukon River. From here she made her way back to European waters and to the opposite side of the treacherous Arctic ice to pick up the intrepid explorers who had succeeded, having experienced the most perilous conditions, in reaching the North Pole. This redoubtable vessel was eventually purchased by the chief engineer, Ken Cameron, who renamed her *Arctic Gael* and, as Sir Ranulph says at the end of his book: 'The *Benjy B*, the remaining link with our memories, was no more'. The last Bowring ship had played her part with the Transglobe Expedition valiantly and had upheld, throughout, the reputation of a distinguished shipping heritage.

In my first message to the Bowring Employees, published with the Annual Report and Accounts for 1978, I said:

> The 1978 results show once again the overall strength of the Group. As you know the whole band does not play all the time and it is a substantial advantage that when there is a halt for breath in one section, another takes up the tune. It is certain that 1979 and subsequent years will be a period of challenge and excitement not least for the insurance side in the development of their new and imaginative relationship with Marsh & McLennan.

As already mentioned there had been earlier discussions with Marsh & McLennan (Marsh) starting in 1973. Jack Regan, the then newly appointed Chief Executive of Marsh, was anxious to buy into a substantial London broker and had approached others as well as

Bowring's with this in mind. Edgar was able to prolong negotiations with Jack Regan long enough for the share price to gain strength following its collapse during the secondary banking crisis. However Regan, notwithstanding the weakness of Bowring shares, hadn't pressed with the negotiations and, in fact spent from 1975 to 1978 buying substantial minority interests in European insurance brokers. In 1978 the Committee of Lloyd's imposed the '20 per cent rule' which was intended to limit the holdings of insurance interests outside Lloyd's to 20 per cent of any Lloyd's broker. In September discussions were resumed between Bowring's and Marsh. What was sought from Bowring's point of view was a more equitable division of the spoils whilst keeping the Marsh connection and maintaining independence. The ultimate goal, as described in *The Daily Telegraph* of 21 September under the headline 'Bowring Group in talks with top US Broker', was to 'bring about co-ordination of the operations and the combination of the results of all their insurance interests'. Put simply, the plan was to put the insurance earnings of the two groups into one 'pot' and then divide them on the basis of an agreed formula. It should be remembered that the connection had not only endured for over seventy years but Marsh had been providing something around one third of Bowring's American business, itself representing a very substantial portion of the Company's overall brokerage. It was confidently and publicly affirmed at the time that any arrangement arrived at would not involve a merger which, theoretically under the somewhat slender Lloyd's 20 per cent rule, would not be permitted in any case. And, as far as most members of the parent company Board were concerned, a merger was unacceptable.

Various alternative relationships were discussed and talks dragged on for over a year. There were signs that some senior members of the staff were becoming restless. Whilst being privy to the fact that discussions were taking place there were many who suspected that something sinister was afoot and it became necessary to publish a statement which, it was hoped, would put their minds at rest. In order to achieve this Ivor Binney, Chairman and Chief Executive of C. T. Bowring (Insurance) Holdings Ltd made an announcement in the Staff News of the Spring 1979 issue of *The Bowring Magazine*. It read as follows:

> At the time of writing, there is still some way to go in formulating the terms of the agreement but this much can be said. Although Marsh & McLennan is about three times the size of the insurance side of Bowring

in terms of profits, an equal voice in management has been agreed for both sides. Co-operation through an advisory committee will be maintained at all times with Marsh & McLennan but in case anyone is in any doubt, no change is contemplated in the present management of C. T. Bowring (Insurance) Holdings Ltd or the underwriting companies.

The two firms combined represent by far the most significant insurance broking co-operation in the world. *The Policy Holder* magazine referred to it as the most important insurance broking event in 1978 and probably in the whole decade. In addition, the insurance underwriting interests represent an important factor, but will continue to be kept completely and entirely separate from the broking side.

I look forward to the future co-operation with Marsh & McLennan with great confidence. People on both sides have proved very compatible and I believe that we shall enjoy and benefit by working alongside each other.

We also expect to meet the needs and requirements of our other clients and intend to give them just as good service as we have in the past.

But the time came when the discussions had reached a point where it seemed clear that further progress could not be made and on 17 December, 1979 C. T. Bowring & Co. Ltd issued the following press release:

Since September 1978 discussions have been taking place between C. T. Bowring & Co. Ltd and Marsh & McLennan Companies, Inc. with a view to implementing proposals for the co-ordination of the operations and the combination of the results of all their insurance interests.

It has progressively become apparent that Marsh & McLennan are unwilling to implement a pooling arrangement as originally envisaged. Alternative forms of structuring an association have been examined, but Bowring have reluctantly concluded that any structure acceptable to Marsh & McLennan could not be regarded as in the best interests of the shareholders of Bowring.

The Directors of Bowring regret that, in view of the long association between the two businesses, Marsh & McLennan have chosen to make a unilateral announcement of their intention to consider an offer for the whole of the share capital and convertible loan stocks of Bowring. If and when any offer is received it will be examined by the Directors of Bowring in the light of their duties to shareholders and staff.

A few days before this announcement Ivor Binney and I went to New York to explain our position to the Marsh & McLennan board. Our explanation of the Bowring decision infuriated Jack Regan who, showing his impatience, stated his intention to make an offer for all the Bowring capital. The gloves were off. An attempt was made to stall the Marsh & McLennan bid by taking out court actions against them in New York and London for restraining orders to prevent them from using confidential information they had obtained during the earlier ill-starred negotiations – but to no avail. Marsh were determined, by whatever means, to obtain 'a seat at the Lloyd's table'.

The extent of the acrimony that quickly built up can be detected in the following extract from the *Financial Times* of 7 January 1980:

> A bitter row has broken out between top executives of C. T. Bowring and Company, the British insurance broker with large Lloyd's of London interests, and Marsh & McLennan Companies Incorporated of the U.S., the world's largest insurance broker, which is considering making a bid for Bowring.
>
> The seriousness of the row is revealed in a letter from Mr Peter Bowring, Chairman of C. T. Bowring to Mr John Regan, Chairman of Marsh. The letter marked 'personal, private and confidential', was sent to the American group immediately after Marsh announced it was considering a bid in the middle of last month.
>
> The letter has been used as an exhibit by Marsh and McLennan as part of its attempt to resist court proceedings instituted by C. T. Bowring in the U.S. to stop Marsh from using confidential information supplied during earlier talks about a pooling of their respective insurance interests in furtherance of a bid.
>
> Mr Bowring says in the letter: 'Any offer made to the shareholders of C. T. Bowring & Co. Ltd, by whatsoever means and on whatever terms, with a view to acquiring all the issued share capital of the Company would be considered by me and my board as an unfriendly act.
>
> 'We are unanimous in our determination to resist any such offer by every means available to us, and this cannot exclude obtaining support in the City of London and elsewhere from whatever institutional bodies are sympathetic to our very strongly held views.
>
> 'I must remind you that on more than one occasion in the past you have assured me that action such as you are now suggesting would never be considered by you. In these circumstances, that you should now suggest approaching shareholders with a view to acquiring all the shares of C. T. Bowring is interpreted by us as a breach of faith which is positively detrimental to the relationship that has existed between our two companies for the past 70 years, a relationship that, as you have stated as

often as we have, should be preserved in the interests of both companies on terms that are mutually acceptable.

'To say that your undertaking no longer holds in view of changed circumstances is frankly nonsense', says Mr Bowring.

'I cannot forbear to mention again the extremely damaging effect that prolonged and fruitless negotiations' – a reference to the 18-month-old talks for a pooling arrangement – 'have had on morale and business generally throughout our Company, and it is not in your interests or ours, as I am sure you will agree, that this intolerable situation should be allowed to continue. Your unilateral announcement [about the possible bid] has served only to exacerbate and to crystallise ill-feeling'.

There were two factors which, for opposite reasons, could have affected the conduct of further negotiations; on the one hand, Lloyd's still adhered to their 20 per cent rule, which would inhibit a total takeover; on the other hand, however, something of the order of 60 per cent of Bowring's shares were now held by substantial institutions whose investment managers would find it difficult to resist an attractive offer for the Bowring shares held in their portfolios.

The battle wore on wearily – and sometimes acrimoniously – for several months. There were times when the situation resembled an infantry battle with two enemy battalions, reinforced by their 'supporting troops' – in this context merchant banks, lawyers and accountants – slogging it out from their long occupied positions – their boardrooms. Regular discussions took place at The Bowring Building, sometimes lasting until late in the evening, in an attempt to discover a means of defeating the 'enemy'. These meetings seemed endless and, most of the time, fruitless. To make the outlook even bleaker, I discovered that one of my most senior fellow-directors was suspected of being in regular contact with the opposition, disclosing, by telephone conversation, information regarding the content of the discussions. I sensed at the time that he was hoping, in the event of an 'enemy' victory, that he would be seen as a suitable candidate for high office bearing in mind his most brilliant career as a Lloyd's broker and recognized leadership qualities. In the event his performance was not admired by Marsh and his aspirations fell well short of fulfilment.

Gil Cooke, who had become Managing Director of Bowring's during Edgar Bowring's chairmanship, and I did our best to obtain the support of the Office of Fair Trading and had a meeting with the Director, Gordon Borrie (later Lord Borrie) whose report to the Trade Secretary, then John Nott (later Sir John), would lead to the latter's decision on whether or not the matter should be referred to the Monopolies and Mergers Commission, where the proposed takeover could have been stopped. Early on the morning of 25 March, 1980, as I entered my office, the telephone was ringing. It was John Nott's representative who informed me that he had decided that the matter would not be so referred – and to all intents and purposes, that was that. There was little we could now do to fend off the predator's assault.

Indeed, there was only the Lloyd's 20 per cent rule that might stand in the way of Jack Regan's single minded assault, but that was of waning significance and under close scrutiny; in any case, had we accepted an offer then, he would have been given several months to comply with it.

It is difficult to explain the extreme disappointment I felt as Chairman at a time when, after nearly 170 years since its creation and five generations after the founder, Benjamin Bowring, had started the Company, it would now almost certainly lose its identity.

Throughout the negotiations I had made a habit of visiting the older Edgar Bowring (my Uncle Egg of the woolly mitten), at his flat in Grosvenor House to bring him up to date. Now well over eighty he always listened patiently to my moans and groans and plied me with sufficient whisky to raise my spirits. When I told him that there was little chance of our surviving any reasonable bid, he said he didn't think it was the end of the world, and expressed his view that, whilst the growth of Bowring's for more than a century and a half had been mainly organic, some of the major milestones of the company's progress resulted from significant acquisitions. As a result we had become an important international concern and, he suggested, it was no surprise that we should have attracted the attention of prestigious predators who 'knew a good thing when they saw one'. He believed we should derive some pride from the fact that we had been singled out by the largest insurance broker in history as a suitable addition to their internationally renowned group. Whilst this view was comforting to me, it was not in accord with the sentiments of other members of the family, some of whom continued for a long time to harbour resentment notwithstanding their greatly increased wealth as holders of Bowring shares, the value of which appreciated beyond their highest possible hopes.

It was not long before Gil Cooke and I were sitting in secret around a table in a secure room at the Ritz Hotel in London with Jack Regan and Bob Newhouse, President of Marsh & McLennan, seeking a better price for Bowring shares and extracting from them guarantees especially concerning our 9,600 wonderfully loyal and patient employees. Eventually, on 14 April 1980, a bid of $419.8 million (at the time £258 million) was accepted by 97 per cent of the shareholders. The offer became final in December, fortunately for Marsh very soon after the Lloyd's 20 per cent rule was abolished. Gil Cooke, Edgar Bowring, Ivor Binney and I were appointed to the Marsh & McLennan Board, of which I became joint Vice-Chairman with Bob Newhouse. He, Jack Regan and, later Marsh's Financial Director, Bruce Schnitzer, joined the Bowring Board.

There were those outside the company who, at the time, expressed the view that Bowring's lost the battle 'because they were too gentlemanly'. It was suggested by some that had the company been more inclined to 'fight dirty' victory might have been achieved. But at what price? It would probably, if Marsh had lost the battle for C. T. Bowring and acquired some other London broker, have resulted in the company losing all the business that Marsh had hitherto put its way for over 70 years. And, in the final analysis, though there were some understandable defections, some of whom started their own insurance broking businesses and others who joined different firms, most of the employees continued to be satisfactorily engaged in the immediate years ahead.

But things have changed and, as I write these words, job security is no longer a certainty. When I joined Bowring's in 1947 my father, Fred Bowring, explained to me that the company never fired any employees – except, of course, for dishonest behaviour, of which there were very few cases. He maintained that, if any members of the staff proved to be inadequate for the jobs allotted to them, that was management's fault for misplacing them; they should be found more suitable occupations. That is not the case today when, without warning, employees can be told that they are redundant and given, at best a few days and sometimes only a few hours to clear their desks and depart – not, of course, without receiving some redundancy pay.

There is no satisfaction to be derived from witnessing the last days of an enterprise, begun by a courageous and patently honest man nearly two centuries ago, who instilled into his successors those same enduring qualities that enabled them, for five generations, to create an international undertaking that lasted for nearly 170 years before its excellence proved to be the cause of its demise. Countless such situations will continue to arise as long as new businesses are created and become successful. But whatever political trends and global developments may dictate in the years ahead, there would always seem to be good reason to recall the words of Benjamin Bowring which he wrote to his sons on the creation of the firm of Bowring Brothers in St John's, Newfoundland in 1841, when he wished them:

> '. . . every success that can be expected to result from combined industry, from careful speculation and from unanimous determination to forget the interest of the individual in the better interest of the whole.

Bibliography

Brown, Antony, *Hazard Unlimited*, Peter Davies, London, 1984

Brown, Cassie, *A Winters Tale*, Doubleday Canada Limited, 1976

Cook, John, *A List of Vessels owned and managed by C. T. Bowring & Co. Limited. and Bowring Brothers 1818–1983*

Cornish, Jim, *The Seal Fishery*, Gander Academy

DMO, HM Treasury and Bank of England Information, *Bank of England History*

Fiennes, Ranulph, *To the Ends of The Earth*, Hodder & Stoughton, London, 1983

Frost, David, *The Bowring Story of the Varsity Match*, Macdonald Queen Anne Press, 1986

Hodson, Godfrey, *Lloyd's of London*, Allen Lane, London, 1984

Keir,David, *The Bowring Story* The Bodley Head, London, 1962

The National Film Board of Canada

O'Neill, Al & Sue, *Historical Newfoundland*

Prowse, D. W., *A History of Newfoundland*, London, 1895

Riggs, Bert, various publications, Memorial University of Newfoundland

Reader's Digest Association, 1987 *Guide to Places of the World*

Ryan, Shannon, *The Ice Hunters*, Breakwater, St John's NF 1941

Ryan, Shannon, *Fish out of Water*, Breakwater, St John's NF 1941

Tarver, Mike, information on *Terra Nova*

Wardle, Arthur, *Benjamin Bowring and his Descendants*, Hodder & Stoughton, London 1940

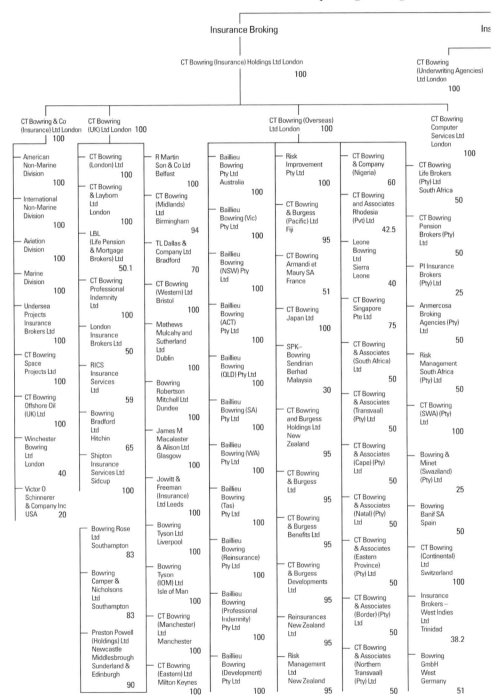

Insurance Broking

Ins

CT Bowring (Insurance) Holdings Ltd London
100

CT Bowring
(Underwriting Agencies)
Ltd London
100

CT Bowring & Co
(Insurance) Ltd London
100

CT Bowring
(UK) Ltd London 100

CT Bowring (Overseas)
Ltd London 100

CT Bowring
Computer
Services Ltd
London
100

American
Non-Marine
Division
100

International
Non-Marine
Division
100

Aviation
Division
100

Marine
Division
100

Undersea
Projects
Insurance
Brokers Ltd
100

CT Bowring
Space
Projects Ltd
100

CT Bowring
Offshore Oil
(UK) Ltd
100

Winchester
Bowring
Ltd
London
40

Victor O
Schinnerer
& Company Inc
USA   20

CT Bowring
(London) Ltd
100

CT Bowring
& Layborn
Ltd
London
100

LBL
(Life Pension
& Mortgage
Brokers) Ltd
50.1

CT Bowring
Professional
Indemnity
Ltd
100

London
Insurance
Brokers Ltd
50

RICS
Insurance
Services
Ltd
59

Bowring
Bradford
Ltd
Hitchin
65

Shipton
Insurance
Services Ltd
Sidcup
100

Bowring Rose
Ltd
Southampton
83

Bowring
Camper &
Nicholsons
Ltd
Southampton
83

Preston Powell
(Holdings) Ltd
Newcastle
Middlesbrough
Sunderland &
Edinburgh
90

R Martin
Son & Co Ltd
Belfast
100

CT Bowring
(Midlands)
Ltd
Birmingham
94

TL Dallas &
Company Ltd
Bradford
70

CT Bowring
(Western) Ltd
Bristol
100

Mathews
Mulcahy and
Sutherland
Ltd
Dublin
100

Bowring
Robertson
Mitchell Ltd
Dundee
100

James M
Macalaster
& Alison Ltd
Glasgow
100

Jowitt &
Freeman
(Insurance)
Ltd Leeds
100

Bowring
Tyson Ltd
Liverpool
100

Bowring
Tyson
(IOM) Ltd
Isle of Man
100

CT Bowring
(Manchester)
Ltd
Manchester
100

CT Bowring
(Eastern) Ltd
Milton Keynes
100

Baillieu
Bowring
Pty Ltd
Australia
100

Baillieu
Bowring (Vic)
Pty Ltd
100

Baillieu
Bowring
(NSW) Pty
Ltd
100

Baillieu
Bowring
(ACT)
Pty Ltd
100

Baillieu
Bowring
(QLD) Pty Ltd
100

Baillieu
Bowring (SA)
Pty Ltd
100

Baillieu
Bowring (WA)
Pty Ltd
100

Baillieu
Bowring
(Tas)
Pty Ltd
100

Baillieu
Bowring
(Reinsurance)
Pty Ltd
100

Baillieu
Bowring
(Professional
Indemnity)
Pty Ltd
100

Baillieu
Bowring
(Development)
Pty Ltd
100

Risk
Improvement
Pty Ltd
100

CT Bowring
& Burgess
(Pacific) Ltd
Fiji
95

CT Bowring
Armandi et
Maury SA
France
51

CT Bowring
Japan Ltd
100

SPK–
Bowring
Sendirian
Berhad
Malaysia
30

CT Bowring
and Burgess
Holdings Ltd
New
Zealand
95

CT Bowring
& Burgess
Ltd
95

CT Bowring
& Burgess
Benefits Ltd
95

CT Bowring
& Burgess
Developments
Ltd
95

Reinsurances
New Zealand
Ltd
95

Risk
Management
Ltd
New Zealand
95

CT Bowring
& Company
(Nigeria)
60

CT Bowring
and Associates
Rhodesia
(Pvt) Ltd
42.5

Leone
Bowring
Ltd
Sierra
Leone
40

CT Bowring
Singapore
Pte Ltd
75

CT Bowring
& Associates
(South Africa)
Ltd
50

CT Bowring
& Associates
(Transvaal)
(Pty) Ltd
50

CT Bowring
& Associates
(Cape) (Pty)
Ltd
50

CT Bowring
& Associates
(Natal) (Pty)
Ltd   50

CT Bowring
& Associates
(Eastern
Province)
(Pty) Ltd
50

CT Bowring
& Associates
(Border) (Pty)
Ltd
50

CT Bowring
& Associates
(Northern
Transvaal)
(Pty) Ltd
50

CT Bowring
Life Brokers
(Pty) Ltd
South Africa
50

CT Bowring
Pension
Brokers (Pty)
Ltd
50

PI Insurance
Brokers
(Pty) Ltd
25

Anmercosa
Broking
Agencies (Pty)
Ltd
50

Risk
Management
South Africa
(Pty) Ltd
50

CT Bowring
(SWA) (Pty)
Ltd
100

Bowring &
Minet
(Swaziland)
(Pty) Ltd
25

Bowring
Banif SA
Spain
50

CT Bowring
(Continental)
Ltd
Switzerland
100

Insurance
Brokers –
West Indies
Ltd
Trinidad
38.2

Bowring
GmbH
West
Germany
51

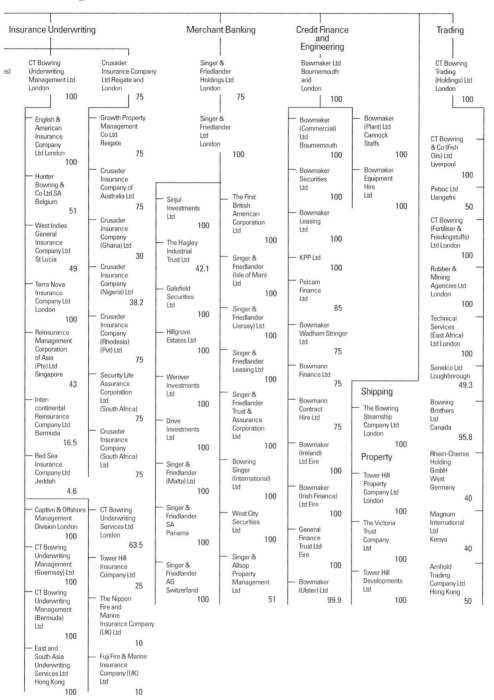

Insurance Underwriting

- CT Bowring Underwriting Management Ltd London — 100
  - English & American Insurance Company Ltd London — 100
  - Hunter Bowring & Co Ltd SA Belgium — 51
  - West Indies General Insurance Company Ltd St Lucia — 49
  - Terra Nova Insurance Company Ltd London — 100
  - Reinsurance Management Corporation of Asia (Pte) Ltd Singapore — 43
  - Inter-continental Reinsurance Company Ltd Bermuda — 16.5
  - Red Sea Insurance Company Ltd Jeddah — 4.6
  - Captive & Offshore Management Division London — 100
  - CT Bowring Underwriting Management (Guernsey) Ltd — 100
  - CT Bowring Underwriting Management (Bermuda) Ltd — 100
  - East and South Asia Underwriting Services Ltd Hong Kong — 100
- Crusader Insurance Company Ltd Reigate and London — 75
  - Growth Property Management Co Ltd Reigate — 75
  - Crusader Insurance Company of Australia Ltd — 75
  - Crusader Insurance Company (Ghana) Ltd — 30
  - Crusader Insurance Company (Nigeria) Ltd — 38.2
  - Crusader Insurance Company (Rhodesia) (Pvt) Ltd — 75
  - Security Life Assurance Corporation Ltd (South Africa) — 75
  - Crusader Insurance Company (South Africa) Ltd — 75
  - CT Bowring Underwriting Services Ltd London — 63.5
  - Tower Hill Insurance Company Ltd — 25
  - The Nippon Fire and Marine Insurance Company (UK) Ltd — 10
  - Fuji Fire & Marine Insurance Company (UK) Ltd — 10

Merchant Banking

- Singer & Friedlander Holdings Ltd London — 75
  - Singer & Friedlander Ltd London — 100
    - Sinjul Investments Ltd — 100
    - The Hagley Industrial Trust Ltd — 42.1
    - Galefield Securities Ltd — 100
    - Hillgrove Estates Ltd — 100
    - Weniver Investments Ltd — 100
    - Drive Investments Ltd — 100
    - Singer & Friedlander (Malta) Ltd — 100
    - Singer & Friedlander SA Panama — 100
    - Singer & Friedlander AG Switzerland — 100
  - The First British American Corporation Ltd — 100
  - Singer & Friedlander (Isle of Man) Ltd — 100
  - Singer & Friedlander (Jersey) Ltd — 100
  - Singer & Friedlander Leasing Ltd — 100
  - Singer & Friedlander Trust & Assurance Corporation Ltd — 100
  - Bowring Singer (International) Ltd — 100
  - West City Securities Ltd — 100
  - Singer & Allsop Property Management Ltd — 51

Credit Finance and Engineering

- Bowmaker Ltd Bournemouth and London — 100
  - Bowmaker (Commercial) Ltd Bournemouth — 100
  - Bowmaker Securities Ltd — 100
  - Bowmaker Leasing Ltd — 100
  - KPP Ltd — 100
  - Pelcam Finance Ltd — 85
  - Bowmaker Wadham Stringer Ltd — 75
  - Bowmann Finance Ltd — 75
  - Bowmann Contract Hire Ltd — 75
  - Bowmaker (Ireland) Ltd Eire — 100
  - Bowmaker (Irish Finance) Ltd Eire — 100
  - General Finance Trust Ltd Eire — 100
  - Bowmaker (Ulster) Ltd — 99.9
  - Bowmaker (Plant) Ltd Cannock Staffs — 100
  - Bowmaker Equipment Hire Ltd — 100

Shipping

- The Bowring Steamship Company Ltd London — 100

Property

- Tower Hill Property Company Ltd London — 100
  - The Victoria Trust Company Ltd — 100
  - Tower Hill Developments Ltd — 100

Trading

- CT Bowring Trading (Holdings) Ltd London — 100
  - CT Bowring & Co (Fish Oils) Ltd Liverpool — 100
  - Peboc Ltd Llangefni — 50
  - CT Bowring (Fertiliser & Feedingstuffs) Ltd London — 100
  - Rubber & Mining Agencies Ltd London — 100
  - Technical Services (East Africa) Ltd London — 100
  - Senelco Ltd Loughborough — 49.3
  - Bowring Brothers Ltd Canada — 95.8
  - Rhein-Chemie Holding GmbH West Germany — 40
  - Magnum International Ltd Kenya — 40
  - Arnhold Trading Company Ltd Hong Kong — 50

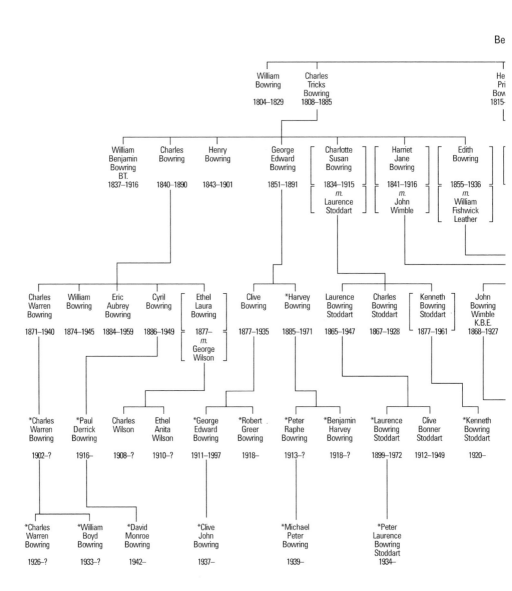

Those who have worked for the company are marked with an asterisk.

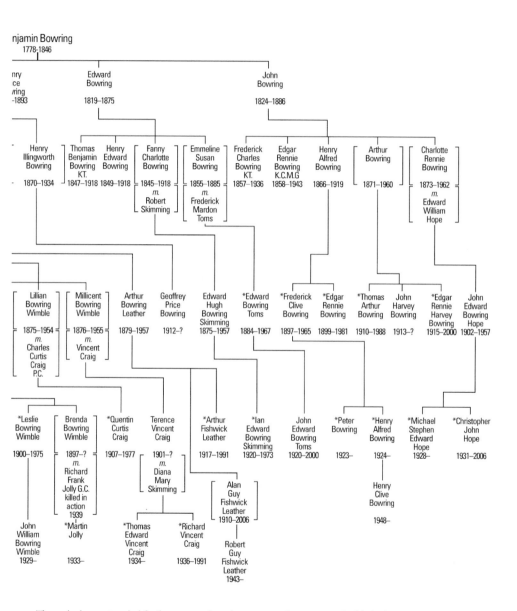

Those who have not worked for the company, but whose successors have, are contained in brackets.

Index of names